TWILIGHT
of
CAMELOT

ALSO BY STEVEN LEVINGSTON

Little Demon in the City of Light: A True Story of Murder and Mesmerism in Belle Époque Paris

Kennedy and King: The President, the Pastor, and the Battle over Civil Rights

Barack and Joe: The Making of an Extraordinary Partnership

TWILIGHT *of* CAMELOT

THE SHORT LIFE AND LONG LEGACY
OF PATRICK BOUVIER KENNEDY

STEVEN LEVINGSTON

GALLERY BOOKS

New York Amsterdam/Antwerp London
Toronto Sydney/Melbourne New Delhi

Gallery Books
An Imprint of Simon & Schuster, LLC
1230 Avenue of the Americas
New York, NY 10020

First Gallery Books hardcover edition February 2026

GALLERY BOOKS and colophon are registered trademarks of
Simon & Schuster, LLC

INTERIOR DESIGN BY KARLA SCHWEER

Manufactured in the United States of America

1 3 5 7 9 10 8 6 4 2

Library of Congress Control Number: 2025949273

ISBN 978-1-6680-3316-6
ISBN 978-1-6680-3318-0 (ebook)

For Suzanne, Katie, and Ben

CONTENTS

TWILIGHT *of* CAMELOT

ONE

"White House—Color It Pink or Blue?"

On April 11, 1963, President John F. Kennedy touched down at Palm Beach airport for the start of his Easter holiday. Local dignitaries turned out en masse to greet him: the town manager, mayor, sheriff, police chief, the county airport director, the county engineer.

But his wife, First Lady Jacqueline, was nowhere to be seen.

Smiling and looking fit and ready for fun, the president climed into a Secret Service vehicle that carried him down the tarmac to a white Lincoln Continental convertible awaiting him near an airport exit. Jack hopped out of the car, and from the shadows stepped Jackie, who had been hiding beyond the range of the news cameras.

What happened next startled observers.

"The president wrapped the first lady in a fond embrace," the Associated Press reported. "She threw her arms around him and they kissed." The famously reserved couple rarely, if ever, acted that way in public. They then got into the convertible and with Jack at the wheel drove off in high spirits toward their borrowed weekend estate. "There was obviously a genuine warmth between them that we hadn't seen that often before," a newsman recalled. "A lot of us got the feeling something was up."

Something *was* up.

For four months, Jack and Jackie had fiercely guarded their secret. But rumors were now circulating. And Jackie grudgingly accepted she had to acknowledge what her body could no longer hide. By the close of the long Easter weekend, the news would be the talk of the nation: the president and first lady were expecting their third child.

To the few already in the know, something else was obvious: that baby was drawing Jack and Jackie closer to each other than they ever had been.

⊱◇⊰

In January, the First Couple had been elated to learn Jackie was pregnant again. But, as always, the joy came with a twinge of fear. Jackie had learned years ago that for her, pregnancy would never be a smooth undertaking. This was her sixth: she had suffered two miscarriages, in 1954 and 1955, delivered a stillborn girl in 1956, and nearly lost John Jr., who was born three weeks early in 1960. Only Caroline was carried to term, arriving without incident in 1957.

Jackie restricted her secret to a very tight circle: family and personal aides. In late January, she dropped a hint to her Secret Service agent Clint Hill while they were strolling the grounds at Glen Ora, the Kennedys' rented residence in Middleburg, Virginia.

"Mr. Hill," she said, "I suppose you have noticed that I haven't been horseback riding like I normally do."

"Yes, Mrs. Kennedy, I noticed that."

He told her he also had noticed she stayed off the water skis on her December visit to Palm Beach.

"I can't keep any secrets from you, Mr. Hill, can I?"

She swore him to secrecy, then confided that she was due in mid-September.

Unable to contain their excitement, Jack and Jackie gave in to spontaneous bouts of celebration. They had never broken Secret Service rules, had never stepped off White House grounds without alerting agents. But one evening in February, in an act of mischievousness, they sneaked out for a quiet stroll together. Frantic agents scrambled and caught up to the escapees as they came out of the Southwest Gate. Jack and Jackie led their protectors on a leisurely, twenty-minute amble north along the west side of the White House outside the fenced perimeter. At Pennsylvania Avenue the parade turned right and reentered the grounds through the Northwest Gate.

The following week they got up to their antics again during an unpublicized, private weekend visit to New York. One afternoon, on their way to lunch at the restaurant Voisin on the Upper East Side, they suddenly hopped out of their unmarked vehicle and walked four and a half blocks along Park Avenue without warning the Secret Service. On the ride back to their hotel they popped out of the car again for an after-lunch constitutional. "It was challenging for the agents," Hill recalled, "but it was wonderful to see them thoroughly enjoying themselves—like they were just an ordinary couple—thrilled to be expecting a child, with so much to look forward to."

⟐

As they kicked off their Easter weekend, Jack and Jackie were, as the newspapers put it, "in a happy holiday mood." With Jackie at his side, the leader of the free world piloted the Lincoln Continental convertible out of the airport along roads closed to traffic and lined with well-wishers. Every now and then, he would snap off his sunglasses and wave at the crowd, sending the vehicle weaving erratically across the road.

For his stay in Palm Beach, the president had the use of the luxurious estate of a family friend, C. Michael Paul, an arts benefactor and oil and finance tycoon. The eight-bedroom mansion, decorated with Gothic tapestries and exotic tropical plants, had a private beach, swimming pool, and enormous inner courtyard where the Kennedys and their friends watched movies on a portable screen.

Press secretary Pierre Salinger promised journalists that barring any domestic or international crises, they could expect a five-day weekend of no news. The president was in sunny Palm Beach for relaxation: yachting, swimming, shopping, fun with his kids, and Easter observances. No official meetings were on his calendar and little, if any, White House business would be conducted.

And so it went. The president strolled the ritzy Palm Beach shopping district on Worth Avenue, played golf, went boating. Jackie, Caroline, and John Jr. decorated Easter eggs at a dining table cluttered with coffee mugs of colored dye: blue, green, red, and purple. Jackie and Caroline wore sleeveless Lilly Pulitzer dresses Jack had grabbed for them on his shopping spree: Jackie in a pink checkered shift, Caroline in a blue dress with white trim and a white barrette clipped into her hair.

Jack adapted his playing style to the age and character of each child. In the pool, he and Buttons, as he called five-and-a-half-year-old Caroline, drifted from one edge to the other, her dad pulling her gently through the water, bouncing her lightly up and down while they engaged in long face-to-face conversations.

John Jr., by contrast, preferred combat. He floated in his foam swimming ring and taunted the president of the United States, calling out

"Silly Daddy" and splashing him. Then he paddled away frantically as his father chased after him. When the boy tried to escape by climbing up the pool's stairs, Jack pulled down the imp's trunks exposing his bottom and dragging him back into the water.

"Naughty Daddy," John Jr. reprimanded his old man.

And the game began again.

Finally, the boy got himself onto the deck, where he turned back and shouted: "Daddy, you are a Foo-Foo Head."

His dad returned the scolding: "John Kennedy, how dare you call the President of the United States a Foo-Foo Head? You rascal, you wait till I get ahold of you."

In the evening, when the Kennedys were hosting seven guests for dinner, the children came in to say good night before bed. John Jr. kissed all the ladies at the table and bowed to all the men and shook their hands.

Before leaving, the two-and-a-half-year-old made sure he had his father's attention, and everyone else's, then delivered a parting shot at the president in a fine stage whisper: "Foo-Foo Head."

Jackie stayed out of public view until Easter morning. With a Secret Service agent at the wheel, the First Family climbed into the backseat of the white Lincoln Continental for the short ride from their vacation home to the Palm Beach villa of Jack's father, Joseph Kennedy Sr., who was incapacitated after suffering a stroke in late 1961. Caroline sat on her father's lap in a white cotton dress with red trimming, clutching her new toy, a stuffed white bunny. Beside them, John Jr., in white shorts, was propped up on his mother's lap.

When the sedan pulled up to the villa about a hundred spectators applauded from across the road beneath the palm trees. A Secret Service agent opened the back door and lifted John Jr. off of Jackie's lap. The first lady climbed out looking resplendent in a pale-pink linen sheath dress, a white lace mantilla, and long white gloves. She took her son by the hand and guided him past a gauntlet of press photographers.

Inside the villa, the president and his family were joined by his father, his mother, Rose, his youngest brother, Senator Ted Kennedy, and Ted's wife, Joan. The Reverend Peter F. O'Donnell of St. Ann Roman Catholic Church in West Palm Beach celebrated a private Mass in the spacious, Spanish-style living room. Lofty windows displayed a sensational view of the Atlantic Ocean, which on this day, according to one account, "was blue and rolling . . . in the brilliant Florida sunshine."

About an hour later, the First Family emerged from the villa to the waiting crowd, now numbering about three hundred, some shouting "Happy Easter." Jack and Jackie and their young children posed briefly for family photos. Jackie directed John Jr. to look toward White House photographer Army Captain Cecil W. Stoughton. But the boy seemed more intrigued by the captain's name, looking up at his mother and repeating it several times: "Stoughton. Stoughton." Jackie urged him gently, "Look at Captain Stoughton."

Before departing, the president, "in a jovial mood," chatted with reporters, then waded into the nearby crowd to shake a few hands.

⸙

The next day, press secretary Salinger strode into the briefing room at the Palm Beach Towers hotel at 5:30 p.m. He looked ill-at-ease. In his hand was a single sheet of paper. Newsmen sat at a bank of tables pushed together in front of the podium. Some had flipped open the cases of their portable typewriters and were already pecking at the keys.

Others stood along the walls of the windowless room with a notepad in hand. Television cameras were directed at a half-dozen microphones.

It was the second briefing of the day. Salinger had met with reporters at his regular 11 a.m. press call when he cryptically announced he wanted to see everyone again in the late afternoon. The unusual second meeting at the tail end of the holiday weekend raised the journalists' news radar.

A reporter had piped up: "Will you give us the subject?"

"No," the press secretary curtly replied.

Over the next six hours, Salinger was silent as reporters scrambled but dug up nothing. One zealous newsman caught up with the president's brother Senator Ted Kennedy on a Palm Beach tennis court. Was Salinger about to confirm that the president would be making a sentimental trip to Ireland in the summer? "No," Ted replied, "it's sexier than that." A disgruntled wire service reporter speculated that whatever the press secretary planned to announce, it was "a matter so sensitive that all official lips were sealed."

Standing at the podium, Salinger knew what he was about to take part in was a rare, possibly unprecedented, moment: Jacqueline Kennedy was going to allow a family secret to be divulged *on purpose*. She would have given anything to avoid such exposure, but she had no choice. The press already had been grumbling about her unexplained absence from public events in recent weeks, and her burgeoning belly threw out hints. Once she'd gone public, Jackie knew—given her pregnancy history—the press would do everything in its power to keep a hot spotlight on her.

Salinger was under intense pressure to ensure the announcement went precisely the way the first lady wanted—that is, he had to divulge only the agreed-upon minimum and not a word more. He had felt the first lady's wrath on more than a few occasions. "One of the treasures of my life is a series of memoranda from Mrs. Kennedy," he wrote later, "asking (usually in outrage—and with justification) why this story or that picture had appeared in the press." His job, in Jackie's eyes, was to keep the press wolf pack at bay, and he had grown to expect his dressing-downs. "After receiving a steady stream of memoranda pointing out deficiencies in my efforts," Salinger remembered, "I received one with a heading: *Don't worry—a nice calm memo.*"

With television cameras trained on him, Salinger, in a jacket, white shirt, and tie, studied the sheet of paper in his hand. "Let me say first," he began, speaking into a cluster of microphones at the podium, "that I will read this at regular speed first. It is a short statement. And then I will go back and read it at dictation speed. After that, I would appreciate it if the cameras cut off and I will read it again."

It suddenly occurred to him that his words might be streaming out to the nation as he spoke. "There are no cameras going out live on this, is that correct?" he said, and was relieved to hear from the room: "We are taping."

Salinger took a moment to study the statement one last time, then began: "The White House announced today"—he glanced down at the page again, then peered out into the room—"that Mrs. Kennedy"—his eyes flicked downward to the text, then back up—"is expecting a baby. . . ."

That was it—the bombshell in one sentence. Salinger paused, as if girding himself for a barrage of questions. But the only sound was the clacking of typewriters.

The press secretary pushed on, adding that the presidential baby was due "in the latter half of August." It was unclear why Salinger gave an August due date. That timeline contradicted what Jackie had told Agent Hill in January, that she expected to give birth in mid-September. The August date implied she was further along in her pregnancy. Perhaps it was meant to underscore smooth progress so far and discourage the press from prying into Jackie's private life.

Returning to his statement, Salinger nervously worked his way through two more sentences outlining Jackie's plans in the coming months. He stopped seven times to check the exact wording on the sheet, as if the first lady was hovering over his shoulder to make sure no stray word slipped in. "Mrs. Kennedy has maintained," he began, "her full schedule . . . for the past few months. . . . Because of this active schedule . . . her physicians have now advised her . . . to cancel all her official activities."

In all, Salinger uttered three short sentences. The news was joyous—capable of lifting hearts throughout the world—but Salinger looked oppressed. His shoulders were hunched as he spoke, he tensely rocked on his feet, and his eyes shifted from side to side with each halting phrase.

Reporters covering Jackie knew the press secretary was shading the truth: the first lady had not maintained a full schedule in recent months, as Salinger asserted. "Actually," United Press International reported, "the first lady had somewhat curtailed her public activities some time ago." Another dispatch went further: "During the past few months, she has been seen in public only rarely. She has pursued her own private life." *The Washington Post*'s society reporter Maxine Cheshire was more sympathetic, noting Jackie's "history of difficult pregnancies," adding that "although she is reportedly in excellent health, her physicians have advised her to take things easy."

Some Jackie-watching journalists were peeved she kept her baby news under wraps for so long. The announcement, one asserted, "was attended by secrecy and suspense usually reserved for the most momentous official pronouncements." Another reporter rated her pregnancy as "one of the White House's best kept secrets—better than some National Security Council meetings."

⊱◇⊰

Only one other first lady, Frances Folsom Cleveland, wife of President Grover Cleveland, had delivered a baby while serving in the White House. She gave birth to a daughter, Esther, in 1893, and another daughter, Marion, in 1895, during Cleveland's second term. Jackie would own a place in the history books if her baby was a boy, as no male child had been born to a sitting president.

Newspapers blanketed the nation in glowing coverage. "First Family Awaits Visit from Stork," cheered one. "News of Jackie's Baby Takes Capital by Storm," declared another. *The Washington Star*'s society columnist Betty Beale enthused: "A prospective little bundle of joy at 1600 Pennsylvania Avenue [is] adding to the sparkle of the sun-sprinkled capital."

The newspaper reports mirrored the joy that Jack and Jackie experienced in these early days. "I would say that they were very happy at that time, very anticipatory, really looking forward to this child," agent Hill recalled in an interview for this book. "Everything was looking up. Really, they were in kind of a giddy state."

Jackie, pictured "in a very chic Easter outfit" holding John Jr.'s hand, led the front page of *The Billings* (Montana) *Gazette* under the headline: "White House—Color It Pink or Blue?" The first lady was described alternately as "radiant" and "aglow." Even Salinger, apparently having survived his crucible unscathed, smiled broadly in a front-page cameo with the caption: "a beaming Pierre."

Newspaper readers were treated to photo montages of the president and first lady and their children. The Hackensack, New Jersey, *Record* published a scrapbook titled "Kennedys Play Waiting Game" featuring ten photos of Jack and Jackie with their adorable brood over the years: Jackie cuddling a giggling John Jr., Jack gazing into the eyes of toddler Caroline; in another shot, an older Caroline sucked on a lollipop; and in yet another, John Jr. showed off his new hairstyle described as a European-type cut favored by his mother.

The glimpses into the Kennedys' family life gave Americans a chance to see Jack and Jackie as ordinary parents just like themselves. Though obviously living in their cocoon of glamour, wealth, and power, the president and first lady came across as a father and mother bursting with the delight of any expectant couple. Summing up the First Family's long weekend, UPI White House correspondent Alvin Spivak observed that "vacations with the Kennedys can produce a bundle of surprises," and on this occasion "the Easter holiday . . . [helped] prove that presidents and their families are really human."

⟡

Bibs, booties, and bonnets poured into the White House. Some women knitted sweaters, others stitched quilts. More than three hundred letters of congratulation from around the world piled up daily in the mail room; a hundred notes from Europe arrived each week, many of them written in French.

Children took to their pens. One young correspondent enclosed a four-leaf clover so Mrs. Kennedy's baby "will be a very healthy one." An opinionated young girl begged Jackie to give birth to twin girls, " 'cause I don't like boys."

A youngster from Far Rockaway, New York, asked the president for "the honor of being the godfather to the new baby. I am 10 years old, if you want to know. And I'll be the happiest and proudest boy in the whole world." The Kennedys graciously declined the boy's offer, noting that "this role is usually filled by a relative or very close friend of the family."

A girl from Marion, Ohio, asked Jackie, "Have you decided what you are going to name the baby? And if so, will you please tell me, if possible."

No names were divulged before the birth. But Kennedy insiders scooped up hints. If the baby was a boy, the family's nanny Maud Shaw had learned, he would be called Patrick. A long line of Kennedys bore the name Patrick: Jack's great-grandfather, his grandfather, and his father, the current family patriarch, Joseph Patrick Kennedy. And if the child was a girl, "Caroline had her own ideas," Shaw recalled. "She wanted the name Susan."

Given her precarious history, Jackie's obstetrician John Walsh prescribed rest and relaxation. In early July, the first lady escaped with Caroline and John Jr. to Cape Cod, where she planned to stay largely out of sight until the birth—now publicly acknowledged as expected in mid-September.

The president rented a rambling, fifteen-room house just a mile walk from the Kennedy Compound in Hyannis Port. Brambletyde, as the place was called, was tucked away down a one-lane gravel road on a spit of marshland known as Squaw Island. It was a grand 1912 estate with airy rooms and pastel-colored walls owned by Louis Thun, a textile tycoon in Pennsylvania. Upstairs were ten bedrooms, each with a fireplace and a panoramic view of the sea. In the back was a private beach where Caroline and John Jr. could play beyond the snooping eye of telephoto lenses.

The Secret Service set up a command center inside a trailer at the end of the driveway. Though Jackie was far from what she described as the "goldfish bowl" of the White House, she still had reminders of her very public life. Wherever she glanced there were bundles of presidential communications equipment and Secret Service surveillance gear threading through the residence.

Dr. Walsh, a former Army surgeon in World War II, took up residence not far from the house. Though he had busy obstetrics practices in Washington and Bethesda, Maryland, he handed his patients over to another physician and settled in for what he called "an indefinite 'vacation,'" checking in on his famous patient almost daily.

In June, Dr. Walsh and White House physician Janet Travell had swept through the Cape on a stealth reconnaissance of local hospitals in search of a first-rate site should Jackie suffer a pregnancy mishap. The doctors weighed the relative advantages of Cape Cod Hospital in Hyannis, a local institution since the 1920s; the new Falmouth Hospital, which had opened in May 1963; and the hospital located on the Otis Air Force Base.

The Otis institution was selected because, in Travell's words, the 551st Hospital, as it was officially known, "provided the best combination of medical service, security, and accessibility." The place looked like what it was, a military hospital: a collection of low, one-story structures that resembled barracks. The grounds were a drab expanse of sandy soil with scrub pine and oak and patches of browned grass. Travell praised the hospital's interior as "rather charming . . . really very pleasant" but deemed the exterior environment as "very shabby."

The Otis hospital presented a stark contrast to Walter Reed Army Medical Center in Washington, the planned site of Jackie's delivery.

Walter Reed boasted stately Georgian Colonial Revival architecture on manicured landscaping. The elegant Truman-Eisenhower Suite awaited the first lady. An arts committee had collected antiques to decorate the quarters' sitting room, dining room, music room, and bedroom. No first lady had ever given birth at Walter Reed (or any U.S. military hospital), and doctors, nurses, and administrators were just as eager as Jackie to hear the first cries of a presidential baby within its walls. Army Surgeon General Leonard D. Heaton had declared that having Mrs. Kennedy as a patient was to be a great moment in the history of the hospital.

Otis also had a VIP suite, Building 3703, a former nurses' barracks that had been converted into a hospital ward in 1961 for use by President Kennedy, if needed, during his vacations to the Cape. After the air base was quietly designated as Mrs. Kennedy's backup site, the staff went to work redecorating and upgrading the suite for a possible emergency birth. The Air Force bought new furniture for Mrs. Kennedy's bedroom and the First Couple's sitting rooms and new appliances for the kitchen. The operating room got new lights and was made safe for the use of cyclopropane, a highly explosive anesthesia preferred by Dr. Walsh.

The Air Force brass, working with the medical staff, drew up an emergency response plan for good and bad weather. Administrators, doctors, nurses, helicopter pilots, ambulance drivers, airmen blood donors all went through repeated drills to perfect the crisis procedures. In military fashion, the Air Force leadership gave their operation a high-priority name: Top Drawer.

⁂

At Brambletyde, Jackie spent tranquil hours upstairs reading, painting, and organizing White House events for the fall. She and her personal secretary, Mary Gallagher, worked in a closed-in porch adjoining Jackie's bedroom. "From here," Gallagher wrote in her 1969 memoir, "we could feel the strong breezes and hear the lashing of the waves against the rocks."

At the start of July, as soon as Jackie was settled in, the president began arriving almost every weekend. So far, Jackie's pregnancy, just shy of its seventh month, was flawless. She was healthy, active, and in good spirits. The president and first lady had no reason to doubt that she would leave the Cape near the end of summer for a September birth in Washington.

"July was the month of bright promise," Gallagher remembered. "Everything seemed so secure, so full of good omens for the future."

TWO

Heartbreak Worth the Pain

Jack and Jackie had come a long way together.

From the moment Jackie first met the Massachusetts congressman in May 1951 at a dinner party arranged by their mutual friends, Charley and Martha Bartlett, she sensed his fear of the wedding altar. At thirty-four, Jack still clung to his bachelor lifestyle. He knew if he wanted to advance in politics he'd have to find a wife, but the prospect did nothing to erase his jaundiced view of marriage. Everything he had seen of it at home made him leery. The union of his millionaire father, Joseph P. Kennedy, and his mother, Rose, was nothing if not a glaring example of the corrosive experience that awaited the betrothed.

Joe Kennedy, with his freckles, red hair, and piercing blue eyes, was a man of all-consuming lusts: money, power, and women. He had dedicated his life and his fortune to lifting his children: the boys, to positions of power in politics; the girls, into the arms of wealthy husbands. He was ruthless in the pursuit of riches, flagrant in his philandering. He was proud of his prowess and saw no need to hide his infidelities. Betty Spalding, a friend of Jack's sisters Eunice and Kathleen (Kick), remembered dinners at the Kennedys' when Joe's young paramours were seated around the table. "The old man," she exclaimed, "having his mistresses there at the house for lunch and supper! I couldn't understand it! It was unheard of."

Mary Pitcairn, a friend of Eunice's, had a casual dating relationship with Jack in his early days as a congressman. She remembered Jack as adorable, thoughtful, and sensitive. "But I was always on my guard," she said. She was interested in a serious relationship but Jack's roving eye stood in the way: "I don't think Jack was ready for deep affection." She worried about his father's damaging influence. In a competition worthy of jungle animals, Joe Kennedy would pursue women Jack was seeing; he'd call them up and take them to dinner. He took Pitcairn for a meal at the Carlton Hotel in Washington and asked personal questions—"*extraordinarily* personal questions," she recalled. Once when Pitcairn was visiting Eunice on Cape Cod, he came into her bedroom when she was in her nightgown and kissed her good night in front of his daughter, who witnessed the scene through the open door of their adjoining bathroom. And it was no fatherly peck on the cheek. Not only that, it was common behavior familiar to the Kennedy siblings. "I think all this confused Jack," Pitcairn said. "What kind of object is a woman? To be treated as his father treated them?"

Jack's mother, Rose, was by her own description "a convent-bred girl." Her life was built on a foundation of piety. "She had found in God someone she could always love and trust," explained historian Doris Kearns Goodwin. Her faith gave her strength to endure the deaths of three sons and a daughter and look past the worst of her husband's behavior. To cope with Joe's reckless philandering, she retreated into a cocoon of denial. "Mrs. Kennedy had this amazing knack for shutting out anything she did not want to know or face or deal with, and conversely of actually believing whatever she wanted to believe," observed a Kennedy employee. When Joe flaunted his highly public affair with actress Gloria Swanson, Rose never acknowledged its reality, insisting his relationship was nothing more than one of his many movie industry business affiliations. "One of the characteristics of my life with Joe was that we trusted one another implicitly," she maintained. "There was never any deceit on his part and there was never any doubt in my mind about his motives or behavior."

She and her husband arrived at a twisted compact: he would carry on with his lovers and she would ignore the dalliances for the sake of appearances. But her private—and not-so-subtle—denial warped the marriage. She upheld an outdated Catholic code decreeing that sex was only for procreation, not pleasure. Following the birth of her ninth and last child, Ted in 1932, she declared: "No more sex," and ever after she and Joe occupied separate bedrooms.

Rose not only kept herself out of Joe's bed but also left him and the children for long periods to shield her eyes from her husband's stream of female conquests. Her repeated disappearances left a sour taste among some of her young kids. When she was setting off for a two-month stay with her sister in California in April 1923, leaving the young ones behind in the hands of maids and nursemaids, governesses and cooks, laundresses and their father, six-year-old Jack spoke up: "Gee, you're a great mother to go away and leave your children all alone."

As Jack pondered a future filled with marriage, kids, and family, his parents' dysfunction darkened his perspective. One night, in the mid-1940s, he was dancing under the Starlight Roof of the Waldorf Astoria Hotel with a woman named Elizabeth Drake, who was engaged to one of his war buddies. As they moved across the dance floor, Drake listened to Jack's despondent soliloquy on the institution of marriage: he couldn't fathom why anyone put their faith in it. "He was always asking me if I thought I really wanted to get married because there were so many unhappy marriages," she told biographers Joan Blair and Clay Blair Jr. Jack never explained to her why he was so averse to settling down. But Drake had an inkling: "I . . . think Jack was looking back in his own head to his own mother and father."

At that dinner with Jack in 1951, Jackie had a telling first impression of her future husband. "In a flash of inner perception," wrote her friend Mary Van Rensselaer Thayer in a 1961 authorized biography, "she realized here was a man who did not want to marry. . . . Jacqueline looked into Jack's laughingly aroused, intelligently inquisitive face and knew instantly that he would have a profound, perhaps disturbing influence on her life." She saw at that moment the possibility of heartbreak "but just as swiftly determined such heartbreak would be worth the pain."

When Jack and Jackie began spending time together, he realized she was unique among the many women he had known. She challenged him with her intelligence, style, and frank humor. "He really brightened when she appeared," recalled Jack's friend and Choate prep school roommate Lem Billings. "You could see it in his eyes; he'd follow her around the room watching to see what she'd do next. Jackie *interested* him, which was not true of many women."

A halting courtship began. He would disappear from her life for weeks, campaigning for a Senate seat in the 1952 election, calling from the road on occasion, as Jackie remembered it, "with a great clinking of coins" into the pay phone. Valentine's Day and Christmas rang in with no gifts, no tokens of his affection. His negligence may not have been a sign of indifference but a lack of experience with anything but fleeting relationships. He didn't know how to court a woman seriously the way other men did. If his attentions didn't involve a quick sexual conquest, he was inept and uncertain; he still had a lot to learn. From the road, Jack sent no love letters. The closest Jackie got was one postcard bearing five words as impassioned as he could muster: *Wish you were here. Jack.*

A voracious reader, Jack gave her books he treasured—perhaps as a way for her to better understand him. One title, *Pilgrim's Way*, a memoir by John Buchan, a former governor general of Canada, gave a potential peek into Jack's veiled emotional life. As journalist and Kennedy friend Laura Bergquist detected, Jack relied on his "cool cat exterior" to hide "a reservoir of emotion" lurking within him. In *Pilgrim's Way*, Buchan described one of his own friends in a way that a careful reader like Jackie might interpret as a coded portrait of Jack Kennedy: "He disliked emotion, not because he felt lightly but because he felt deeply."

Like him, Jackie immersed herself in books, and she presented Jack with volumes on French history and collections of poetry as passageways to understanding her. She discovered they shared a love of Shakespeare, and she admired his knowledge of the plays and his ability to quote long passages. Gradually they crept closer, recognizing they were of similar disposition—both keenly observant and somewhat shy with a quick wit and a taste for gossip. Later, perceiving their intellectual compatibility, Jackie explained, "We both have curious, inquiring minds—that's a reason we chose each other."

If books and intellectual pursuits drew them toward each other, their life journeys, especially their difficult paths through childhood, established a deep affinity. Jack began a lifelong battle with illness at age three when he contracted scarlet fever. Through his teens into adulthood, he spent long periods in school infirmaries and hospitals. His catalogue of ailments was encyclopedic: hives, fevers, pink eye, fatigue, blurry vision, declining weight, and severe abdominal pains. He came down with baffling, sometimes terrifying, conditions: an infection from a skinned knee at prep school landed him in the hospital near death with what was at first diagnosed as leukemia but later dismissed. During a semester at an all-boys Catholic boarding school in Connecticut, thirteen-year-old Jack endured a long bout of ill health that kept him cooped up in the infirmary. In his eight months at the school, all the while grappling with a range of ailments, his father and mother visited him once. His mother, in particular, was stingy with physical affection, a dispassion that seemed particularly cold for a boy as ill as Jack. "My mother never really held me and hugged me. Never. Never," Jack told artist Bill Walton, a close friend of his and Jackie's.

His parents' attention was heaped on Jack's older brother, the most beloved, eldest son, Joe Jr. Jack's father placed all his hopes for family greatness in Young Joe, whose dominance over his siblings in family lore ran the gamut from the physical to the social to the intellectual. "Emotions resonated between young Joe and his parents that none of the others would ever know, that none of the others would ever forget," historian Kearns Goodwin observed.

Jack chafed at his secondary status and competed to triumph over Joe Jr. He escaped into himself, plowed through books, and proved his intelligence superior to that of his brother. Jack tested higher in his IQ exams than Joe Jr. did but Rose never believed it. She lectured the children on the primacy of education but criticized Jack's most beloved reading material, which she deemed as "romantic and idealistic." When she saw him repeatedly reading *King Arthur and the Round Table*, she was displeased he found joy in the legends; she warned his reading tastes demonstrated a lack of seriousness: "he was inclined to be somewhat of a dreamer." Jack was falling short of her expectations. "I often had the feeling," she wrote in her memoir, "his mind was only half occupied with the subject at hand, such as doing his arithmetic homework or picking his clothes up off the floor, and the rest of his thoughts were far away weaving daydreams." She prized order and punctuality and decorum, and Jack was persistently untidy and late for meals and irreverent. Rose was "a tough, constant, minute disciplinarian," Lem Billings observed. "This went against Jack's natural temperament . . . so there was friction, and, on his part, resentment." As a result, Jack and Rose were never close. "Toward his mother," Goodwin concluded, "he developed a lifelong detachment."

Jackie didn't fare much better in her youth. Her mother, Janet, hot-tempered, hyper-critical, and status-conscious, created an explosive environment for her two children, Jackie and her sister, Lee. Janet, a chain-smoker who bit her fingernails, was described alternately as "a monster" and "utterly charming," "highly strung" and "very kind." "She expected so much from each of us," Lee recalled. There was a constant, general harping on "excelling and perfection. . . . But that may have been her unhappiness with herself."

The girls' home life in their preteen years was disrupted by their mother's bitterness toward their father, Jack Bouvier, a vain, swarthy seducer who wore a thin Clark Gable mustache and had a silk handkerchief poking from his jacket pocket. Known as "Black Jack," he also was called "The Sheik," in reference to a 1921 silent movie starring Rudolph Valentino. Like the Kennedy patriarch, Black Jack was an irrepressible adulterer; but unlike the millionaire Joe Kennedy, Bouvier drank too much and frittered away his wealth, incensing his social-climbing wife. Black Jack and Janet's tempestuous relationship was doomed. He was a hollow, flashy figure who thrust his wife into a state of constant humiliation. An accomplished horsewoman, Janet was once captured in a photograph sitting on a fence in her riding clothes while Black Jack stood beside her blatantly holding the hand of an attractive woman. Whatever his sins, Black Jack charmed his daughters, who preferred his company to their mother's. The girls' friends told biographer Sarah Bradford that Jackie and Lee hated their mother and resented her violence: Janet at times erupted in such rage over her own circumstances, she struck the girls.

The marriage collapsed in 1940 when Jackie was eleven. It was a nasty public divorce played large in the newspapers: Black Jack's parade of women was displayed in photographs. In those days, divorce left a painful stigma. For a sensitive, shy girl of Jackie's age, the sadness and spectacle were character-forming. As historian Bradford put it, "In public Jackie developed a protective shell of reserve, so none of her school friends or teachers seem to have realized the hurt that lay behind it. . . . It was now that Jackie developed the capacity to shut out things she didn't want to hear, to block out pain, which stood her in good stead later in life."

Two years later, when Jackie was thirteen, Janet married Hugh D. "Hughdie" Auchincloss, an old-money investment banking attorney and Standard Oil heir. Hughdie came with not only a solid fortune but also two splendid estates. Merrywood, in McLean, Virginia, surrounded by fifty acres of woods with dazzling vistas of the rushing Potomac, gave Jackie the seclusion she craved and a broad expanse of countryside for horseback riding. Hammersmith Farm in Newport, Rhode Island, was built in 1887 and featured a twenty-eight-room mansion overlooking the waters of Narragansett Bay. The residents and staff padded along crimson-carpeted hallways. Fourteen fireplaces promised warmth on chilly days. The vast grounds supported a working farm and stables for sixteen horses. Jackie took comfort in painting and composing poetry in the quiet gardens designed by Frederick Law Olmsted, the architect of New York's Central Park.

Janet and her daughters also acquired in Hughdie his backstory of complicated family relationships. Before taking up with Janet, his third wife, Hughdie had had a series of marital catastrophes. His first wife was a woman of Russian descent, Maria Chrapovitsky, who had "noble blood lines" reaching back to Peter the Great. It was said she had an ancestor who, as Catherine the Great's private secretary, composed the empress's letters to Voltaire. Hughdie, who was known as kindly but stuffy and boring, couldn't hold on to Maria, who deserted him to take up with a lover.

His second wife was Nina Gore Vidal, the daughter of Oklahoma senator T. P. Gore, and mother of writer Gore Vidal by a previous marriage. The acid-tongued writer had a contentious relationship with his stepfather and was wickedly ungracious in his literary depictions of him. Among Vidal's more generous images was his characterization of Hughdie as "large, cumbersome, [and] stammering." In his memoir, *Palimpsest*, Vidal lampoons Hughdie as an impotent sexual bungler with a stash of pornography that Nina demanded he pitch into the Potomac. Vidal concocts a satirical tale that Nina was able to conceive the two children she had with Hughdie only by spooning sperm into herself. Like his first wife, Nina left Hughdie to be with her lover.

Despite Jackie's new, posh surroundings, the pain of her parents' divorce lingered. Scarred by the turmoil and the loss of the regular presence of her father, Jackie turned inward, escaping into her books, poetry, and horses. An excellent equestrian—she'd won a prize in family competition with her mother at age five—she threw herself into the physical intensity of riding. On horseback, Jackie found her courage and competence. Sally Roche Higgins, who attended Miss Porter's prep school with Jackie, noticed her classmate's aloofness. Describing the teenage Jackie, Higgins told biographer Laurence Leamer, "She was so shy, so insecure, so removed from everyone and everything, interested primarily in her horse."

As she moved into her teens, Jackie retained her adoration of her father despite his failings, and he doted on her, favoring her over her sister. Black Jack's dangerous charm and mischief were thrilling to Jackie. When he was around, she was never bored. Jackie even had an overdeveloped acceptance of her father's sexual meanderings. As a student at Miss Porter's, she regaled her classmates with tales of his exploits, even recounting the time he cheated on her mother during their honeymoon. Jackie created such a rakish portrait of this alluring charmer that when he came to take her away on weekends, the schoolgirls lined up outside waiting to sneak a peek at him.

So blinded by her love of Black Jack, Jackie failed to appreciate the figure he cut in public. The girls at Miss Porter's were curious, certainly, but also merciless in their ridicule of him. A school friend of Jackie's, Ellen "Puffin" Gates, described her father as a "cartoon example of a dirty old man." When Black Jack came to the school, Gates recounted, "what we liked to do was run around and shake our behinds at him because he was an absolute lecher." Gates knew Jackie was amused by the impact her father had on the girls. "But I don't think she was aware . . . of the extent to which we were teasing her father and making fun of him," she explained. "This man was decidedly repulsive."

Jack Kennedy's courtship of Jackie dragged on for two years, eliciting her wisecrack to a friend: "I don't know if I'll live long enough to marry him." Yet he did propose in June 1953. He was ill-prepared for marriage and, in no small measure, was surrendering to it for political reasons. He had won a Massachusetts U.S. Senate seat in 1952 and already had an eye on the White House. It was imperative in any future campaign to have a wife at his side. Jackie was clear-eyed enough to know how she fit into the picture. She wrote about Jack to a confidant, Father Joseph Leonard, saying if he did marry her "it will be for rather practical reasons—because his career is this driving thing with him."

Some observers have made much of certain similarities between Jackie's father and Jack Kennedy. Though the two men differed in substantial ways—Black Jack loved prizefights, and gambling, and betting on horse races and the stock market, Jack preferred world affairs and deep reading—they converged in one glaring respect: both were handsome, insatiable womanizers. Kennedy friend Charles Spalding sought a psychological explanation for Jackie's passion for both men. "She wasn't sexually attracted to men unless they were dangerous like old Black Jack," Spalding said. "It was one of those terribly obvious Freudian situations. We all talked about it—even Jack, who didn't particularly go for Freud but said that Jackie had a 'father crush.' What was surprising was that Jackie, who was so intelligent in other things, didn't seem to have a clue about this one."

But it was one thing to have a father who was a womanizer and quite another to have a husband who kept roaming outside the marriage. Writing to Father Leonard before Jack proposed, Jackie took pause over the potential similarity between Jack and her father. "He's like my father in a way—loves the chase and is bored with the conquest—and once married needs proof he's still attractive, so flirts with other women and resents you," she told the Irish priest whom she had befriended on a trip to Dublin in 1950. "I saw how that nearly killed Mummy."

There was something else that attracted Jackie to both her father and to Jack: she was sympathetic to their private struggles. In the case of her father, it was his obsessive vanity, his drinking, and his frittering away of his wealth. In Jack's case, Jackie was sensitive to the way pain and illness had dominated his life since he was a child. Jack was easygoing and uncomplaining, but she saw what lay beneath the strong façade. In her own words, she was deeply moved by "this little boy, sick so much of the time, reading in bed, reading history, reading the Knights of the Round Table." As historian Kearns Goodwin put it, "His vulnerability aroused her deepest interest."

If there was a special understanding between Jack and Jackie, it was, in the eyes of Lem Billings, an appreciation for what they each had overcome to glide smoothly through life with charm and aplomb. They gleaned from each other how to re-create themselves for success. "They had both taken circumstances that weren't the best in this world when they were younger," Billings observed, "and learned to *make themselves up* as they went along. . . . They were both actors and they appreciated each other's performance."

Their wedding on September 12, 1953, just three months after Queen Elizabeth II's coronation, gave rise to whisperings that Jack and Jackie were America's royal couple. A *Life* magazine article on their June engagement had created a portrait of a glamorous lovestruck couple frolicking with the Kennedy clan at the family's summer home in Hyannis Port. The cover photo showed the smiling couple out for a sail, Jackie clutching a mast for support, her hair wind-ruffled. Jack was pictured on shore skipping stones along the water, demonstrating, as the caption read, a "manly skill" on the family's private beach. America got a look at Jackie the sportswoman engaging in robust Kennedy athletics: attempting an "end run" in a game of touch football and displaying an "unorthodox but vigorous batter's style" in a softball game on the estate's broad lawn. In a *Life* solo shot, Jackie leaned back on a veranda in a sun hat posing like a model and showing lots of leg. A few lines of text characterized the Cape Cod scenes as an Everyman's love story: "The handsomest young member of the U.S. Senate was acting last week like any young man in love."

In *Life*'s depiction, Jack Kennedy was an Everyman who also just happened to be American royalty. The magazine reminded readers that Jack's father, Joseph P. Kennedy, had served as ambassador to the United Kingdom; its photo spread included a shot of Jackie examining portraits of the Kennedys and British royalty posing together. The wedding a few months later, also featured in *Life*, was attended by six hundred diplomats, senators, and society figures. The reception on the sprawling three-hundred-acre grounds of Hammersmith Farm was a lavish fete for twelve hundred guests. One partygoer gushed the event was "just like the coronation."

⸻

But there the fairy tale ended. In its first three years, the marriage steadily deteriorated. Jack spent long hours away from home working into the night. On weekends, he traveled, often to see constituents in Massachusetts or to speaking engagements around the country. "I was alone almost every weekend," Jackie recalled. "It was all wrong. Politics was sort of my enemy and we had no home life whatsoever."

During this period, Jackie had the two miscarriages, which not only saddened her but also alarmed her. As Jack's close aide Ken O'Donnell explained: "Jackie . . . learned that carrying and delivering a child would always be difficult for her." And of course there were the other women, lots of them. Jackie wasn't naïve about her husband's sexual proclivities: she had married him fully aware of his reputation. A life with him, she realized, would require strategies for coping, as she acknowledged to a friend: "How can you live with a husband who is bound to be unfaithful but whom one loves?"

It all took its toll. "After the first year they were together," reported a friend of Jack's, "Jackie was wandering around looking like the survivor of an airplane crash." Jack gave a cryptic assessment of that first year, saying: "We didn't fully understand each other."

Jack confronted a severe health crisis the following year, putting further strain on the marriage. The crisis struck when two conditions aggravated in adulthood conspired to nearly kill him. One condition arose in London in 1947, when Jack at age thirty was laid low by a spike in temperature, a drop in blood pressure, extreme fatigue, and skin discoloration. He slid so close to death that a priest hovered nearby to give him last rites, if necessary. The diagnosis was Addison's disease, an adrenal insufficiency that inhibits production of certain hormones. Addison's, which Jack never publicly acknowledged throughout his political career, raised the prospect of a significantly shortened life. Anticipating an early death, Jack flung himself into a race against time. He had witnessed the cruel fate of shortened lives: he lost his older brother, Joe Jr., in 1944 in World War II at age twenty-nine, and beloved sister Kathleen (Kick) in a plane crash in 1948 at age twenty-eight. "The point is," he told his friend George Smathers, "you've got to live every day like it's your last day on earth. That's what I'm doing."

Despite treatment, his Addison's disease flared repeatedly in following years. In 1951, on a visit to Tokyo, he was raced in a military aircraft to a U.S. naval hospital on Okinawa with Addison's symptoms and a temperature of 106 degrees. Again he came close to death and survived.

The second condition, which plagued him from birth, was his compromised spine. His debility was aggravated in World War II when the PT boat he commanded was rammed by a Japanese destroyer. Since then, back pain was his companion. He was a year into his marriage when he experienced searing pain from the collapse of his fifth lumbar vertebra. In response, he submitted to risky spinal fusion surgery, confronting a sharply raised chance of a fatal infection because of his Addison's. Three days after the procedure, his temperature shot up and infection swept through his body. He fell into a coma, was given last rites, then crept back from the edge. He embarked on eight months of recuperation; during that time, he succumbed to another infection and wound up back in the hospital for a second operation to remove a metal plate that had been implanted in his back during the initial procedure.

During recovery, Jack had an eight-inch-long, pus-oozing incision in his back that Jackie learned to dress after a few lessons from a nurse. Writer Gore Vidal noted her devotion to her ailing husband. "There is no doubt that Jackie came through for Jack," he said. "She did everything she had to do when it came to nursing him. She lived up to her end of the marriage contract."

Jackie's devotion, however, went largely unappreciated: Jack's mind was on a woman other than his wife. During his long convalescence, he pined for a young Swedish woman he had met in the summer before his wedding when he had fled to the Riviera for a last blast of bachelorhood. There he was introduced to a twenty-one-year-old blonde, Gunilla von Post; they dined together on matching orders of sole meunière at a fashionable restaurant called Le Château, overlooking the hills and valleys of Haute-de-Cagnes. Their conversation was teasing and intimate. "For the moment," she told biographer Donald Spoto in 1999, "there was no mention of a fiancée." As the night wore on, they wound up at a popular nightclub called Jimmy's Bar. Jack cringed from back pain while dancing with her but insisted on keeping at it until two in the morning, as von Post recounted in her memoir. Then they joined another couple for a drive to Cap d'Antibes and sat alone above the sea listening to the water crash against the rocks. In von Post's telling, they kissed beneath the stars and Jack whispered that he'd fallen in love with her. Then came his confession. "I have to tell you something," he said. "I'm going back to the United States . . . to get married." He told her that if he had met her earlier, he would have canceled the wedding. When he took her back to her lodging, Jack suggested a nightcap inside her room but she declined. The night ended, in her words, with a "long, deeply passionate kiss."

While convalescing the following year, Jack—now married—wrote to her and phoned her repeatedly. When he was strong enough, in August 1955, he jetted off to meet her again, this time in the Swedish resort town of Båstad. Author Garry Wills, an incisive critic of the Kennedys, has contended that Jack's poor health—compounded by his carpe diem philosophy—supercharged his pursuit of sex. "With a truly staggering willpower Kennedy refused to acquiesce in his own debilities," Wills argued in his book *The Kennedy Imprisonment: A Meditation on Power*. "There was a testing of himself, his potency." Drawing on the musings of the sixteenth-century Renaissance philosopher Michel de Montaigne, Wills wrote that the ill or the aging often relied on "the tickle of lust" to rejuvenate themselves. So it was with Jack, Wills surmised. "It is only fair to assume," Wills concluded, "that Kennedy's constant self-testing, the lashing of his body back to a sense of its powers, contributed to his continual, almost heroic sexual performance—a way of cackling at the gods of bodily debility who plagued him, 'I'm not dead yet.'"

On his arrival in Båstad, he and von Post immediately fell into bed in his hotel room. "His back trouble was always a critical factor," she recalled. Later, when Jack and his lover joined others for dinner at a restaurant overlooking the harbor, he displayed the consequences of his vigorous escapade: as von Post recounted, "Jack came in on crutches." By the end of their week together, he had promised to divorce Jackie and marry von Post. But nothing came of it—that was the end of their romance.

After his dalliance in Båstad, Jack went to meet Jackie, who was vacationing separately that summer in Antibes. She was suffering through the miserable start of their marriage and wasn't naïve about his gallivanting in Sweden. Among her crowd in Antibes, which included Jackie's sister, Lee, and her first husband, Michael Canfield, among others, there was a "rumor that Jackie had left her husband, if not forever then for a trial separation," historian Sarah Bradford reported. Jackie had confided to a companion that she was done with Jack: "I'm never going back."

But when Jack arrived, William Douglas Home, a politician, playwright, and son of the Earl of Home, noticed that he and Jackie looked genuinely happy to be back together. From Douglas Home's vantage point, there was something vital in their companionship, something abiding and shatterproof, even if the wounds went deep. "She did love him," he observed, "and they had this relationship which was fun." People who closely observed them sensed their deep connection when they "exchanged eyes," as Dave Powers described it. Jackie's half-brother Jamie Auchincloss believed that no matter how twisted their love may have been, Jack and Jackie were bound together by "an intensity, an electrical current between them."

THREE

Marriage in a Shambles

However intense their attraction to each other, Jack and Jackie had to see their way through still darker times ahead. By 1956, Jackie was pregnant again. In August, in her eighth month, she accompanied Jack in the sweltering heat to the Democratic National Convention in Chicago. Over four days, Jack mounted a vigorous, though unsuccessful, campaign for the vice presidential slot on the November ticket. Afterward, he abandoned Jackie at her family's estate Hammersmith Farm in Newport and fled to the South of France to sail the Mediterranean. His cruise, according to biographers Peter Collier and David Horowitz, was a "bacchanale," with a gaggle of beautiful young women "getting on and off the boat at its ports of call."

On August 23, Jackie awoke from an afternoon nap hemorrhaging and in severe pain. Raced to the hospital, she required blood transfusions during an emergency caesarean that left her in critical condition. When she regained consciousness, she learned the devastating news: she had delivered a baby girl who was not alive at birth. Jack, still at sea, was unreachable, despite frantic efforts by his family—his forty-foot yacht had no ship-to-shore radio. *The Washington Post* declared on its front page: "Sen. Kennedy on Mediterranean Trip Unaware His Wife Has Lost Baby."

Though their daughter never took a first breath, Jackie and Jack had chosen a name for her: Arabella, after the flagship vessel in the eleven-ship fleet that brought John Winthrop, future colony governor, to Massachusetts Bay in 1630.

Three days after the baby's death, Jack sailed into port at Genoa and learned the news over the phone. At first, he thought, what was the point of racing home? The baby was lost; nothing he did now would change anything. When a friend urged him to leave immediately, he shot back: "Why the hell should I go now?" Biographer Laurence Leamer saw in Jack's reaction his "terrible obtuseness, his awesome, willful insensitivity." In Leamer's view, Jack had "little apparent regard for Jackie and her anguish."

It was only after a friend bluntly warned him about the peril to his political career that Senator Kennedy changed his mind. "If you want to run for president," the friend advised him, "you'd better get your ass back to your wife's bedside, or else every wife in the country will be against you."

He raced home.

Just shy of forty, Jack was in many respects still immature for his age. Garry Wills noted that one of Kennedy's favorite books, *The Young Melbourne* by Lord David Cecil, depicted the lascivious and sophisticated youth of William Lamb, who later as Lord Melbourne became Britain's prime minister. In the book, Cecil portrayed the future prime minister as a "slow maturer" in much the same terms that applied to Jack. Writing of young Melbourne, Cecil might have been describing John Kennedy: "He was the sort of character that, in any circumstances, does not come of age till middle life. His nature was composed of such diverse elements that it took a long time to fuse them into a stable whole."

Others have attributed Jack's behavior to his complicated and elusive personality. In this reading, Jack was devastated by Arabella's loss but was ill-equipped to confront a personal and family crisis: it was easier to lock away his emotions and keep his distance. "Surely no one would suggest that John Kennedy was without feeling for his wife and for their loss," observed Spoto in his book *Jacqueline Bouvier Kennedy Onassis: A Life*. Jack was, Spoto added, "shocked and saddened" but reluctant to throw himself into the public spectacle waiting for him at home. "When tragedy struck—he wanted to deal with it in solitude."

David Ormsby-Gore, a confidant of Jack's, believed his friend's heartbreak was undeniable. Ormsby-Gore knew Jack wrestled with "deep emotions and strong passions" beneath his aloof exterior. "When his friends were hurt or a tragedy occurred or his child died," Ormsby-Gore explained in an oral history, Jack "felt it very deeply. But somehow public display was anathema to him."

It was the closest Jack had yet come to a child of his own, and his grief, historian Kearns Goodwin believed, was just as keen as Jackie's: "For Jack too, the loss of the baby was a wrenching experience." His anguish, however, arose perhaps more from his sorrow over the baby's death than from his empathy for Jackie. "Children evoked in all the Kennedy sons the strongest emotions they would ever know," Goodwin explained.

Prep school buddy Lem Billings witnessed up close over many years the way Jack and his brothers favored their children. "They were all oriented toward their kids far more than their wives," he said. "This was true for Bobby and Teddy as well as for Jack."

⁂

The loss of Arabella was not only personal, it was a mark against Jack and Jackie in the Kennedy baby hierarchy. The family set impossible standards for childbearing. Kennedy daughters and wives were expected to pump out offspring at a rapid pace, beginning in the first year of marriage. Jack's mother, Rose, set the bar high, delivering five children in the first six years of her marriage, eventually finishing with a brood of nine.

Competition among the siblings and their spouses was intense. The clear champion, and challenger to Rose, was Ethel, wife of Jack's brother Robert, who had four children in the first five years after her marriage in 1950. Two weeks after Jackie's stillbirth, Ethel delivered her fifth child. By the time Ethel completed her sprint in the baby sweepstakes, she would walk away with the title, beating Rose, with eleven children over eighteen years. In another sign of Jack and Jackie's inadequacy, Patricia, who married Peter Lawford in 1954, gave birth to her second child two days after Jackie was rushed to the hospital in Newport. "Though the Kennedys never mentioned it to her," Lawford said, "there was always the uncomfortable feeling in the air when [Jackie] was around, that as far as childbearing went, she had rather let them down."

Jack and Jackie, still childless after three years, were the odd ones out at family get-togethers. Luella Hennessey, the family's private nurse who looked after new Kennedy mothers since 1937, observed, "It was terribly hard to be Aunt Jackie and Uncle Jack to so many babies when they had none of their own."

Jack's execrable behavior along with the devastation over Arabella left Jackie bitter and the marriage in a shambles. After Jackie recovered from her surgery she fled to London for nearly the entire month of November. She stayed with her sister, Lee, and her husband, Michael Canfield, the private secretary to the U.S. ambassador. Before returning home in early December Jackie and Lee treated themselves to a four-day jaunt to Paris.

Jackie's extended disappearance stoked gossip she was considering divorce. Historians seeking to puzzle out the truth have had to wade through speculation without agreeing on a reliable conclusion. The rumors had it that Joe Kennedy, fearful that divorce would render a death blow to his son's political career, offered Jackie a million dollars to stay put. When that story gained currency, according to some biographers, Jackie got Joe on the phone and jokingly "called him a 'cheapskate. Only one million? Why not ten million?' "

Accounts of this traumatic time portrayed Jackie as uncontrollably needy, demanding, and simply impossible, and Jack as pathologically indifferent, each frustrated and unable to understand the other. Biographer Spoto believed the gossip oversimplified the circumstances. Both Jack and Jackie were still grappling in their own way with their grief over Arabella and questions about their marriage. "By all accounts, there was no malice—only a terrible sadness with which each of them coped differently," Spoto noted. "Wounded by their pasts, Jack and Jackie had few resources to cope with their present."

David Nasaw, author of *The Patriarch*, an exhaustive biography of Joseph P. Kennedy, believed it was unlikely that Jackie and Joe discussed divorce or any special financial accommodation. "As for Joe paying off Jackie, there is no evidence of that anywhere," Nasaw said. He pointed out that neither Jack nor Jackie, as Catholics, was inclined to consider divorce an option.

In the midst of their turmoil, Jackie sent an emotional letter to Father Joseph Leonard. She affirmed her faith in God and expressed a wish, or prayer, that hope would eventually emerge from the tragedy. "Don't think that I would ever be bitter at God," she assured him. She wanted to move forward and acknowledged that she could "see so many good things that come out of this—how sadness shared brings married people closer together."

Jack gradually realized he had made a colossal mistake by abandoning Jackie and hesitating to race home after Arabella's death. He wished to make amends. But Jackie resisted. The influential columnist Drew Pearson spoke with Jack about the tensions in his marriage and recalled the conversation in a 1966 column. Jack wanted to mend their rift, according to Pearson, but Jackie was having none of it. Regardless of the spirit of hope Jackie displayed in her letter to Father Joseph, she was lost in a fog of bitter anger, disappointment, and depression. "She . . . had a will of her own," Pearson reported. "At times she could be imperious." With Jack, "she had experienced some stormy scenes." In his conversation with Jack, Pearson had elicited that "for a long time she wouldn't listen to his overtures for a reconciliation."

In that conversation, Jack expressed remorse and a sense of responsibility for his marital impasse. Many of his friends and colleagues had known Jack to learn from his mistakes and evolve, though often his progress was slow and inconsistent. There was a hint in Pearson's column that this grieving father and oblivious husband had awakened to the need to do better. Pearson put it simply: "He blamed himself for the estrangement."

FOUR

"At Last a Baby We Both Love"

The marriage survived. In 1957, Jackie was expecting again. Through her largely trouble-free pregnancy, Jack was on the road, in Massachusetts campaigning early for his Senate reelection in 1958 and in a multitude of other states introducing himself to Americans ahead of an expected run for the presidency in 1960.

During this time, his personal secretary Evelyn Lincoln noticed something different about her boss. "As the Senator crisscrossed the country in his travels," Lincoln recalled, "I could tell he was worried about Jackie . . . [and] their much-wanted baby. He would caution me each time he left to 'keep in close touch with Jackie in case you need me in a hurry.'"

While Jackie gave birth in a planned caesarean delivery on November 27, Jack was in the waiting room, and as jittery as any first-time father. "He paced the corridor in a terrible state of anxiety," recalled nurse Hennessey, who had come to look after Jackie. He was nerve-racked over his wife's health, worried about the baby's condition, impatient over the lack of news from the operating room. When Hennessey approached the family after the delivery, Jack "pounced" on her with an onslaught of questions: "Where's Jackie? Why isn't she with you? Has something gone wrong?" He relaxed only when Jackie's physician assured him that mother and baby girl were both well. When the doctor told Jack that his daughter was "very pretty," Jack drew a breath, Jackie's mother, Janet Auchincloss, recalled, and the tension drained from his face. "I will always remember the sweet expression on his face and the way he smiled."

Jackie had given birth to a healthy seven-pound, two-ounce girl soon to be christened Caroline Bouvier Kennedy after Jackie's sister, Caroline Lee, and her father, Jack Bouvier.

The new father was smitten. Many close friends marked Caroline's birth as a life-changing moment for Jack. He had suddenly woken up to the emotional joys of fatherhood. In 1953, the year he married Jackie, Jack had been not only wary of settling down but even warier of kids. Before his trip to the altar, "Jack seemed completely indifferent to children," observed his friend Paul "Red" Fay, a father of two. Fay remembered Jack challenging him, "I don't understand how you can get such a big kick out of your children, particularly when they are only about one and three years old. Certainly nothing they are going to say is going to stimulate you."

With Caroline's birth, Jack discovered how wrong—and naïve—he had been. Phoning Evelyn Lincoln with the news of Caroline, the new father rattled off her physical details: length, weight, eye color. "And not just because she's mine," Jack boasted, "but she is the prettiest baby I have ever seen."

On the phone, friends heard the euphoria in his voice. "Jack was more emotional about Caroline's birth than he was about anything else," Lem Billings remembered. "His voice cracked when he called to tell me the news, and when he showed me the baby he looked happier than I had seen him look in a long time."

Jack dragged Billings to the nursery to peer through the glass pane at rows of bassinets. "Now Lem," he demanded, "tell me, which one of the babies in the window is the prettiest?" When Billings innocently pointed to the wrong infant, Jack was so indignant he didn't speak to him for two days.

Tiny as she was, Caroline exerted extraordinary power over her father, observed Betty Spalding, the wife of Kennedy's friend Charles Spalding. "I don't think he really knew what loving someone was like until he had Caroline," Spalding said. "It was the first time he ever revealed any kind of emotion. It was fascinating to watch him grow in this capacity."

Dr. Travell, who at the time was treating Jack's ailing back and later would become his White House physician, watched his baby girl cast her spell on him. Jack wasn't the man he had been before her birth. She asserted: "Being Caroline's father had made him different."

In an undated letter to Jack—written probably in 1957 or 1958—Jackie posed the notion that their infant daughter had worked magic on their marriage. She was confident now that the worst between them was over. In her letter, Jackie celebrated what fate had bestowed upon them: "at last a baby we both love."

⁂

But Jack's progress as a devoted husband and father was anything but straight and smooth. Immediately following Caroline's birth, her father was away for long periods, first to secure his Senate reelection, then to pursue the golden ring of the presidency. He missed much of Caroline's first three years. But whenever he came home, either after working late in his office or after a campaign trip, he insisted on having a moment with his girl.

"No matter how tired he was, how terribly overworked," nanny Maud Shaw recalled, "he always found time for that . . . quick peek at Caroline, and to have a word with me about his daughter's progress."

Though he swept in and out, he managed to catch a few milestones in Caroline's early development. "He was delighted to be rewarded with her first smile when she was about four months old," Shaw remembered. "She was lying on her tummy and just lifted her head to turn and smile at him."

But as Caroline grew older, her father's absences confused her and disheartened her mother. "This life is very hard on a little child," Jackie explained to a reporter during the 1960 campaign. "She kisses her daddy good-night, and when she looks for him in the morning, he's in Oregon or some place." Caroline wondered where her father was and waited for him to come home. "Every time a plane goes over she asks if daddy is on it," Jackie said. "She asks where he is, and I have to say Alaska, or California."

FIVE

"I'm Never There When She Needs Me"

On November 8, 1960, Jackie was weeks away from giving birth to another child when Jack was elected president of the United States. Senator John Kennedy won the presidency by the smallest margin in the popular vote since 1884, beating Vice President Richard Nixon by just 118,574 votes; he captured 303 electoral votes to his opponent's 219.

On the following day, Jackie joined her husband inside the packed Hyannis Port Armory for the president-elect's victory speech. At the rostrum, Jack was shuffling through the pages of his speech when he realized that Jackie was standing too far away from him. He motioned for her to come up close. She crept over and for a moment was hidden behind him. Then she stepped into view at his right, her baby bump pressing against her buttoned purple coat. Someone called out unintelligibly from the floor, and Jack smiled, took her arm, and said: "She's all right, she's all right right here."

His remarks were brief. He gave thanks to Nixon and President Dwight Eisenhower for their congratulation notes and to all Americans no matter how they voted, and expressed optimism over the challenges that lay ahead. In closing, the president-elect smiled and said: "So now my wife and I prepare for a new administration and for a new baby."

Jack had seventy-two days before taking office and needed to fill hundreds of positions in his new administration. He jetted off to Florida to set up his transition team's headquarters at his father's Palm Beach estate. Jackie, seven and a half months pregnant, would remain at their Georgetown house to await the birth.

After twelve days in Palm Beach, Jack returned to Washington for a quiet Thanksgiving with Jackie and Caroline and a few friends. Throughout the holiday meal, Jackie was in good cheer, recalled friend Bill Walton. "Jackie never looked more beautiful," he observed. "She was full of bounce, getting up and down from the table to help serve dinner."

But afterward when Jack announced he was returning to Palm Beach, her heart sank. Jackie had hoped he would stay home until her planned caesarean delivery at New York Hospital in December. But he still had too much to get done: he set off that evening.

About two hours into Jack's four-hour flight to Florida, nanny Maud Shaw, who was also a trained nurse, heard Jackie call out from her second-floor bedroom.

"Can you come quickly, Miss Shaw?"

Shaw hurried downstairs to discover Jackie was hemorrhaging nearly a month before her child was due. An ambulance sped to the N Street home, and the crew hustled upstairs to find Jackie lying in bed in a white sweater and white wool socks. Her pink nightgown was mostly hidden beneath a red tweed overcoat. "She looked so tiny in her big coat," driver Willard Baucom remembered.

Dr. Walsh bounded upstairs minutes after the ambulance arrived. Jackie was terrified: the last time she hemorrhaged she delivered her stillborn daughter, Arabella. She pressed Walsh: "Will I lose my baby?" After a quick examination the doctor determined Jackie was only lightly hemorrhaging and her pain wasn't severe. "Everything's going to be fine," he assured her, "don't you worry."

Raced to Georgetown University Hospital, Jackie was taken to a surgical suite on the fourth floor. Dr. Walsh scrubbed up and began an emergency caesarean at 11:45 p.m., assisted by a resident obstetrician, two nurses, and Kennedy family pediatrician Edward Broocks. Pediatric resident Ira Seiler, who happened to draw the short straw to work Thanksgiving Day, was also around the table; he had been on duty for twelve hours when he was ordered to assist on Mrs. Kennedy's delivery. "I was the low man on the totem pole," explained the thirty-two-year-old resident. "If anything went wrong, be it my fault or not, the blame was probably going to fall on me."

On board his private plane the *Caroline*, a buoyant president-elect spent the first half of the flight discussing the pros and cons of potential cabinet members, reading through documents, riffling through some mail, and chatting with the pool reporters. After a snack of soup, pie, and milk, he retreated to his private compartment in the rear for a short nap.

About an hour from Palm Beach, Jack was handed a radio message from the cockpit containing scant information: Jackie had been rushed to Georgetown Hospital. Jack was visibly jolted. After the loss of Arabella, he and Jackie had hoped her smooth pregnancy with Caroline signaled an end to premature births and bitter sorrows. Jack intended to be at Jackie's side for this birth: he was set to return to Washington on December 5, ahead of her planned mid-month delivery.

But now, Jackie was alone confronting the trauma of another early birth. "[Jack] became tense and very nervous and restless, stricken with remorse because he was not with his wife," recalled aide Ken O'Donnell. Kennedy regretted his needless departure that evening, telling O'Donnell: "I'm never there when she needs me."

⁂

At 12:22 a.m., Jackie's newborn boy was lifted into the world. He didn't squall. The chief of anesthesiology hoisted the baby by the ankles and slapped his behind. Nothing. He slapped him again and for good measure a third time, but still nothing.

Jackie's son was yet to take a breath. He was silent and his face was turning blue.

Seiler, watching the crisis unfold, spoke up. He told the chief of anesthesiology the obvious: the baby needed assistance breathing. The standard procedure at the time was to pass a thin tube through the baby's mouth into the trachea and then breathe air into the lungs.

Protocol demanded that such a high-level intervention be carried out by the head of anesthesiology—someone of far higher status than Seiler—but the designated doctor wasn't acting, perhaps flustered by the fame of his tiny patient. "He handed the baby to me," Seiler recalled. And the young resident went to work: "I passed a tube into the trachea."

Acknowledging his status, Seiler then handed the baby back to the anesthesiology chief, whose responsibility then was to breathe into the tube and bring the child to life. But this senior physician "was nervous and inadvertently knocked the tube out," Seiler said.

There was a sense of escalating alarm in the operating room.

"I took the baby from the chief," Seiler recounted, "and put the tube back into the baby's throat and started to blow air into the lungs."

With a steadiness beyond his years, Seiler puffed oxygen into the newborn's premature lungs for six minutes. It seemed an eternity. But Seiler calmly persisted: puffing and puffing until—to everyone's relief—the infant wailed. At last, baby Kennedy was breathing on his own.

The newborn was handed to attending nurse Carol Forman, a twenty-six-year-old mother with a daughter the age of Caroline. She placed the boy into a warmed incubator infused with oxygen. "It was a very tense moment for all of us the moment he was born," she remembered. "Our hands were trembling and even the doctor was perspiring."

Confident the littlest Kennedy was out of danger, doctors moved him to the premature infant nursery.

The president-elect landed at Palm Beach Airport at 12:23 a.m., unaware his son had been born one minute earlier. He was directed to an open phone inside the terminal. Awaiting him on the other end was a nurse at Georgetown Hospital. She had little to impart: only that Jackie was in surgery. It was too soon for her to know about the drama in the delivery room.

The president-elect raced back out to the tarmac and commandeered the press plane, a DC-6, because it was faster than the *Caroline*, a Convair 240. After thirty minutes on the ground, the DC-6, fully packed with reporters, the president-elect, and his close aides, shot down the runway and was airborne for Washington. A female White House correspondent, unhappy at the chaotic turn of events, groused over the mess the president had created. "Why was he going to Palm Beach in the first place when his wife is back home pregnant," she wanted to know. "If it had been me ready to have a baby and my husband went away to have a good time, I'd be sore as hell!"

Eleven minutes into the flight, the president-elect was in the cockpit wearing a pair of radio headphones when he heard the news from Georgetown Hospital. A smile crossed his face. Press secretary Pierre Salinger followed the president-elect back into the main cabin. "We have just been advised by radio that Mrs. Kennedy has given birth to a baby boy," Salinger announced to the planeload of journalists over the public address system. "Both mother and son are doing well."

The cabin burst into cheers and applause.

Jack waved and bowed. Feeling generous—and cheeky—he urged Salinger to give cigars to all the newsmen "out of your regular supply."

⁂

At 2:15 a.m., Jackie regained consciousness in the recovery room and immediately asked about her baby. Learning her son was healthy, she looked immensely relieved and happy, recalled night supervisor Jeanette Robinson. She didn't say a word, Robinson said, "she just smiled."

Dr. Walsh released the news to reporters still hanging around the hospital. "The mother is resting comfortably and is in excellent condition," he announced. Dr. Broocks, Jackie's pediatrician, said he examined the infant an hour after his birth and "pronounced him healthy in every respect." Though he knew of the baby's breathing difficulties, he mentioned nothing about it. Walsh added that he was satisfied by the baby's size: six pounds, three ounces. "It was premature by date but not by weight," he said. The newborn demonstrated a "lusty cry," he told newsmen, perhaps referring to the baby's wailing after Seiler breathed life into him. Walsh noted the boy was "a very good-looking and healthy youngster . . . a very handsome young fellow."

As Jackie was being wheeled from the recovery room at 2:50 a.m., an Associated Press photographer named Tony Freeman leaped out of a linen closet, his camera clicking. "Three beautiful shots—bang, bang, bang," he said later.

Jackie muttered: "Oh, no, not that."

A Secret Service agent pounced on the photographer and tore the camera "right off my neck," Freeman said. When his camera was returned to him later, the film inside was gone: his prized photos were lost to history. His stealth attack was a warning to Jackie of the brutal invasions of her privacy that awaited her as first lady. She was already bracing for life as the president's wife. With surprising bluntness, she told *Time* magazine soon after the election: "I feel as though I have just turned into a piece of public property. It's really frightening to lose your anonymity at 31."

When the DC-6 touched down at National Airport at 4:04 a.m., Jack bounded across the tarmac and climbed into a white sedan that set off at high speed for Georgetown Hospital. Upstairs in her room on the third floor, he found Jackie still groggy for their quiet reunion, which lasted less than ten minutes. Jack then headed off to the premature baby nursery to gaze at his son through the thick windowpane. A nurse briefly lifted the newborn out of his incubator like a prized trophy for the father to claim.

Jack was described as looking "jubilant" when he told a crush of reporters: "the baby is fine . . . my wife is fine." A nun who got a glimpse of him said, "He was all smiles."

Weary from an exceedingly long day, Jack went home just before dawn. Outside his house were the all-night stalwarts: reporters, police, and Secret Service agents. The president-elect, speaking of the long night, lowered his voice to a near-whisper: "It was really something, wasn't it?" The men on duty—the police officers and his Secret Service agents—"softly called out their congratulations," wrote UPI's White House bureau chief Merriman Smith.

Standing on his doorstep at almost five in the morning Jack was "tired but unable to stop smiling," Smith observed. The birth of his son, Smith said, turned this imposing personage John F. Kennedy into one of the boys: "The president-elect seemed much more like a young father than a potentially powerful world figure." Someone asked, do you have a name for your son? "Why, it's John F. Kennedy Jr.," he said. "I think she decided—it has been decided. Yes—John F. Kennedy Jr."

⸻

The day after the birth, Jackie described her harrowing experience to private nurse Luella Hennessey, who had rushed to the hospital. "I was so terribly worried about the baby," Jackie told her. "They *say* he's fine. But I haven't *seen* him. Perhaps something is wrong—"

On her way to Jackie's room, Hennessey had popped in for a look at young John F. Kennedy Jr. "Well," she comforted Jackie, "*I've* seen him, and he's adorable and perfect. He's quite a bit early and he's little, so he's having some oxygen to get him off to a good start. But he's fine."

When the president-elect came to visit, Hennessey stepped out of the room to greet him. She was taken by the crush that surrounded him: Secret Service men, doctors, nurses, patients, and visitors. "Jack always seemed so terribly worn and harassed when he arrived," Hennessey remembered. Entering Jackie's room changed his demeanor from world-leader-in-waiting to father and husband. "When the door of that hospital room closed, the weariness dropped away and hustle and bustle were left outside. Here there was only quiet and peace and happiness."

Before slipping out of the room to give the couple their privacy, Hennessey caught the tenor of their conversation together—nothing about international turmoil or cabinet appointments. Instead, a wife speaking to her husband: "Jack, are you taking time out for regular meals? How much sleep did you get last night? What does Caroline say about the baby?"

At 5:15 p.m., Jack was back at the hospital to escort Jackie down the hall to the premature baby nursery for her introduction to her son. "I just walked along with her," he told reporters, revealing little. When asked what his wife said on seeing her son for the first time, the president-elect just "shook his head and grinned."

Leaving the hospital, Kennedy disclosed for the first time, without divulging any details, that John Jr. had experienced troubles at birth. He noted that the baby was suffering a slight respiratory ailment but was coming along well. He pointed out that premature babies often had initial breathing difficulties and that his son would remain in an incubator for at least another day or two.

Now a father of two, President-elect Kennedy visited his wife and newborn son in the hospital twice a day—sometimes three or four times, if possible, during the first week. In the nursery, Jack brimmed with questions on his son's progress: How much formula was he drinking? How much did he weigh? If doctors told him John Jr. had gained a half-ounce, he was thrilled.

Outside Jackie's room, he grilled Secret Service agent Hill about her condition: Was she recovering from her surgery? How did she sleep at night? "It was obvious he was sincerely concerned," Hill remembered, "and despite the endless decisions that needed to be made as he prepared for the presidency, the well-being of his wife and son was uppermost in his mind."

Five days after his birth, John Jr. was moved from the premature infant nursery to a private room a few steps away from his mother. He remained in an incubator, but it was no longer infused with oxygen. Pediatrician Broocks said the baby was active, his color was good, he was taking formula without difficulty, and he hadn't had any oxygen for thirty-six hours. Dr. Walsh had only good news about the boy's mother: "Everything's beautifully normal."

Though her strength was returning, Jackie was still weak. She needed time off her feet and an extended period of recovery. But from her bed, she was working on her plans for serving as first lady, preparing for the inauguration and for the move into the White House. She made phone calls, dictated letters to her personal secretary, Mary Gallagher, looked over final sketches of her inaugural outfits, and ironed out details for her coming convalescence in Palm Beach.

"But what she really was interested in was the little boy across the hall," said nurse Hennessey, who assisted Jackie on the brief journey to his private room. When Jackie held baby John, Hennessey recalled, "she was so radiant with joy, as she cradled him gently in her arms and whispered silly little nothings to him, that it seemed an intrusion to watch. I'd say, 'I'll leave you alone with your young man,' and tiptoe out of the room."

Jack, too, couldn't get enough of infant John. Each time he arrived at the hospital, his first stop was the baby's room. After visiting with his wife, Jack would want to slip by John Jr.'s room a second time on his way out. He wondered aloud to nurse Hennessey, "Do you think it would be all right if I asked the nurses to show him to me again?" When he walked across the hall to his son's room, the president-elect knocked before entering. He cracked open the door and asked the attending nurse: "May I have another look at my baby?"

Neither Jack nor Jackie ever publicly acknowledged John Jr.'s scrape with death in the delivery room. Nor did either parent ever identify by name the young doctor who saved their newborn's life.

The closest the president came was a couple of veiled references to the press. Though doctors described the birth as perfectly normal and the baby's health as excellent, Jack cryptically told reporters after his first hospital visit, "I am very very grateful it has all turned out so well."

On another visit, Jack hinted at how worried he was about his newborn. In response to a reporter's ironic twist on the age-old question "Did this father want his son to grow up to be president?" the president-elect said: "I haven't thought about it. I just want for him to be all right."

Jackie slipped an allusion to the baby's crisis at birth into a *Ladies' Home Journal* article published in April 1961. She had collaborated with a friend, society columnist Mary Van Rensselaer Thayer, on a three-part series for the magazine chronicling her life before the White House. The article recounted a presidential campaign event in October 1960, when a very pregnant Jackie rode with her husband in a ticker-tape parade through New York's financial district perched on the backseat of an open car. One million people were estimated to have lined the route. At one point, spectators broke through police and Secret Service cordons, shook the car, and grabbed at Jackie. "It was one of the greatest moments of John Fitzgerald Kennedy's life, but terrifying to his wife," Thayer wrote. "She knew her strength had been overtaxed. A few weeks later when John Fitzgerald Kennedy Jr. decided to arrive a month ahead of schedule, only a matter of minutes, luck and a wonderful doctor saved him."

Privately, the president-elect acknowledged Dr. Ira Seiler's fast-thinking heroics. On Jackie and John Jr.'s release from the hospital, he sent the pediatric resident a note thanking him "for the many kindnesses shown to Mrs. Kennedy." Zeroing in on Seiler's contribution, he added: "Your wonderful care has contributed greatly for her and my new son to leave . . . in the very best of health."

The president-elect also made sure the young doctor and his wife received an invitation to his inauguration and tickets to the Inaugural Ball, and all of the receptions and concerts. At the inauguration ceremony, Seiler was seated next to former Illinois governor and two-time Democratic presidential nominee Adlai Stevenson. Seiler's wife, Gloria, had a spot reserved for her beside former first lady Eleanor Roosevelt. When Seiler later told a Georgetown Hospital nurse that he attended the ceremony, she let him know that she had written to the inaugural committee. In her note, she told the committee that if Seiler "had not been there John F. Kennedy Jr. would have died."

SIX

A Bewildering Portrait of a President

On January 20, President-elect John F. Kennedy placed his hand on an 1850 family Bible and took his oath of office. Bright sunshine defied the twenty-two-degree chill. Then, in stirring rhetoric, President Kennedy let it be known "that the torch has been passed to a new generation." Here was the promise of youthfulness and hope, a pledge that spoke to the nation but also symbolized Jack's embrace of his own new generation: Caroline and John Jr.

At the close of the inaugural ceremony, Jackie hurried to catch up to her husband in the crush of dignitaries filing off the platform. She wanted to congratulate him on his brilliant address. "I was so proud of Jack," she recalled. "There was so much I wanted to say!" She closed in on him in a corridor near the Capitol Rotunda. "I so badly wanted to see him . . . alone."

Unlike President Eisenhower, who kissed Mamie after his swearing in, President Kennedy maintained his trademark restraint. "Everyone says, 'Why didn't Jack kiss you after?'—which of course, he would never do there," Jackie explained.

When she stopped Jack for their quiet moment together, she respected their personal protocol. "I could scarcely embrace him in front of all those people, so I remember I just put my hand on his cheek and said, 'Jack, you were so wonderful!' And he was smiling in the most touching and most vulnerable way. He looked so happy."

A photographer caught the moment, his flashbulb throwing a bright light on Jack's face. The photo, which caromed around the country, became an iconic, romantic image of the president and first lady. Here they were displaying their natural charm and style just as they were sweeping into the White House. "There's a picture where I have my hand on his chin and you know, he's just looking at me," Jackie recalled. "I mean, that was so much more emotional than any kiss because his eyes really did fill with tears."

Moving into the White House brought the family close in ways no one had anticipated. Jackie had fretted over the impossibility of a normal life. "I used to worry," she explained, "thinking all the things anyone thinks. It'll be a goldfish bowl, the Secret Service, I'll never see my husband."

But settling in, she got a welcome surprise. Jack mostly worked at home in the Oval Office on the first floor. The family lived in the private residence on the second floor. Caroline's schoolroom was in the Solarium on the third floor. The children's playground was on the South Lawn within view of their father's office. Though she mostly left him to his business during the day, Jackie sometimes had lunch with Jack alone, and saw him when he came upstairs for his afternoon nap. The White House lifestyle had its advantages, she recalled: "I didn't realize the physical closeness of having his office in the same building and seeing him so many times a day."

Jackie realized her initial hesitance was unfounded. "My life here," she wrote to Bill Walton in June 1962, "is now under control and the happiest time I have ever known—not for the position—but for the closeness of one's family."

Typically family togetherness began in the morning. Once John Jr. was big enough, he and Caroline would burst into Jack's bedroom and blast cartoons on the television: *The Flintstones, Mr. Magoo, The Jetsons, Deputy Dawg.* Sometimes it would be Jack LaLanne, that "awful exercise man," as Jackie described him. Caroline and her brother thought it was hilarious to get down on the floor and mimic LaLanne's gyrations. No noise or commotion perturbed the president. He sat reading his briefing books and newspapers while the kids flopped on the floor or climbed all over him. "He loved those children tumbling around him," Jackie remembered.

When Jack went to soak in the tub, John Jr. would follow him. Jack had pleaded with Jackie to find something "to amuse John" while he was bathing. And each morning, father and son would find a battalion of rubber duckies, pink piggies, and other animals lined up on the rim of the tub. While Jack soothed his back and read his briefing reports in preparation for his day, John Jr. happily pushed the duckies and piggies round and round on the surface of the water.

After his bath the president would head downstairs to the Oval Office, escorted by Caroline, who would then race back upstairs to her classroom. During recess, Caroline and her fellow students would sprint to a playground on the South Lawn, where an array of amusements awaited: a barrel tunnel, leather swing, slide, treehouse. Nearby was a rabbit hutch, lamb pen, and pony stable.

The president, catching sight of the kids, would break from his work and get a moment of fresh air. "He often stepped out to shrieks, hugs, quacks, barks, cackles, bleats, and all sorts of commotion," recalled chief White House usher J. B. West. "He seemed to delight in the mad scene." Sometimes, he would clap his hands and the kids would streak across the lawn to the White House, then dart away again, each with a piece of candy in their fist.

In the evenings, after his day in the Oval Office, Jack checked in on Caroline and John Jr. "for about a half an hour before dinner," Jackie recalled, and again before their bedtime. If the president and first lady were entertaining guests, it didn't matter if it was a small or large affair, Jack insisted on spending some time with the kids beforehand "in their pajamas," Jackie said. "He really would play with them first, even if it was a state dinner. . . . He'd get on the floor, then he could really roll around with them."

By their nature, the kids were eroding the old Jack and bringing into being a man more affectionate, more emotionally engaged, more loving than he had ever been. "Nothing alters a man more, I think," reflected Jack's friend Alastair Granville Forbes, a journalist and cousin of Franklin Roosevelt, "than this added ingredient to life, you know, the children." Jack unabashedly adored Caroline and John Jr., journalist Laura Bergquist observed, and they couldn't get enough of him. "There is a rapport there," she said, "a serious attention, so much naked intensity of feeling."

If Jack was embracing fatherhood, he was still less than committed to his role as a husband. Feelings between husband and wife were not nearly as pure as they were between father and children. In the first two years of his presidency, tension knifed through Jack and Jackie's relationship, caused in no small part by his continued compulsive womanizing.

Jackie was fully aware of Jack's sexual excesses and at times expressed her bitterness with surprising verve. Once, as she walked past Evelyn Lincoln's desk with a reporter from the magazine *Paris Match*, she noticed one of Jack's young White House lovers sitting nearby. Turning to the reporter, she said in French, "This is the girl who supposedly is sleeping with my husband."

The reporter, a friend of Jackie's, related the incident to a White House staffer, Barbara Gamarekian. "I've always wondered why Mrs. Kennedy said this," Gamarekian recalled. "Whether she thought since she was talking to a Frenchman, this was something he would understand and accept or whether she was trying to shock him or whether she was bitter enough so that this just came out."

Mostly, however, Jackie was subtle in her disapproval. She adopted the strategy her mother-in-law, Rose Kennedy, used to cope with the many transgressions of her husband, Joe. She ignored, or denied, the importance of Jack's infidelities and the hurt and disappointment they inflicted on her. Like Rose, Jackie fled for periods of time, staying away from the White House at their home in Hyannis Port, and at Glen Ora, the estate in Middleburg, Virginia, or taking extended vacations in London to see her sister or in other locations in Europe.

Jack tactlessly regarded his assignations as something separate from his marriage. Jackie's sister, Lee, who repeatedly confronted Jack for his conduct, was appalled he showed no remorse. "He'd have absolutely no guilty conscience," Lee told her friend British photographer Cecil Beaton in 1968. According to Lee, Jack insisted: "I love [Jackie] deeply and have done everything for her. I've no feeling of letting her down because I've put her foremost in everything."

Jackie ultimately reconciled herself to her Jack's profligacy by casting his conduct as typical among people of their elite lifestyle. Both her father and his were flagrant womanizers. As biographer Bradford explained, "She could accept the infidelity. It was standard behavior in the international circles in which she . . . moved."

No matter how widely her husband wandered, Jackie persevered by convincing herself she remained first in his heart. "She had brought up the subject of Jack's mistresses from time to time with no apparent discomfort or distress," singer/songwriter Carly Simon wrote in her memoir of her relationship with Jackie. "In a cheerful but resigned way, she told me that of course she knew about them—she just didn't mind their presence as much as she might have because she knew he loved her more, much more, than any of his dalliances."

⸻

The president in his first two years in the White House presented a bewildering portrait of a man sweetly doting on his children, manically philandering, and incautiously taking excessive doses of questionable drugs for his health conditions. His White House physician Janet Travell administered daily shots of cortisone, a steroid hormone, for his Addison's disease. She also was overseeing pain treatments for his back, administering two or three injections a day of procaine, an anesthetic.

Unbeknownst to the White House medical staff, a celebrity doctor named Max Jacobson, known as Dr. Feelgood, was giving the president shots of the addictive stimulant methamphetamine mixed with other ingredients—possibly steroids and vitamins—but never fully identified. Jacobson promised the injections would increase the president's energy and focus.

While Kennedy had a strong innate sexual appetite, his ingestion of cortisone and amphetamines—both known to stimulate the libido—could have played a potent role in his sexual antics in the early years of his administration. As historian Alan Brinkley has written, and as other scholars have concurred, "One of the many side effects of daily cortisone treatments was increased sexual desire." Likewise, a side effect of amphetamines is hypersexuality. Historian Robert Dallek noted that Jack's lifelong sporting pursuit of women only intensified during these years: "Kennedy's womanizing had, of course, always been a form of amusement, but it now also gave him a release from unprecedented daily tensions."

Amphetamines also can cause side effects not advisable in a world leader: nervousness, belligerence, irritability, impaired judgment, and overconfidence. Visitors to the White House in the first two years were greeted by a fidgety president, prone to pop out of his seat in the middle of a conversation and pace restlessly about. Historian William Manchester spent time with Kennedy up-close as his presidency was taking shape. Though he never mentioned any drug use by the president, and was probably unaware of it, he depicted Kennedy as exhibiting hyperactive behavior possibly caused by the effects of amphetamines. Interviewing Kennedy in his study upstairs at the White House a year into his administration, Manchester observed: "His right hand, which is never still—it almost seems to have a life of its own—drums on a matchbook, on the rocker arm, on a shaving scar, on his teeth. His eyes are hooded." The president was given to mood swings, a side effect of amphetamine use. Manchester wrote that cabinet members struggled to keep up with the president's frenetic behavior, observing that his top staff was "displaying symptoms of Kennedy hypomania." Kennedy admitted to Manchester that he was not happy being "always on the edge of irritability," then, the author noticed, "the hand makes a sudden, spastic fist."

The president's amphetamine use was believed in some later accounts to have played a role in his poor performance at his Vienna summit with Soviet premier Nikita Khrushchev in June 1961. Kennedy was jacked up on amphetamine shots during the tense and combative meetings. The summit did not go well. "We cannot discount the impact of Jacobson's chemicals on him," Dallek noted. Khrushchev overpowered Kennedy; the president couldn't hold his own against him. Afterward, Jack was distraught. "He treated me like a little boy, like a little boy," he said of Khrushchev, adding: "he just beat the hell out of me."

The month before his debacle at the Vienna summit, President Kennedy suffered a severe back injury at a tree-planting ceremony in Ottawa, Canada. With an excess of bravado, he had grabbed a silver-plated shovel and scooped at least eight spadefuls of soil onto the base of a twelve-foot red oak. He was left on crutches and so debilitated that later at an economic conference in Washington he had to speak while seated.

The accident, as painful as it was, proved fortuitous. It initiated a thorough revamping of the president's medical treatments. Over the next year and a half, Kennedy entrusted his care to two doctors, George C. Burkley, his assistant White House physician, and Hans Kraus, the future father of sports medicine. After careful examination, Kraus suspected that Dr. Travell's excessive injections of the anesthetic procaine were in fact weakening the president's back muscles. Dr. Nassir Ghaemi, a professor at Tufts University School of Medicine, analyzing the president's treatment years later, speculated that Travell's injections had caused a "probable long-term worsening" of his condition.

Kraus implemented a new approach: a physical regimen that exercised the president regularly in the White House pool and gym beginning in October 1961. He guided his patient through weight-lifting sessions three times a week, daily swims, massage, and heat therapy. "Within months, the improvement was dramatic," concluded a study in the *Journal of Neurosurgery: Spine* in 2017. "Kraus's management of Kennedy's back problems ushered in a period of sustained and remarkable improvement in the health of JFK's back." As he gained strength, the president was seen engaging in activities that earlier had been impossible for him, among them: bending over to hug his children and playing golf.

Kraus was alarmed when he became aware of the heavy amphetamine doses Jacobson was pumping into the president. He was so disturbed that he warned Kennedy in December 1962 that he would publicly reveal the drug use if the shots weren't discontinued. "No president with his finger on the red button," Kraus told Kennedy, "has any business taking stuff like that."

By the start of 1963, Jacobson no longer had a role in the president's care. By June 1963, Travell had been relieved of her management of the president's health. Kennedy quietly moved Burkley into the role of chief White House physician. He kept Travell on his medical staff and allowed her to still be identified as a White House physician, moves intended to discourage retribution and ensure her silence on the true nature of his health. She would join Dr. Walsh on the Cape as a second medical eye on Jackie during her pregnancy.

The president soon was feeling better than he ever had, and was inordinately grateful to his new medical team. His personal secretary Evelyn Lincoln had witnessed his many health struggles during the decade she worked for him. "One day when Dr. Kraus was in the office," she recalled in her memoir, "I overheard the President say to him, 'I wish I could have known you years ago.'"

As the calendar flipped to 1963, a spirit of hope and promise took hold in the White House. Jackie had had a run of high-profile international achievements in the previous year. In March 1962, she had collected accolades as she swept through India, Pakistan, and Italy. In April, she and the president hosted forty-nine Nobel Prize winners at the White House. Two weeks later, the first lady entertained the French minister of culture, André Malraux, and convinced him to loan the *Mona Lisa* to the United States for display at the National Gallery and the Metropolitan Museum of Art in 1963.

In the new year, Jackie turned inward, praying for a private triumph. As she and the president anticipated the birth of their third child, Secret Service agent Hill believed that after Jackie's public successes in 1962, "it seemed that 1963 was only going to be even better."

The president entered 1963 humbled but savvier and more confident than when he first entered office. Over his first two years, the young leader had been sharply tested on the global stage. In April 1961, the Bay of Pigs disaster had threatened to mark his presidency as a failure before he even got his footing. And just two months later at the Vienna summit, he got kicked around by Soviet premier Nikita Khrushchev. But in October 1962, he reversed his fortunes by staring down Khrushchev during the Cuban Missile Crisis, earning plaudits for yanking the world back from the brink of nuclear Armageddon.

President Kennedy had grown increasingly optimistic about America's future and his role as its leader. His two close aides Ken O'Donnell and Dave Powers noticed that a change had come over him in 1963. "He seemed to us to be more forceful and sure of himself, and more relaxed and happier than we had ever seen him," they observed in their joint memoir, *"Johnny, We Hardly Knew Ye."*

In his State of the Union address, Kennedy alluded to his success in his Missile Crisis showdown with Khrushchev, boldly asserting that "the tides of human freedom [are] in our favor.... We have every reason to believe that our tide is running strong." Commenting on the speech, James Reston of *The New York Times* saw in Kennedy a man who was now "buoyantly hopeful." Reston observed: "The truth is that President Kennedy is more optimistic now than at the beginning [of his term] because he feels more on top of his job and can now see the promised land beyond the wilderness."

When James M. Cannon of *Newsweek* visited the White House in April, he found no hint of the fidgety, moody president who greeted William Manchester two years earlier. Instead, on entering the Oval Office, he was struck by "the serenity of the surroundings and the self-possession of the principal." In conversation, the president "was casual. He was affable. He was unhurried, unbadgered," Cannon jotted in his notes on his interview. "In this man, at this moment, there was no evidence that he was worn with the cares of office."

When Cannon asked how things were going, the president replied with a big smile, "Well, I think it's going well. As you know we do have our ups and downs, the tides ebb and flow.... [But] in general, I think things are going well."

Writer E. B. White was intrigued by the balance that had come into Kennedy's life. Here was a president caught in the constant whirlwind of life-and-death decisions that shook the White House. Yet he had grounded himself in the daily humors of fatherhood. White happened to read a brief account of Jack and John Jr. leaving the Oval Office together one day; just as they were stepping out, the father instinctually pulled a white handkerchief out his pocket and wiped his boy's nose.

Inspired by that casual act, White found poetry in the president's days:

One crisis ebbs, another flows,
And here comes John with a runny nose.

⁂

Something else seemed to be taking shape as the months rolled by in 1963. The president was off the amphetamines. His health was vastly improved. He had grown closer than ever to his two young children, and a third was on the way. He and Jackie had eased the frictions that hobbled their marriage and were finding pleasure in each other's company. As a sign of how extraordinary a break 1963 was from his past, Jack began tidying up certain aspects of his extracurricular sex life. He was stepping away from his liaisons with two of his favorite mistresses, Mary Pinchot Meyer and Mimi Beardsley.

Meyer, a sister-in-law of *Newsweek*'s Washington Bureau chief Ben Bradlee, had been Jack's lover since early 1962. She was a forty-two-year-old sophisticated beauty from a wealthy politically prominent family. Jack was dazzled by her "flamboyant eyebrows, piercing green-blue eyes, fine-boned face" and her "amused, arrogant, aristocratic" demeanor, as one acquaintance described her. After at least a dozen visits to the White House (according to entry logs), and possibly many more than that, Meyer had gained a special place in Jack's life. As historian Robert Dallek concluded, "there was no doubt that Meyer meant something more to him than many of the other women did."

But in 1963, Meyer was gradually evolving from a bedmate into a friend whose opinions and perceptions Jack valued. "He could talk in ways she understood, and their trust was mutual," explained historian Herbert Parmet. "She understood all about the pompous asses he had to put up with. When he was with her, the rest of the world could go to hell."

Beardsley, a Wheaton College sophomore, began sleeping with the president when she was a summer intern in 1962 and returned for the summer of 1963. On her second stint, she worked near in the press office and saw the president almost every day he was in the White House. In her 2012 memoir, she detailed the cooling off of her affair in the summer and fall of 1963. "I didn't sleep over in the residence anywhere near as often as I had the year before, because Mrs. Kennedy was expecting another child," she wrote, "and the President spent much more time with her and the children in Hyannis Port."

Beardsley revealed that their sexual relationship wound down through the summer "and it was President Kennedy who had taken the lead." She was young, twenty years old, and happy just to be around the president. She hadn't even noticed she wasn't winding up in his bed as frequently as she once had. "The President was changing the relationship," she said, "and I wasn't seeing it."

SEVEN

Signs of a Healthy, Full-Term Delivery

The summer on the Cape during Jackie's pregnancy kicked off in high spirits over the July 4th weekend. The president had just completed a triumphant European jaunt to Germany, England, Italy, and Ireland, and he and Jackie hadn't seen each other for nearly two weeks. When he stepped off his helicopter on the lawn at his father's Hyannis Port house, Jack embraced his wife with uncommon tenderness in the presence of reporters.

In the evening, the Kennedy clan gathered on the lawn at Joseph Kennedy's home to watch fireworks streak into the sky from nearby Kalmus Park. It was a festive night: bells ringing, bonfires blazing, fireworks exploding, drums beating, fifes and bugles blaring. *The Boston Globe*, straining the English language to capture it all, reported, "Thursday had to be one of the ding-dongiest Yankee Doodling days of 'em all."

In the midst of the celebration, Ethel Kennedy departed for St. Elizabeth's Hospital in Boston, where she gave birth to her eighth child, Christopher George. Ethel, with her hardy childbearing constitution and fierce athletic prowess, played tennis the day before she delivered; and when she arrived at the hospital, she refused a wheelchair, insisting on walking to the elevator that took her to the maternity ward. Two months earlier, Joan Kennedy had suffered a miscarriage in her fifth month of pregnancy. Their outcomes, Ethel's and Joan's, were polar opposites—reminders of pregnancy's stark uncertainties, while Jackie awaited her own day in the coming weeks.

As proof of his renewed fitness, the president played golf over the weekend—just five holes—for the first time in more than two years. Although he bogeyed all five holes at the Hyannis Port Club, he sank a twenty-foot putt, eliciting a smile from Jackie, who watched from a golf cart with her German shepherd Clipper at her side. Back at his father's house, Jack, a joyous prankster, was driving Jackie across the lawn in a golf cart when he spotted a water sprinkler at work. As *The Boston Globe*'s Frank Falacci reported: "He made one careful pass as the moving spray of water looped across the lawn and gave his wife a light dousing."

On Monday, Jack returned to Washington tanned and invigorated and told Ken O'Donnell that he'd just had the "greatest Hyannis Port weekend in many years." He recounted his delight at playing golf, taking cruises on Nantucket Sound, and tumbling around with Caroline and John Jr. "He reported that Jackie, in her seventh month of pregnancy, was healthy and happy."

⸻

The following weekend the president was back. When he touched down at Otis Air Force Base on Saturday, July 13, he was surprised to see his two-and-a-half-year-old son alone, waiting for him with a Secret Service agent. There was no sign of Jackie or Caroline.

John Jr. had persuaded his mother to allow the agent to drive him to the base to welcome his dad. Dressed in light blue shorts, a white shirt, and white shoes, the boy barreled across the tarmac as the president came off of Air Force One. Moving with purpose, the toddler was intercepted by his father, who swept him up and held him in his arms. A short distance away sat the president's helicopter, its rotor blades whirling, ready to ferry him and his chopper-crazy son to Hyannis Port. A photo in the newspapers the next day captured the moment of the father-and-son reunion: the sweet embrace.

But Jack was wise to the reality behind that image. "Every mother in the United States is saying, 'Isn't it wonderful to see that love between a son and his father?'" Jack quipped to his buddy Paul Fay. "Little do they know that that son would have raced right by his father to get to that helicopter but his dad stepped into his path and grabbed him."

In late July, President Kennedy won a hard-fought victory he had pursued since the terrors of the Cuban Missile Crisis. At the close of negotiations in Moscow, representatives of the United States, Britain, and the Soviet Union agreed in principle to slow the proliferation of nuclear weapons. The Limited Test Ban Treaty still faced a difficult path to ratification in the U.S. Senate. But even the Soviets had awakened to the dangers of nuclear Armageddon. During the negotiations, a Soviet representative had declared that nuclear weapons cooperation was essential now that the world had felt "the breath of death" during the Missile Crisis.

While the president understood the threat nuclear weapons posed to the entire world, he felt a particular responsibility to ease the nightmares of children. Schoolkids were all too aware of the stakes. At the height of the crisis, a girl in Massachusetts wrote to a friend, "Can you imagine not seeing another Christmas, Thanksgiving, Easter, birthday, dance, or even Halloween? We're just too young to die."

People closest to the president noticed that his concern for children informed his viewpoint on nuclear weapons. David Ormsby-Gore, Kennedy's friend and British ambassador to the United States, remembered that Jack's approach on nuclear disarmament initially had been the same as it was on any national or international issue: "logical and unemotional."

Then came the thirteen-day standoff with the Soviet Union. "That's when he finally realized that the decision for a nuclear holocaust was his—and that final decision was just over the horizon," Ormsby-Gore said. "He saw it in terms of children—his children and everybody else's children. And then that's where his passion came in, that's when his emotion came in."

When the president escalated tensions on the sixth day of the Missile Crisis by initiating a U.S. naval blockade of Cuba, he happened to see Caroline and her classmates playing outside the Oval Office on the South Lawn. He stepped out onto the portico and clapped his hands to summon Caroline. But she didn't come running as usual, and the president couldn't wait: he had to rush to an emergency meeting in the Cabinet Room.

Racing over about five minutes later, Caroline stopped at Evelyn Lincoln's desk. "Where's my daddy?"

"He's in a meeting in the Cabinet Room, but I wouldn't go in there," Lincoln advised.

"But I *have* to."

When Caroline threw open the Cabinet Room door, she came

upon somber men sitting around a table fretting over the possibility of a nuclear missile fusillade directed at the United States. "Daddy, I would have come sooner," she blurted. But, she explained, her teacher Miss Grimes wouldn't let her go.

Five-year-old Caroline broke the tension. Everybody laughed.

And the president, perhaps reminded by her presence that peace with the Soviets was the only path, said simply: "That's all right, Caroline."

On Friday, July 26, 1963, the day after the Test Ban Treaty was initialed in Moscow, the president spoke to the nation from Washington live on radio and on the three major television networks. He somberly hailed the agreement, reminding Americans that since the creation of nuclear weapons "all mankind has been struggling to escape from the darkening prospect of mass destruction on earth." He repeatedly stressed the importance of protecting children in a world haunted by weapons of mass destruction. "This treaty is for all of us," he said. "It is particularly for our children and our grandchildren, and they have no lobby here in Washington." Today's kids and future generations, he asserted, "are not merely statistics toward which we can be indifferent."

⸻

In late July, a small firestorm broke out over the refurbishments of the VIP wing at the Otis Air Force Base hospital. Several news outlets reported that the Air Force had spent $12,000 (nearly $120,000 in today's dollars) on various upgrades including air-conditioning units, an electric dishwasher, and a garbage disposal. Worse, the special wing in Building 3703 was gussied up with fancy furniture for Jackie's bedroom and the sitting rooms from the posh Jordan Marsh department store in Boston.

The president was furious. He was facing a tough appropriations battle with Congress and couldn't afford the terrible look of excessive Air Force spending on hospital quarters for his own wife.

What most outraged him was a photo in his morning newspaper of a smiling Air Force officer posing beside Jackie's expensive new bed.

The red-hot president phoned Assistant Secretary of Defense Arthur Sylvester and demanded to know what the furniture cost and if the bills had already been paid. "I'd just like to send that goddamn furniture back," he fumed. "I'd love to send it right back to Jordan Marsh in an Air Force truck this afternoon." He ranted about sending the captain in charge of the refurbishing on the truck, too. And he had a plan for the Air Force officer in the photograph. "That silly fellow who had his picture taken next to the bed, have him go up to Alaska."

Next the president got his Air Force aide, General Godfrey McHugh, on the phone.

"See that fellow's picture by the bed," Kennedy said, referring to the newspaper.

"Yes, sir," McHugh said, in a rather subdued voice for a general.

With penny-pinching lawmakers in mind, the president exploded: "Now you know what that's gonna do? . . . You just sank the Air Force budget!"

In a near-mumble, the general said: "Sir, I'm appalled but—"

Kennedy cut him off. "Well, I'm appalled too. I mean, he's a silly bastard." The penitent general tried to explain: "Why, sir, this is obviously—"

The president roared: "Well, this is obviously a fuckup!"

The political firestorm the president feared never ignited. The brouhaha quickly dissipated. But his anger was telling. What most worried Jack may have had nothing to do with politics. He did not want to be reminded of the fallback hospital site at all. Its existence implied a pregnancy crisis and an emergency deviation from Jackie's planned birth at full term at Walter Reed. That was something neither the president nor first lady wished to contemplate.

During the media storm, Frank Falacci of *The Boston Globe* provided a note of prophecy, observing: "If the stork should decide to fly over Squaw Island ahead of schedule . . . Bldg. 3703 at nearby Otis Air Base will catapult into international prominence."

❧

On Saturday, July 27, the president flew to the Cape to celebrate Jackie's thirty-fourth birthday the following day. It was another raucous weekend for the Kennedy clan. "Children almost too numerous to count were running over the Kennedy family compound, the President's leased house on Squaw Island, and the two White House yachts that were here for the occasion," *The New York Times* wrote. When Jack stepped off his helicopter, Caroline and her cousins swarmed him. Caroline called out: "It's my daddy's turn! It's my daddy's turn!"

The children piled onto a golf cart with him for a ride to the candy store. "The kids all yelling 'Uncle Jack! Uncle Jack,'" recalled *Look* magazine photographer Stanley Tretick. "Everybody had heard about the candy store and really wanted [a spot on] the golf cart."

Jack was no longer the forlorn childless uncle. He was now beloved Uncle Jack. He showed special interest in each of the young Kennedy cousins. "He spent a lot of time with them," journalist Laura Bergquist recounted. "I remember one of them would tell him some big long story of something that happened that week, and the President would say, 'Now is that a fact?' treating them very adultly."

Jack's friend Alastair Granville Forbes detected a trait that especially appealed to kids. "The one thing they can't stand is being talked down to," Forbes said. Jack was natural and direct with them. "One of his most amiable characteristics was to say really what was on the tip of his tongue to everybody," Forbes observed, "and children value that more than anything."

As Jack and kids filed into the candy store, he called out: "What's the limit? What's the limit?"

Caroline set him straight: "Everyone gets five cents worth."

Typically without cash, Uncle Jack turned to a Secret Service agent: "Anybody got a buck?"

To which, the ever-attentive Caroline chided her father: "Daddy, did you take us to the store with no money?"

And in the straight talk that the kids loved, he admitted: "Oh Caroline, I've goofed again."

Over the weekend, Caroline was seen cannonballing off the presidential yacht the *Honey Fitz*, as her father and his guest David Ormsby-Gore bobbed in the water, watching. Jackie joined a cruise on the *Honey Fitz* smoking cigarettes in a flowery shift and sunglasses. "Friends at Cape Cod say she has never looked more beautiful or happy," United Press International reported. "She is approaching the time to have her baby in confident anticipation." The wire service noted that Jackie "had excellent care" from two doctors always on the Cape: her obstetrician John Walsh and White House physician Janet Travell. As if wishing to encourage continued good progress, the report added that "if all goes according to plan," the first lady would leave the Cape for Washington to give birth at Walter Reed Army Hospital.

In the afternoon before her birthday party, Jackie hosted a cake and ice cream fete for Caroline and John Jr. and their cousins. In the evening, she took center stage at a small, family dinner in her honor. Strict privacy prevailed. No one spoke to the press. No details emerged about the festivities, about her gifts, and even her cake. The *Globe* led its coverage of the day with lighthearted ribbing over its exclusion: "One of the best kept secrets on Cape Cod is what President Kennedy gave his wife as a 34th birthday present Sunday." The headline topping the story read: "JFK Gift to Wife? CIA Not Told."

Jackie's personal secretary, Mary Gallagher, had combed the shops of Hyannis Port agonizing over a gift for her boss. When she finally found something appropriate, she prevailed upon the first lady's personal maid to slip it onto her Sunday morning breakfast tray. Gallagher, who was not invited to the birthday party, was overjoyed to hear later that her selection delighted Jackie. In her memoir, Gallagher described the piece as "a lovely ceramic pitcher" decorated with figurines "expressing the love between mother and child." It was perfect for the moment, Gallagher knew, as Jackie's "big event" was coming soon.

With her baby's due date fast approaching, Jackie urged chief usher West to complete construction of the White House nursery. She wanted it in a tiny space in the residence known as the "high-chair room" where John Jr. and Caroline often dined—and to keep it simple. Before she lost Arabella in 1956, Jackie had thrown herself into elaborate pre-birth decorating. Ever since, she pursued the low-key and practical in nursery construction.

In a May memo, she had instructed West: "All I want . . . is a pair of curtains like Johns [*sic*] room & . . . white glass curtains you can still see through—like Johns [*sic*]—& a white rug not wall to wall." She wanted someone to purchase "a rather shaggy inexpensive one at Sloanes [*sic*] which we can throw in washing machine—& a rubber pad beneath it."

Looking past the birth, Jackie stepped up planning on a slew of state dinners and White House social events coming in the fall and winter. With Mary Gallagher taking dictation and chasing down details, Jackie organized menus and entertainment. She sorted through possible performers: Margot Fonteyn and Rudolf Nureyev, Maria Callas, Leontyne Price, Alfred Lunt and Lynn Fontanne. She wondered whether she should ask choreographer Jerome Robbins to create a new ballet to be performed at the White House.

Hoping to regain her pre-pregnancy figure, Jackie asked Gallagher about a machine that helped new mothers get back in shape; unsure what it was called, she described it as "a vibrator with a big strap." She wanted to know the brand and where one could be purchased.

She had begun working with fashion designer Oleg Cassini on a "post-natal wardrobe." But she didn't limit her search to Cassini. She had an aide "ask quietly" if designer Gustave Tassell "had anything she might like—especially something she could wear to the baby's christening."

She also was throwing herself into planning for her tenth wedding anniversary in September. Working with usher West, she was overseeing production of three sophisticated scrapbooks as a present for Jack, charting his years in the White House. "Enough work went into those scrapbooks to qualify them as fine art books," West said.

During the summer, Jackie sometimes ignored her doctor's edict to avoid vigorous activity and instead gave in to her spirited sense of play. Before her pregnancy, West had seen her romping at the White House with Caroline and John Jr. "Jacqueline Kennedy enjoyed playing as much as the children did," he wrote in his memoir. She played "exactly as a child plays." Seeing Jackie "so happy, so abandoned, so like a little girl who had never grown up," West observed, "*this* was the real Jacqueline Kennedy."

West also saw Jackie in her role as first lady, performing "with such grace and authority." But at those times, he believed, "she was just pretending. She really longs for a child's world, I thought, where she can run and jump and hide and ride horses. I thought of her as an actress—constantly playing a role."

On Squaw Island, she couldn't resist the urge at times to play freely. One afternoon Mary Gallagher was working alone in the upstairs office at Brambletyde when she glanced out the window. There in a shallow inlet behind the house was Jackie late in her pregnancy standing up in a canoe. Caroline and John Jr. were seated waiting for the fun to begin. Jackie was slowly moving the canoe along, pushing the paddles into the shallow bed first on one side, then the other. Mother and children were alone playing in complete privacy. Panicked, Gallagher tracked down a Secret Service agent. "Will one of you men please go out there and get Mrs. Kennedy off that canoe?" she instructed.

Agent Lynn Meredith raced to the rescue. He sprinted out back, kicked off his shoes, and waded into the water. By then, Jackie and her young seafarers had become stuck in the mud. To Gallagher's relief, Meredith "soon had Jackie and the children back on dry land."

On Friday, August 2, the president landed on the Cape for his fifth straight weekend visit. When he stepped off of his Marine helicopter at the family compound in Hyannis Port, Caroline and John Jr. raced up to their father, still in his suit looking presidential.

Little John attached himself to his father's legs and bounced up and down as Jack patted him on the bottom. The president bent over a little stiffly and wrapped an arm around Caroline's waist as she grabbed him around the neck to give him a big hug. Jackie, in a pink, sleeveless maternity dress, gave Jack a peck on the cheek, and he briefly took her hand—both small gestures but in previous years unseen.

With each passing week, the president and first lady had many reasons to celebrate the approaching birth, not the least of which was that all signs pointed toward a healthy, full-term delivery.

Only once was there a moment of panic. It was either on this weekend or the previous one: Jack's friend Assistant Secretary of the Treasury James Reed recounted the incident in a Kennedy Library oral history but wasn't sure on which of the two weekends it occurred.

In the morning, Reed recalled, Jackie awoke feeling ill. Jack sat with her, held her hand, and comforted her. "President Kennedy was extremely solicitous of Jackie," Reed recalled. "He was quite concerned about her."

Reed and a small posse set off to hunt down Dr. Walsh. But when the ad hoc search party could not locate him for nearly an hour, the president became "very, very upset," Reed remembered.

At last, Walsh showed up, with a reasonable explanation for being out of reach: he was out on a walk. He quickly examined the patient and delivered the good news: Jackie was just fine.

But Jack was shaken. The scare revealed just how tense these final weeks were. He and Jackie were all too familiar with the sudden trauma of premature birth. With uncharacteristic severity, the president instructed Walsh: "I just hope that if you do go off for a walk for any period of time that you always tell someone where you are, how you can be reached immediately, in case I do have to get in touch with you."

Just days after Jackie's scare, the president invited Mary Meyer to the White House for an evening visit. What occurred between them on August 5 is a matter of debate between scholars. Barbara Leaming, who has written biographies on a range of figures, from Orson Welles to Winston Churchill, asserted that Meyer's visit resulted in Jack "thoughtlessly carousing with another woman."

But Leaming also noted that at this point in his life Jack was in the process of transformation. "He was a man who had been taught to take his pleasures as and when he wished, without guilt of any kind," she wrote in *Mrs. Kennedy: The Missing History of the Kennedy Years*. "In August 1963, Jack Kennedy was no longer the same man. Most important, of course, he had had the experience of loving two children of his own." Leaming acknowledged that Jack had changed so much that this particular assignation with Meyer elicited something new in him: "he was feeling an emotion with which he had theretofore had little acquaintance: guilt."

Sally Bedell Smith, author of *Grace and Power: The Private World of the Kennedy White House*, among others, also believed that Jack was evolving in the summer of 1963. But she suggested a different interpretation of his rendezvous with Meyer. Smith conveyed through the comments of artist Anne Truitt that Kennedy and Meyer spent several hours together that night in innocent camaraderie.

Anne was married to James Truitt, a journalist and executive at *The Washington Post*, who moved in high circles in Washington. Through him, she was introduced to figures in the Kennedy world and was entrusted with certain confidences. She told Smith that by the summer of 1963 Jack viewed Meyer as "a friendly familiar diversion." The suggestion was that by then Jack appreciated Meyer more for her conversation than for other pleasures. Truitt believed that Jack's relationship with Meyer was transforming "from what it might have been in terms of sexuality into friendship." For Jack, this kind of progression in a relationship was not extraordinary. He kept on good terms with former lovers whose company he enjoyed. "Certain women from his past," observed biographer Sarah Bradford, "remained his friends and close to him long after anything sexual between them was over."

EIGHT

"This Baby Mustn't Be Born Dead"

On the morning of August 7, nanny Maud Shaw was preparing for a day off, but a glimpse of the first lady gave her second thoughts. Shaw was a diligent, sixty-year-old English nanny and nurse, a gentle disciplinarian standing five-foot-two and typically attired in a white uniform. "I noticed that Mrs. Kennedy was looking rather pale and worn-out," she recalled. She offered to stay home and look after Caroline and John Jr. But Jackie wouldn't hear of it.

"Oh no you don't," she insisted. "You go off and enjoy your day off."

So Shaw, as she later put it, "rather against my judgment," went to meet a friend in the village of Sandwich to relax on the beach and swim in Cape Cod Bay.

At the White House, President Kennedy started his Wednesday morning as he did most every other day when he was in Washington.

His longtime valet George Thomas tapped on his bedroom door at 7:45 and entered with the president's breakfast and a stack of newspapers. Seated in an armchair, Kennedy ate poached eggs and crisp bacon from a tray, sipped orange juice and coffee, and pored over the newspapers and his briefing books.

Shortly after 9 a.m., the president went downstairs to the Oval Office for his first meeting, with Kentucky Democratic congressman John C. Watts, a tobacco grower. Watts, whose district included Bourbon County, was a strong advocate of whiskey distillers who felt threatened by a possible surge in imports. In the visitor log, the meeting was stamped "OFF THE RECORD."

President Kennedy then walked to the Cabinet Room for his most important session of the morning. Around the table were twelve men who made up a newly formed private group called the Citizens Committee for a Nuclear Test Ban. After its signing, the treaty had entered its precarious uphill battle for ratification. A strong public campaign was needed to bring pressure on balking senators and other high-profile opponents.

One chief critic was the "troubled genius" Edward Teller, a dominant figure in the creation of the hydrogen bomb; others were former defense chiefs of staff and some members of the military. Critics feared the treaty would give the Soviet Union an edge in nuclear weapons and would harm America's defense. Standing in the way of the treaty's wide acceptance were countries wishing to build or expand their arsenals.

Enactment of a test ban was, in the words of the president's aide Ken O'Donnell, Jack's "cherished ambition." But the treaty scarcely registered with the public. Americans who had been terrified by a U.S.-Soviet nuclear confrontation ten months earlier seemed to have moved on. The president had learned that letters pouring into the White House mail room showed by a large margin that Americans had less interest in a possible humanity-saving nuclear test ban treaty than in the care and feeding of Caroline's pony Macaroni.

To raise awareness and galvanize the public, Kennedy that morning presided over an off-the-record conversation with the Citizens Committee for a Nuclear Test Ban, composed of business leaders, public relations specialists, and prominent figures. Among its members were Walter Reuther, the powerful president of the United Auto Workers, and nuclear disarmament advocate Norman Cousins, who served as a private conduit between President Kennedy and Soviet premier Khrushchev. Also around the table were several administration figures, including aide and speechwriter Ted Sorensen and the president's brother Attorney General Robert Kennedy.

Over a half-hour, the citizens group discussed strategies to sell the treaty to Americans and leaders across the globe and to bring pressure to bear on senators such as Barry Goldwater of Arizona and detractors serving in the military.

An energized Kennedy took a personal role in directing the participants, advising them on which senators to target, how to rouse their constituents, which business leaders to mobilize, and how to sway Americans who remained unconvinced. The president even reviewed and approved the group's newspaper and TV advertisements.

On the Cape, Secret Service agent Paul Landis pulled up to Brambletyde to chaperone Caroline to her horseback-riding lesson. Landis was filling in for Clint Hill, Jackie's primary agent, who had a day off. Usually at Jackie's side working long hours, on this day in the dead of summer, Hill was catching up on his sleep inside the small cottage he rented near Hyannis Port.

Agent Landis, at twenty-eight, was the youngest member of the children's detail entrusted to protect the president's kids. In the previous administration, the unmarried Ohio native had been assigned to the so-called Kiddie Detail and charged with looking after President Eisenhower's grandchildren. Code-named Debut, a nod to his youth, Landis was playful and boyish, more like a young uncle to the Kennedy kids than a Secret Service agent.

Stopping in front of the house, Landis was surprised to see Mrs. Kennedy come out holding her daughter's hand. He expected her to stay close to home on this warm, sticky day late in her pregnancy. Only once, in mid-July, had she accompanied Caroline to her riding lesson. But today she chose to climb into the backseat of the Secret Service Ford sedan along with her daughter. The trio—Landis and the two Kennedy females—went slowly down the gravel driveway, followed by Special Agent Lynn Meredith, head of the Kiddie Detail, in a second vehicle. Meredith was a musician and bore the Secret Service code name Drummer. A much-loved traveling companion, he liked to bring donuts on long rides and to sing with the kids.

The two-car caravan bumped along rutted roads for for about fifteen minutes until it rolled to a stop in a dust cloud at the Allen Farm in Osterville. Mrs. Kennedy, in a summery cream-colored maternity shift, sunglasses, and straw hat, walked toward a farmhouse that overlooked the riding ring. "Mr. Landis," she said, "I'm going to be sitting here on the porch."

Caroline trotted off to the stables and soon reappeared astride her pony Macaroni. Her trainer led her into the ring, and the five-and-a-half-year-old went through her paces. Landis and Meredith positioned themselves along the fence surrounding the ring.

After a short time, Mrs. Kennedy came down from the porch and walked slowly toward the riding ring. "Mr. Landis, I don't feel well," she informed him. "I think you better take me back to the house."

Caroline was intently focused on her horsemanship and hadn't noticed her mother's movements. "If we could just sneak off quietly," Mrs. Kennedy whispered, "we should do that."

As Landis escorted Mrs. Kennedy to the sedan, she betrayed no sense of urgency, no trace of panic. The agent ruled out an immediate trip to the hospital. Instead, the best option was to get the first lady swiftly back to Brambletyde, where Dr. Walsh could have a look at her and make a ruling. "She did not seem distressed at all," Landis recalled in an interview for this book. "She was being very calm."

When he pulled onto the country road, Landis grabbed the car's communication radio. Whenever Mrs. Kennedy or the children were in transit, their movement had to be reported to the Secret Service's command center outside Brambletyde. Ensign George Dalton, an assistant to President Kennedy's naval aide, was on duty inside the trailer. Dalton was a master of transportation logistics for the White House; if you needed to launch a crisis operation, he was the one you wanted in charge.

Landis filled Dalton in: he and Mrs. Kennedy were leaving the Allen Farm for Squaw Island, Meredith was staying behind with Caroline. Then came the agent's bombshell: "I think she's going into labor."

Dalton was to notify Dr. Walsh and get him over to the house. Agent Hill had to be tracked down; he was needed at Brambletyde. In the event Mrs. Kennedy needed urgent transport to the nearby 551st Air Force Hospital at Otis, Landis instructed Dalton: "Call and have a helicopter on standby."

From his perch inside the Secret Service trailer, Dalton began pulling the levers on a well-rehearsed emergency plan.

Agent Hill was in a deep slumber when the phone jangled in his

Hyannis Port cottage. He brought the receiver to his ear and recognized Ensign Dalton's voice: "Clint, Mrs. Kennedy is going into labor. You better get over here."

Hill threw on some clothes, grabbed his credentials and his gun, and jumped into his car. He sped toward Brambletyde.

Dalton kept dialing, one call after another. A crew of doctors, nurses, medics, ambulance drivers, helicopter pilots, Secret Service agents, White House staff, and Jackie's close aides had all repeatedly drilled for just such a scenario. "No member of the 551st Hospital really believed that the First Lady of the country would have her baby at Otis Air Force Base," recalled the hospital commander Dr. Paul Stavig. But that hadn't stopped Stavig from running the emergency exercises. Since the first lady would most likely arrive by helicopter, ambulance crews had performed test runs to and from the landing pad. Ambulance drivers had also mapped out the safest and fastest road routes to Squaw Island should bad weather prevent air travel.

A fleet of three helicopters was always at President Kennedy's disposal at the air base. Dalton placed a call, and in minutes a chopper was airborne to Squaw Island.

Participants across the base started moving into position. Donors with Jackie's fairly common blood type, A-1 RH positive, had already been identified among the airmen; they were ordered to the hospital to open a vein should Mrs. Kennedy need a transfusion.

Whenever Jackie was away from Brambletyde, her personal secretary Mary Gallagher migrated from the porch upstairs to a desk inside the Secret Service trailer down the driveway. She was there tallying Jackie's expenditures when Landis's voice crackled on the communication radio.

Her ears pricked up. Listening in, she realized Mrs. Kennedy was possibly going into labor "several weeks ahead of schedule!" The Otis base hospital was certainly not Walter Reed Army Hospital. Would it be up to the task? She worried, "Would everyone at Otis be on duty?"

Glancing at Ensign Dalton hard at work on the phones, Gallagher saw the reality hitting him: "His face was almost white."

⸻

His anxiety intensifying, Landis guided the Ford sedan carefully along the bumpy road. "I was going about as fast as I dared go," he recalled in his interview for this book. Too much speed "and your stomach would go up to your throat and then back down like a roller coaster."

He kept glancing in the rearview mirror, checking on his passenger. But her eyes told him nothing. "She was wearing sunglasses," Landis explained. "She always had sunglasses."

But then a hint came from the backseat: "In that hushed, whispery voice, she said, 'Mr. Landis, can we please hurry? Can we go a little faster?'"

Brambletyde was still several miles away, and Landis had no idea if matters were progressing in the backseat and, if so, how swiftly. In panic, he laid his foot on the accelerator. "So, there I was," he recalled, "a bachelor, the youngest agent on the protection detail, alone, in a car racing down a country road . . . with the First Lady of the United States in the backseat, and she's having labor pains."

When he reached Craigville Beach northwest of Squaw Island, Landis hit the brakes: the posted speed limit was ten miles per hour, enforced by speed bumps. The sedan crawled along, dodging beachgoers darting across the road. With a few miles still to go, Mrs. Kennedy sounded increasingly distressed. "She keeps saying, 'Mr. Landis, a little faster, please go a little faster.'"

Landis suddenly realized—should it come to it—he had no idea how to deliver a baby. He once read something in a survival book: if you were ever in a car with a woman in labor, it was best to get her into the backseat; then, have her put her feet up against the front seat and push. But at this moment, Landis had a hard time imagining such a scenario: "I'm thinking to myself, in an emergency here, the two of us could be in a rather intimate situation." The last thing he wanted was to be coaching the first lady through childbirth at the side of a country road. "I did not quite envision myself being with her and saying, 'Okay, Mrs. Kennedy, one, two, three—push! One, two, three—push!'"

His only recourse, the agent realized, was to beg the Almighty for deliverance. "Please God," he prayed, "don't let her have this baby in the car. Please let me get to the house in time."

Liz Mumford and her mother, longtime residents of Hyannis Port, were out on Nantucket Sound for a morning sail when they spotted a chopper scudding overhead toward Brambletyde. Though they weren't friends of the Kennedys, the women were aware that Jackie was on Squaw Island resting through the summer until her baby's expected birth in September. Liz's mother had an ill feeling. "Jackie's gone into labor," she told her daughter. "She's gone into labor, and it's way too early."

⁂

Turning onto Squaw Island Road, now minutes from the house, Landis caught sight of the helicopter overhead. He was glad to see it descending toward a clearing beside the residence. He slowed to a stop at a sentry post on a narrow causeway providing the only access to the six estates on the Squaw Island marshland. The officer, recognizing Landis and his passenger, waved them through.

Landis drove Mrs. Kennedy along the gravel road leading to

Brambletyde. When he passed the Secret Service trailer at the end of the driveway, he began to relax. At last, he came to a stop at the front porch. Seconds later, Landis saw Dr. Walsh rolling up behind him. Off to one side, the chopper was settling onto the ground, its whirling blades kicking dirt skyward.

"Wow," he sighed to himself. "We made it. Perfect timing."

Dr. Walsh hurried toward the car as Landis ran around to open the back door for Mrs. Kennedy. The agent eased her out and handed her off to Walsh.

"I think I'm going to have the baby," she told the doctor.

Walsh supported Jackie by the arm, assisting her up the steps. They went through the front door into the high-ceilinged entry hall and crossed the dark pine floor to the staircase. Walsh took her slowly up to the second floor, where they entered her bedroom and the door closed. Inside, the doctor began a brief exam.

In the Secret Service trailer, Mary Gallagher heard the cars crunching along the driveway and the roar of the chopper touching down. She swept her ledgers, bills, and pads into her briefcase and pushed it to the side of the desk.

"I felt there must be something I could do—certainly not sit here, working at figures," she recalled.

She ran out with a shorthand pad and a pencil in hand, ready to take notes, if Mrs. Kennedy asked. She trotted up the driveway with Ensign Dalton and found Landis seated in the sedan still recovering from his close call at midwifery.

Gallagher had debated what to wear that morning. Expecting another warm day, she first thought of pulling on a pair of comfortable slacks and Keds. She could dress down because Jackie would be away at the stables and she'd be cooped up in the trailer.

But something told her to reconsider her outfit. Instead of the slacks and Keds, she chose a light dress and heels. As it turned out, she was properly attired should Jackie need her by her side as the day progressed. Commending herself for her "feminine intuition," Gallagher went inside the house and waited in the front hall for Dr. Walsh and his patient to come down the stairs.

When the first lady, now dressed in a pink and orange print dress, made her way down leaning on Dr. Walsh, she smiled at Gallagher.

"Hi, Jackie," Gallagher chirped, "if there's anything you need or that I might do . . ."

"Oh, no, thanks, Mary," Jackie replied wearily.

Upstairs, Dr. Walsh confirmed that this baby wasn't waiting for a September delivery at Walter Reed in Washington. Once again, Jackie was entering the harrowing uncertainty of premature childbirth.

⸙

Hospital commander Stavig had plans to go fishing in the afternoon. But his chances of an outing had shrunk to near zero as he fielded a flurry of calls from presidential aides, doctors, and Navy personnel. The dispatching of a helicopter to Squaw Island confirmed that a potential emergency was in the making.

When he picked up his office phone, Stavig wasn't surprised to hear Dr. Walsh's voice on the line from Brambletyde: "I'm bringing Mrs. Kennedy to the hospital."

Key personnel were swiftly moving into action. Major Mary Waters, the chief nurse at the base, unlocked the doors of Building 3703, the VIP suite. She was joined by Captain Catherine Adams, who oversaw the maternity ward. The two women scrambled to get the suite ready for Mrs. Kennedy, the president, and their entourage. Two other nurses hurried over to the ward: Lieutenant Barbara Goodwin, who was to look after Mrs. Kennedy from 3 p.m. to 11 p.m., and Lieutenant Nancy Lumsden, who would take the overnight shift, 11 p.m. to 7 a.m.

Dr. Charles Sanislow, the hospital's chief of surgery, was at home picking up two fishing rods for his boss Stavig, who had asked to borrow them for his afternoon outing. On his drive back, Sanislow's hospital radio sounded with the alert that Jackie was on her way. Dr. Sanislow, who would assist Walsh during the delivery, sensed a sudden end to his quiet summer day. "I went right to the hospital, made sure everybody was ready for the delivery," he said in an interview for this book. "I got the operating room crew, the scrub nurse, and everybody else ready to take care of her when she arrived."

By coincidence, it was "Caesarean Wednesday," the day each week that the obstetrical team scheduled caesarean procedures. A delivery had just wrapped up and the operating team already had begun preparing for the arrival of First Lady Jacqueline Kennedy.

Outside Brambletyde, Dr. Walsh helped Jackie cross the lawn toward the waiting chopper, explaining to Landis: "We need to get her to the hospital right away."

Watching the scene, Gallagher felt terrible: "I couldn't stand to see her going off alone." She hurried to Jackie's side: "Impulsively I asked, 'Would you like me to come along?'" When Jackie's eyes brightened, Gallagher fell in with the procession to the helicopter.

While Jackie was still within earshot, Dr. Janet Travell came out the front door. From the top of the steps, she hollered into the roar of the chopper blades: "Mrs. Kennedy! Would you like me to call the President?"

It wasn't clear why Jackie chose to answer the way she did. But she made her wish clear. Before boarding the helicopter, she answered Travell in a single, unequivocal word: "No!"

Agent Landis was hurrying toward the chopper when he realized

Agent Hill hadn't turned up at the house. "No Clint!" he thought. He turned and shouted to Ensign Dalton: "Get ahold of Clint, tell him what's happening, and where we're going!"

Landis, the last to board, dropped into a seat behind Jackie and Dr. Walsh. "By the time I buckled in, it was wheels up," he recalled. As the aircraft lifted over the Cape, Landis looked out the window "and watched Brambletyde grow smaller and smaller."

Dalton dashed down the driveway to the Secret Service trailer. Agent Hill was speeding toward the house when he grabbed his car radio phone.

Dalton updated him: "Clint, they're taking the helicopter to Otis."

Hill hit the brakes, turned the car around, and headed toward the hospital.

"Okay," he said, "I'll meet them there."

As her chopper sailed over the Cape, Jackie fell into a panic. "Dr. Walsh," she pleaded, "you've just got to get me to the hospital on time! I don't want anything to happen to this baby."

Walsh took her hand and patted it. "We'll have you there in plenty of time."

Her longtime obstetrician was known for his kind, self-effacing manner. Though often swarmed by reporters, he strove to keep out of the media circus. After delivering John Jr. in 1960, he acknowledged to the press that he was uncomfortable in the presence of cameras and microphones, admitting he was "far more at ease in the operating room."

While boaters and swimmers frolicked on the idyllic seascape below, Jackie was haunted by her tragic stillbirth several years ago that suddenly seemed horribly present again. Dr. Walsh could do little to calm her nerves.

"This baby," she begged him, "mustn't be born dead."

Despite Jackie's protest, Dr. Travell hurried down the driveway to the command trailer and phoned the White House.

Jerry Behn, head of the president's Secret Service detail, took her call at 11:40 a.m. and immediately walked over to the president's personal secretary Evelyn Lincoln just outside the Oval Office. Lincoln caught the urgent look on the agent's face. Behn was a husky forty-five-year-old, whose jaws were often in motion chewing gum, his prescription for relieving tension.

"They called me from up at the Cape," he whispered to Lincoln, "and told me that Mrs. Kennedy was on her way to the Otis Air Force Base Hospital."

Lincoln's heart sank.

"Did she say she wanted the President to know?" she asked.

"No," Behn said.

Lincoln immediately phoned Brambletyde in search of Mary Gallagher. Unable to track her down, she spoke with a worker in the kitchen who happened to pick up the call. Gallagher wasn't there, the worker explained; she went with Mrs. Kennedy to Otis hospital.

"Why did she go to Otis?" Lincoln asked.

"To have the baby, I guess," the worker answered.

After his third meeting of the morning, a brief chat with departing Ecuadorean ambassador Neftalí Ponce Miranda, President Kennedy came out of the Oval Office and stopped at Lincoln's desk to shuffle through some papers. At the edge of her desk sat a well-stocked candy dish that tempted all passersby: cabinet secretaries, members of Congress, generals, and Caroline and John Jr. It had been a favorite stop of Caroline's since her early days in the White House. When John Jr. learned to walk, he was quick to discover the sweets awaiting him. He plunged his hand into the dish, *Time* magazine's Hugh Sidey observed, as soon as "he could navigate to the Oval Office on his own two energetic legs."

For Jack, the dish was a sentimental tradition: first Caroline, then John, and now it awaited a new sibling. As the days ticked off toward the birth, the excited president often reminded his personal secretary: "Mrs. Lincoln, soon you will have three coming over to get candy from your candy dish."

While the president hovered over the desk, Lincoln and Behn remained silent. Neither wanted to be the one to divulge the news. The two exchanged a glance, and Lincoln realized it was up to her.

"Jerry tells me," she began, "that Mrs. Kennedy is on her way to Otis."

The president took it calmly.

His first instinct was to get ahold of Dr. Walsh. But he quickly corrected himself: "No, he will be with her. Call the house."

Lincoln phoned Brambetyde and got the same kitchen worker who had no further information. But he helpfully pointed out, "Dr. Travell is here. Maybe you can talk to her."

He ran off to track her down.

When Travell came on the line, Lincoln handed the phone to the president. Travell confirmed that Mrs. Kennedy was in a helicopter with Dr. Walsh on the way to Otis.

She signed off, promising to come back shortly with more information. Scarcely two minutes later she was on the line again: Dr. Walsh, she said, was preparing to perform an emergency caesarean.

"Mr. President," Travell said, "don't worry, Jackie will be all right."

"I'm coming up," he told her, "as fast as I can."

⁂

The president tossed aside the rest of his agenda for the day.

A sudden burst of activity erupted around Lincoln's desk. Aides and

Secret Service agents converged, then ran off, throwing together plans to rush the president from the White House to the Otis Air Force Base hospital.

With Jackie's condition unknown and the baby still unborn, President Kennedy wanted to keep a tight lid on the news. But his instructions got lost in the morning's chaos.

When Ken O'Donnell learned of the emergency, his reflex was to inform the White House press office. And press secretary Pierre Salinger, expecting a story of this magnitude to spread fast unofficially, immediately began putting together a news bulletin.

The president didn't reiterate his wishes to his press secretary when he phoned him a short time later, assuming he understood the delicacy of the situation and would protect Jackie. Kennedy mentioned only that Salinger needed to get himself ready for a swift departure to Otis.

"I was in my office," the press secretary remembered, "when the President called and told me to be ready to leave the White House in five minutes."

Salinger then rushed "cigar in hand . . . into the lobby of the Executive Wing calling for the wire services and other newsmen," *The New York Times* reported.

UPI White House correspondent Helen Thomas remembered: "Salinger burst into the West Lobby announcing that Kennedy was leaving in five minutes for Hyannis Port. Jackie was on her way to the hospital at Otis Air Force Base for a caesarean section."

In minutes, the news flashed across the country. Newspaper editors saved space in their afternoon editions for coverage of the birth.

Maud Shaw had finished her morning swim with a friend in the waters off of Sandwich. On their way back, she turned on the car radio and heard the bulletin: Jackie, in premature labor, "had been rushed" to the hospital. Shaw had had a premonition the moment she looked into Jackie's drawn face that morning at Brambletyde. Now she put an end to her day off and hurried back to Squaw Island.

From his desk in the Oval Office, President Kennedy himself phoned the Anacostia Naval Air Station in Washington. Three twelve-passenger helicopters were on twenty-four-hour alert whenever the president was in town. A pilot and a copilot, dressed in flight suits, and two cabin crew members sat in a ready room poised to fly into action at a moment's notice.

The men knew the procedures almost by reflex. One of the pilots would take the incoming call while the other immediately raced out to begin powering up a chopper. The aircraft were just a twenty-second sprint away, ready, if necessary, to whisk the president to a top secret secure location in the event of an impending attack on Washington.

On this day, there was no attack but an emergency nonetheless.

With the helicopter en route, the president phoned his Air Force aide, General Godfrey McHugh. He wanted to know how long it would take to get a presidential jet ready to fly.

"Thirty minutes," McHugh told him.

"I want to fly now," the president insisted. "So get ready."

But there was a hitch: Air Force One was not available.

The president had three fully equipped jets at his disposal. But all three were out of position. No one had anticipated an emergency, of course, and the president had no plans to fly anywhere today.

"We had trouble finding a plane," Ken O'Donnell remembered. "One of his Air Force jets was in Moscow with a group of test ban treaty negotiators, another was being repaired and a third one was on a flight a half-hour away from Washington."

McHugh advised the president that the Air Force had several small, four-engine JetStar aircraft as possible stand-ins. But these aircraft were slower, had just twelve seats, and were not outfitted with the communications gear the president needed.

Since Kennedy's entourage included not just his closest aides but many others, he'd need a small fleet of JetStars.

"We'll need three of them," he told McHugh. "On the ramp within ten minutes."

The president then called Larry Newman, his longtime friend and Cape Cod neighbor. Newman was an affable journalist who had worked for the Hearst newspapers and had known Jack since 1945. He threw the first cocktail party in Hyannis Port celebrating Kennedy's election in 1960. "Here he was for years just a boy running around the neighborhood," Newman recalled, "and all of a sudden he's one of the most powerful men in the world."

Jack had a favor to ask of his buddy.

Newman had noticed the chopper coming in to land at Brambletyde. He already surmised that Jackie had been taken to Otis to give birth.

"I want you to go over there and just sit in the lobby of the hospital until I get there," Jack requested. He wanted Newman "just to be there for Jackie."

"I'll go right away," Newman assured the president and jumped into his car.

The helicopter from Anacostia Naval Air Station floated onto the White House lawn six minutes after the president had placed his call. Minutes later, Jack and his closest staff hustled through a drizzle toward the whirling blades and were airborne. Traveling with him were Evelyn Lincoln, Pierre Salinger, Ken O'Donnell, Jackie's press secretary Pamela Turnure, General Godfrey McHugh, and two Secret Service agents. Two more helicopters would arrive shortly to transport other White House aides and members of the president's entourage to the waiting jets at Andrews Air Force Base.

Elspeth Rostow, a foreign policy expert, presidential scholar, and the wife of Kennedy's special adviser Walt Rostow, showed up early for an Oval Office meeting. But the president was nowhere to be found.

"I've never seen anything so disorganized," she told biographer Sarah Bradford. "Evelyn Lincoln wasn't there and the Secret Service, as I checked in, said, 'We don't know what's happened.' But then we suddenly saw the chopper going off."

Touching down at Andrews Air Force Base, the president and his entourage quickly crossed the tarmac to a TriStar jet, which soon was hurtling down the runway and lifting into sky.

The mood aboard was somber.

"We all sat in silence," Lincoln recalled.

Pamela Turnure remembered: "It was a very quiet trip."

The president sat alone.

Turnure kept an eye on him: "He was very withdrawn. He just kept staring out of the window."

NINE

"Please Let the Baby Be All Right"

When Jackie's helicopter touched down at Otis Air Force Base, an ambulance was waiting. Jackie was lifted into the vehicle, the rear door was closed, and Staff Sergeant Nelson Stevens sped his patient to the emergency entrance in three minutes. The converted barracks on the scrubby terrain was far from luxurious. But appearances were deceiving: the Otis hospital staff was of the highest caliber. Medical corpsmen rushed forward to help Jackie onto a stretcher. "She did not lie down," Gallagher noticed, "but sat on the edge, smiling bravely."

Agent Hill reached the hospital just in time to see Jackie sitting up on the gurney. Where Gallagher had imagined bravery, Hill sensed a "deeply worried" mother in premature labor. He kept close to the first lady as she was rolled toward the entrance.

"It's going to be okay, Mrs. Kennedy," he assured her.

He placed a hand on her arm, and the first lady and the agent had a quick comforting look at each other.

"We both knew what the other was thinking," Hill recalled in his book *Mrs. Kennedy and Me*, written with Lisa McCubbin. "Please God . . . please let the baby be all right."

Inside the hospital, Jackie's first stop before surgery was the prep room. "You clean the patient up and try to shave what you need to shave and put a catheter in her bladder," Sanislow explained in an interview.

Jackie, concerned about her privacy, drew attention to a bare window high on the wall about eight feet up. Sanislow believed it was nearly impossible for anyone to see in. "But," he added, "I understand her reacting that way." Staff was ordered to climb up and cover the window.

Jackie had another request.

"She wanted a cigarette," Sanislow recalled. "But she didn't want any cigarette. She had to have a Newport."

But no one had a Newport. Since cigarette machines were banned inside the hospital, the closest place to buy a pack was the base PX or the flight line where aircraft were parked and serviced. Somebody raced out and quickly returned with the Newports needed to satisfy Jackie's craving. She then was fixed with an IV line and given her first blood transfusion.

Dr. Eugene McKee, a general medical officer assigned to the Otis pediatric service, was attending to a just-delivered jaundiced newborn when he heard clattering in the adjoining operating room. He poked his head through the swinging doors to find a nurse preparing for an emergency caesarean.

"Why don't you hang around?" the nurse said.

A minute or two later, Dr. McKee recalled, Jacqueline Kennedy was rolled into the room. "Devoid of makeup, her face pale in the overhead light, she betrayed little anxiety as she was transferred to the operating table," McKee recounted. He had imagined Jackie as "a delicately featured, fragile lady," but now he "was struck by the strong facial structure, broad shoulders, and sharply defined muscles of her upper arms."

When the surgery team was assembled, Dr. Walsh asked: "Who's here for the baby?" His assisting nurse nodded at McKee, noting that he was on the pediatric service. "No longer a spectator," McKee recalled, "I got myself ready." He quickly scrubbed up and donned his gown and gloves.

Jackie and Dr. Walsh had a brief conversation, then surgery commenced. He was assisted by Sanislow and an Air Force team of about a dozen physicians and nurses. The anesthesiologist, Oklahoman Major Frank Mahan, performed his task, later saying Jackie experienced a "beautiful, normal" anesthetic, explaining that "beautiful" meant "uneventful."

Agent Hill stationed himself outside the operating room door, pacing back and forth, trying not to think about what was happening inside. He kept his mind on tasks he had to organize once Jackie emerged. "Who needs to be contacted? What will she need and want from the house? How do we keep the damn press away?"

Mary Gallagher had trailed Jackie as far as possible through the corridors toward the prep room until medical staff turned her away. She retraced her steps and found a lounge, where she fielded calls from Kennedy family members. But there was only silence from the operating room, and she had nothing to report. "The next hour," she recalled, "was excruciatingly long." She did the only thing left to her: "I kept watching the clock."

About 1 p.m., Dr. Walsh, still in scrubs, emerged briefly from the delivery room. Mrs. Kennedy, he told Hill, gave birth to a boy at 12:52 p.m. She was doing fine.

As for the baby, Walsh said, "We have some concerns about his breathing."

"What do you mean?" Hill asked.

"We've put him in the incubator and we'll know more in a little while."

⟡

The boy, born six weeks early, was underweight at four pounds, ten and a half ounces and somewhat undersized at seventeen inches in length. He was a well-formed child with light brown hair. But as he was lifted out of the womb headfirst, he mustered only a weak cry.

The newborn was handed to Dr. McKee. "Immediately, it was apparent the infant was in distress," he recalled.

Doctors tried to ease his labored breathing. But suctioning his mouth and nostrils didn't help much. The infant still fought for air. His skin was bluish. A stethoscope placed on his chest detected shallow, rapid breaths. Doctors wrapped him in warmed blankets and placed him into an oxygen-infused incubator. The team would keep him under close observation, suction the mouth and nose to keep the passageways clear, and hope his breathing improved.

None of the modern tools routinely deployed today to treat premature babies was available. No respiration devices to assist breathing. No special drugs to address lung deficiencies typical of premature infants. Medical science still didn't understand the physiology of babies born before full term. Well-intentioned doctors and nurses had no reliable strategy to ease the suffering of newborns like the Kennedys' and guide them to health.

McKee was pleased that the modest interventions—suctioning, supplemental oxygen—brought some improvement: the baby was grunting a little less as he strained to breathe. "Then, most welcome," McKee noticed, was "a short, shrill cry which repeated intermittently." Since the Kennedys' son had modestly improved, the team prepared to transfer him to the nursery, which was under the charge of Captain William Jablonski, chief of pediatrics.

On the baby's chart, a doctor jotted an initial medical finding: idiopathic respiratory distress syndrome. It was less a diagnosis than an early-stage preliminary assessment of most pre-term babies, raising few alarms yet providing little comfort. Its meaning was simply "difficulty in breathing for reasons unknown."

Nurse Mary Waters tracked down Mary Gallagher in the lounge and delivered the news: "Mrs. Kennedy has given birth to a baby boy! Born 12:52."

Gallagher now had a headline to pass along but nothing more. Nurse Waters conveyed only a standard good-news report: that mother and child were doing well. Mrs. Kennedy, she said, would be coming back to her room shortly.

Gallagher recalled: "We were all excited and happy."

Word of the birth spread quickly through the base. The wives and children of servicemen began streaming toward the hospital, congregating behind ropes set up on the scrub brush outside Jackie's VIP suite. The crowd, full of good cheer, watched the comings and goings, hoping for a glimpse of the president.

The spectators had fun proposing names for the infant. One woman thought it appropriate to call the child Otis; another offered Andrew or Joseph or some "nice, old fashioned" name. A thirteen-year-old boy named Harvey Delaware knew exactly what the newest Kennedy should be called: Harvey, of course.

⸻

The president touched down at Otis Air Force Base at 1:28 p.m., unaware he had missed his son's birth by thirty-six minutes. Hustling into the hospital's VIP wing, he came upon his friend Larry Newman. Overcome with emotion, Jack began to awkwardly embrace him but caught himself, and the men shook hands.

"We'd known each other for so long," Newman recalled, "but I'd never seen this depth of feeling before. He was very emotional and deeply worried."

The president set off with Agent Behn in search of Jackie. In the lounge, he found Mary Gallagher, who leaped up to greet him. She shook his hand and offered her congratulations. "His eyes were wide, eager for information," she recalled.

She blurted: "I'm happy to announce that you are the father of a new baby boy!"

He smiled weakly and thanked her, but his mind was elsewhere.

He wanted to know, "How's the baby?"

She told him the latest report: both mother and child were doing well. She added encouragingly: "I'm sure he's just fine."

The president blurted: "Where's Jackie right now?"

When she told him Jackie hadn't come back from the delivery room, "he took off like a flash."

President Kennedy came upon Agent Hill outside the operating room. Mrs. Kennedy, the agent told him, was still under sedation. Hill chose to keep silent about the baby's condition and advised the president to have a word with Dr. Walsh.

"I didn't know how much he knew at that time," Hill recounted, "and I didn't want to be the one to tell him there might be a problem with his newborn son."

Dr. Walsh let the president know of his son's breathing difficulties; the infant, Walsh said, was being closely monitored. It was too early to know how his condition would play out.

⁂

When nurses and medics wheeled the still-sedated first lady toward her room, the president was at her side. He watched from the corridor as the medical staff moved his wife from the gurney to her bed. When her door closed, he joined his sister Jean in the lounge. Jean, who was vacationing on the Cape, had dashed to the hospital the moment she caught the news on the radio. Mary Gallagher, still fielding phone calls, was repeating over and over that as far as she knew the first lady and the baby were both in good condition.

Waiting for his wife to awaken, Jack and his sister fell into conversation about the Kennedy family's birthing history as if, Gallagher surmised from her eavesdropping, "they were trying to pinpoint and understand Jackie's troublesome births."

Some in the family, including the matriarch Rose Kennedy, laid the blame on Jackie's heavy smoking, a habit she took up in Miss Porter's school. Though some doctors had begun pointing to cigarette smoking as a potential danger to developing fetuses, a general public warning hadn't yet been issued. The landmark surgeon general's report on smoking would be published in January 1964, still five months away.

Jack may have contributed to his wife's difficult pregnancies as a result of his active sexual behavior over many years. While a senior at Harvard in 1940, he contracted a venereal disease that presented the symptoms of chlamydia which persisted for years. Today, chlamydia in pregnant women is known to cause premature labor, low birth weight, and fetus development outside the uterus resulting in miscarriage.

Biographer Sarah Bradford asserted that the cause of Jackie's birthing troubles "was almost certainly chlamydia, contracted from Jack." Bradford speculated that Jack in all likelihood hid his condition from Jackie not just because he was reluctant to talk about his health but because he didn't want her to know he had a transmissible venereal disease. "Although in fairness she should have been the first to be told," Bradford wrote, "he would almost certainly have preferred her to be the last."

When Jackie regained consciousness, Jack was ushered to her bedside. She was still groggy after a traumatic childbirth that required two transfusions. She was in no condition to hear troubling details about the state of her son's health. Her recovery, her husband and doctors believed, would be aided by a compassionate parceling out of concise updates. So Jack kept the information to a minimum. Jackie knew that prematurity challenged a baby's lungs, and Jack assured her that doctors were keeping a close eye on their son's breathing.

After his brief visit, the leader of the free world was in such a rush to see his newborn son that he wound up alone wandering aimlessly in search of the nursery. He had no one to guide him—no doctor, nurse, aide, Secret Service agent—until he bumped into twenty-five-year-old Air Force medic Richard Petrie.

"The next thing I knew," Petrie recalled, "The President of the United States is staring me in the face."

The president shook the medic's hand, asked him his name and where he was from.

Lexington, Massachusetts, Petrie told him.

And the president said: "Ah, a Lexington boy."

The president, clearly lost, said he was looking for his son.

"Come on," said the young medic, "I'll show you the way."

Petrie escorted the president to the nursery door.

On his way back, the young medic was intercepted by an agitated Secret Service agent.

"Have you seen the President?" the agent snapped.

"Sure," Petrie told him.

He described his pleasant encounter and his delight at leading the worried father to his son. The agent, it seemed, was under intense pressure for having lost the president—and for his own service to the commander in chief, Petrie earned a snarling reprimand: "You can't just walk the President around unsupervised!"

Inside the nursery, the president found Dr. Walsh and a team of doctors and nurses gathered around his son's incubator. The isolette, as it was called, was a warmed plexiglass rectangular box with a mechanism at the base that pumped in oxygen; two portholes on either side permitted staff to tend to the baby with minimal oxygen escaping.

After shaking hands with each staff member and thanking everyone for their dedication, the president stepped up to the incubator. He rested his chin in his palm and gazed down at his ailing son for the first time. Through the clear top, he studied his boy's tiny arms, his feet and his hands, the perfectly shaped head, the light brown hair. He watched his son working hard to draw each shallow breath. As his boy sucked oxygen into his lungs, his nostrils flared. Exhaling, he drove out the tiny amount of air he inhaled, pinching his vocal cords together, creating a distinctive, high-pitched noise that filled the room. Some doctors called it "grunting." Others said this was the sound of a baby "singing."

The president noticed a bluish tint to his son's skin. In place of a healthy reddish tone, the infant had a translucent grapelike coloring, warning of an insufficient flow of oxygen to nourish the body. The ailment was known as cyanosis, a combination of the Greek terms *cyan*: blue, and *osis*: process, or abnormal condition.

Since the baby's early hints of improvement, doctors had detected a slight deterioration: his breathing had become more rapid and more labored, requiring an increase in the oxygen pumped into the incubator. The level had to be carefully calibrated. Too much oxygen risked blindness while too little could cause brain damage. While the baby's condition was unstable, the outlook among his doctors remained "cautiously optimistic."

Hovering over his fragile son, Kennedy was both president and parent: the charming world leader who looked, in the eyes of Dr. McKee, "tanned, shorter than I had thought, with a sun-induced auburn tint to his hair," but also any pained father "standing in profile by the incubator, arms folded, one hand cupping his chin, gaze focused on the frail wisp of humanity lying before him."

In the sweltering afternoon heat, press secretary Pierre Salinger, dressed in a suit and tie, crossed the stark grounds outside Building 3703 and stopped in front of three standing microphones. Staked into the ground some distance away was a spindly wood sign: "USAF Hospital," bearing a medical red cross. A lone scrub pine fluttered in a light sea breeze.

Reading from a sheet of paper, Salinger spoke in a monotone to a cluster of reporters: "Mrs. Kennedy has given birth to a four pound ten-and-a-half-ounce baby boy. The baby was born at 12:52 here at the Otis Air Force Base hospital."

There was no joy in his voice.

He said the child was premature, having arrived five and a half weeks early, which conflicted with the six weeks that doctors had indicated. He did not mention the infant's respiratory distress.

"The baby's condition," Salinger read, glancing at his script, "is described by the doctors as good and Mrs. Kennedy's condition is described as good."

⁂

Before leaving the nursery, President Kennedy had a brief conversation with Dr. Walsh. Like all premature infants, the First Couple's son was born before his lungs were fully developed. His fate, Walsh explained, would be determined over the next forty-eight to seventy-two hours. His lungs needed time, and luck, to build enough strength to function outside the womb.

When the president asked for the odds of survival, Walsh gave him the sobering truth: the boy had a fifty-fifty chance.

The president hurried off in search of Agent Hill.

"Clint," he said, approaching him in a hallway. "Find the base chaplain. We need to baptize the baby right away."

The boy in his incubator was rolled out of the nursery into a private room for the ceremony. Father John Scahill, a Roman Catholic priest, delivered an abbreviated liturgy, as was common for babies at risk of imminent death. As a small assembly looked on, he reached through the portholes to splash holy water on the baby's forehead while murmuring the rites in Latin.

Jack and Jackie's son was christened Patrick Bouvier Kennedy. He quickly became America's baby, suddenly so well-known and so beloved he was spoken of in familiar terms. The headline on a *Boston Globe* story about Patrick's doctors declared: "They're on Pat's Medical Team."

After the baptism, Patrick was rolled back to the nursery for continued observation. As the incubator went by, Agent Hill got his first look at the newborn and was moved by the perfectly shaped head and tiny hands and feet. "He was beautiful," Hill recalled. "But he was clearly fighting for each breath, as his poor little chest struggled to get the oxygen he needed to survive."

A father of two boys, Hill wanted to protect the infant but knew there was nothing he could do except pray. "As soon as I saw him, tears welled in my eyes," he recounted. "He looked so alone in the sterile incubator."

In the corridor, the president again ran into the obliging young medic Richard Petrie and pulled him aside confidentially.

"What do you know about televisions," Jack asked in a low voice.

"Well, sir, I can turn one on and off," he said.

The president told Petrie there was a television in Mrs. Kennedy's room, and he was concerned that news coming out of that box might upset his wife.

Nothing more needed to be said. The medic beelined to the first lady's room. While nurses were attending to her, Petrie slipped behind the television and took care of the president's request. He silently destroyed a vacuum tube or two, then tiptoed from the room.

When he found the commander in chief, Petrie was pleased to report that the set was "no longer working, sir."

In Washington, the Senate was debating an appropriations bill when Democratic leader Mike Mansfield of Montana asked his colleague Senator Joseph Clark Jr. of Pennsylvania to yield the floor.

"I yield," Clark said.

"The good news has just reached the Chamber," Mansfield announced, "that President and Mrs. Kennedy have announced the birth of a son."

Senators rose to their feet in applause.

Seated next to Mansfield, filling the position of Senate president pro tempore, the chamber's temporary presiding officer, was Senator Ted Kennedy.

"It is coincidental and historic," Mansfield explained as the president's youngest brother stood next to him applauding the announcement, "that on this happy occasion, the . . . uncle of the newest Kennedy, is in the chair."

In mid-afternoon, Dr. James Hughes, the chief resident in pediatrics at the Children's Hospital Medical Center in Boston, took a call from Otis Air Force Base. On the line was a man who identified himself as Dr. John Walsh. Hughes, who among his duties oversaw new admissions, assumed the call would be like any other: a routine inquiry seeking advice on an ill child or a transfer to Children's.

The caller, speaking in a calm, businesslike tone, told Hughes he was the obstetrician for First Lady Jacqueline Kennedy. He explained that Mrs. Kennedy had gone into premature labor and had given birth at the air base hospital on Cape Cod. The infant, Walsh said, was in respiratory distress. "I would like to transfer him up to Children's. Can you arrange that?"

"Yes, sir, we can," Hughes replied.

Hughes promised Walsh he'd get on it immediately.

But as soon as he hung up, he froze: "Could this be a hoax?"

He wasn't up on the latest news: he didn't even know the president's wife was pregnant. Before possibly blundering into a bad joke, he grabbed the phone again.

"The first call I made was to my wife," he recounted in an interview for this book.

She was fully up-to-date on the Kennedys' day and she set him straight: yes, Jackie was pregnant and she had just delivered a premature boy.

Hughes set to work: he alerted the hospital's admissions staff and the chief of hospital services to prepare for a new patient: the son of the president of the United States.

During its 103-year history, Children's Hospital had established itself as a world-famous institution known for its cool efficiency and topflight care. Just a month earlier, doctors had performed successful open-heart surgery on a seven-day-old infant. Boston was home to some of the world's finest doctors and, if additional specialists were needed, they could be quickly located within the city's vibrant medical community or flown in from other locations. Young patients from around the world flocked to the hospital. Over the previous year, nearly 150 children from Africa, Asia, Europe, and Central and South America came for treatment of ailments ranging from congenital defects to cancer and leukemia. Princess Madawi Abdullah, an eight-year-old niece of King Saud of Saudi Arabia, was at the hospital receiving therapy for polio. She was seen on the ward wearing leg braces and taking small steps with the aid of crutches and a nurse.

Patrick was assigned to a private room, No. 2534, on the fifth floor of Farley Building across the hall from the nursery. Orderlies cleared out a large supply closet next door to the room and hauled in a bed, dresser, and chair so the president could sleep near his son, if he wished.

In each room along the corridor were two to four older children suffering from a range of illnesses or recovering from accidents.

⸻

Dr. James Drorbaugh, a leading expert on infant respiratory ailments, was busy seeing patients at his Boston pediatric practice when an urgent call came in from Children's. Drorbaugh, known for his "quiet authority," was forty-one years old with degrees from Princeton and Columbia University College of Physicians and Surgeons. He had studied the pulmonary physiology of newborns under the father of the field, Clement A. Smith at Boston Lying-in Hospital. He also served as an instructor and attending physician at Lying-in and was an associate in pediatrics at Harvard Medical School.

Drorbaugh listened as Dr. Hughes described the condition of the First Couple's newborn on Cape Cod. The president, Hughes said, had requested that Drorbaugh himself fly immediately to the Cape to advise on care and to escort his son to Children's.

Drorbaugh at first didn't seem to absorb the import of the call. Or perhaps he was stunned. "Well," replied the busy pediatrician, "I've got a lot of patients in the office. . . ." Then it hit him: Hughes was talking about the president of the United States, his baby was in crisis, and he, James Drorbaugh, was to race to the Cape for a consultation, then oversee care of the ailing infant at Children's.

Once Drorbaugh grasped the gravity of the president's request, Hughes recalled, "he managed to get somebody else to take care of his other patients."

After the call, Drorbaugh took a moment to collect his thoughts. "The first thing I did," he recounted, "was take out the shoe shining kit I had in my desk drawer and shine my shoes. I think that was a reflex action to give myself a chance to adjust to what just happened." Then his professionalism kicked in: "I grabbed my doctor's bag and went outside to hail a cab." He told the driver to head quickly to the National Guard hangar at Logan Airport. There he was met by uniformed Air Force personnel who hustled him onto a military helicopter. In minutes, the doctor in his light-colored summer blazer was racing toward Cape Cod.

Amid the day's tumult, the president had forgotten to eat. While waiting for Drorbaugh's arrival he asked around if there was anything in the suite that might serve as lunch. His dutiful medic buddy, Richard Petrie, took up the call. He raced to a small kitchen, which was minimally stocked and outfitted and, so far, apparently unused. Opening a cabinet, Petrie saw the shelves were bare except for some brand-new china—and one can of tomato soup. He found a saucepan, got the stove working, dumped in the soup and some water, and waited.

Once the soup was heated, he confronted another crisis: "No soup bowls, no salad bowls, nothing," he recalled. And the president was waiting. "So I grabbed a dinner plate, put the saucepan on it, grabbed a soup spoon, and brought it to him."

It was no way to serve the president of the United States, the young medic knew, but he had no choice. He presented Kennedy with the soup still steaming in the saucepan and handed him the spoon. "I'm sorry, sir," he said, "but we have no bowls."

In Petrie's eyes, the president became in that instant a common man, just like himself, grateful for even a meager lunch. "He just smiled," the medic remembered, "and ate the soup out of the pan."

When Dr. Drorbaugh landed at Otis Air Force Base he was hurried off the chopper and driven to the base hospital, where President Kennedy came outside to greet him. The doctor, his medical bag in hand, followed the president into the VIP wing to Patrick's room. Peering into the enclosed incubator, Drorbaugh perceived that the infant "was in significant respiratory distress." He saw that baby Patrick was breathing at a rapid rate "and grunting, with lots of effort going into each breath."

There was no doubt, both doctors Walsh and Drorbaugh concurred: Patrick needed to get to Children's as soon as possible. The Boston hospital offered no magical cures and no revolutionary, life-saving treatments—none existed for lung-compromised premature infants—but there were top specialists on site or nearby. And just across the street at Boston Lying-in Hospital was a blood gas machine, one of the few in the nation, that read oxygen and carbon dioxide levels in the blood. It was an excellent tool for monitoring fluctuations in the baby's condition.

President Kennedy agreed that Patrick would be better off at Children's. But he worried about separating the baby from his mother. He wondered, could the specialists and instruments in Boston be transported to the Cape? Drorbaugh told the president that to replicate at Otis the many advantages of Children's Hospital and its environs was impossible. Time was of the essence. Bringing in specialists and equipment would require long hours and knotty logistics.

At 5:25 p.m., President Kennedy and Dr. Drorbaugh walked alongside Patrick's incubator as a nurse wheeled him through the hospital corridors toward Jackie's room. Jack had the delicate task of introducing mother and son for the first time, then informing her that Patrick was leaving for treatment in Boston.

Dr. Drorbaugh kept the explanation for the move to the bare facts. He told the first lady that Patrick had some breathing difficulty and that the best care was available at Children's. Jack tried to soften the blow by reminding Jackie that John Jr. also had lung issues common to premature newborns, and he overcame them.

So far, Jackie had been given only slender, hopeful reports on Patrick's health. Now she confronted a stark reality: if her son was being rushed to Children's, then his condition clearly was much worse than she had been led to believe.

⁂

Jackie was granted a few rushed minutes to get to know her son. His incubator was rolled to her bedside. She saw Patrick's labored breathing for herself. A porthole was opened to permit a painful, brief moment of intimacy. Jackie slipped her hand inside and touched his delicate skin and moved her fingers through his hair. Then the porthole was closed, and she watched as her baby was rolled out of the room. In minutes, he would begin his journey to Boston.

Jackie was left in a fog of unanswered questions. Marooned in her room, she was, according to those close to her, "very distressed."

Press secretary Salinger approached reporters hanging around outside the entrance to the VIP wing. Patrick, he told them, was leaving Otis for Children's Hospital. Reporters had ferreted out on their own that the baby was suffering from a respiratory ailment. Salinger provided no additional details, explaining only that the Boston institution was better equipped than Otis to treat the newborn. The transfer to Children's was, in Salinger's words, "a precautionary move."

Agent Hill was torn over whether to travel with Patrick to Boston or stay with Mrs. Kennedy at Otis. Over their three years together, the Secret Service agent and the first lady had developed an ironclad bond. The strapping thirty-one-year-old Hill grew up in a loving family in a tiny town on the plains of North Dakota. His mother was hearing-impaired, a disability that made him an attentive son: "I learned to anticipate her needs and was always protective of her," he explained. The trait served him well when attending to Jackie: he had learned to interpret the first lady's wishes from a flicker of the eye. Hill felt a tremendous loyalty to both the mother and her ill child. But he decided to stay with Mrs. Kennedy while she recuperated from surgery and grappled with her anxiety over her son's uncertain future. "I had to be there for her," he concluded.

Agent Landis was designated as the baby's escort. But nobody had informed him specifically why Patrick was leaving Otis. "I didn't know what kind of condition he was in, how serious things were," Landis said in an interview. He just assumed the president's child could expect top-notch care at Children's.

Mary Gallagher got a quick peek into the incubator as Patrick was wheeled out: "He lay on his back, almost motionless." He was so tiny his oversized hospital name band dangled on his wrist.

With Patrick's departure, a pall fell over the hospital wing. What began as cheers over his birth and overstated declarations of his good health now succumbed to the sobering truth. "It was a very sad, shocking moment for all of us . . . to know how sick the baby was," Gallagher recalled, "and from that moment our cheerfulness was forced."

TEN

"He's a Kennedy—He'll Make It"

At 5:50 p.m., Patrick was placed into a dark blue ambulance. The president watched alongside Dr. Sanislow, the chief of surgery at Otis. Even in the most trying of moments, the president was stirred by his natural curiosity.

Kennedy turned to Sanislow and asked: "Is that a Cadillac?"

"No, Mr. President," Sanislow replied. "It's a Pontiac."

Dr. Drorbaugh climbed in back next to the incubator. Agent Landis took his place in the passenger seat beside the driver. Helicopter transport had been nixed because of uncertain weather conditions.

The ambulance with its single, rooftop emergency light rotating pulled away from the hospital in a caravan of police cruisers and motorcycle cops. Spectators stopped to watch as the motorcade headed north along Route 28 over the Bourne Bridge, ending up on the Southeast Expressway to Boston.

"I recall seeing crowds of people on nearly every overpass," Drorbaugh said.

As Dr. Hughes awaited Patrick's arrival at Children's Hospital, his pager went off, calling him to the phone. When he picked up, a voice said: "Dr. Hughes, are you the chief resident responsible for the Kennedy baby's admission?" He acknowledged he was and the voice said: "The President of the United States wishes to speak to you."

President Kennedy came on the line to check on his son. Hughes informed him that Patrick hadn't arrived yet, a room was being prepared for him, and, as far as he knew, the baby's condition was stable. The doctor spoke to the president as he would any inquiring parent. He wanted to be "respectful and aware of the pressure upon him as a father having a sick baby."

As the ambulance approached the city, Metropolitan District Commission Police were waiting at the Roy C. Smith Bridge at the Milton–Boston line to take over escort duties. Three MDC cruisers and two motorcycle patrolmen guided the ambulance through the thinning rush-hour traffic on the expressway to the Storrow Drive exit.

Traffic officers were in position on Boston streets at Leverett Circle and at Back Bay intersections to smooth the motorcade's passage along Boylston Street and Park Drive along the Fenway to Avenue Louis Pasteur then on to Longwood Avenue. By then, five more police cruisers had joined the parade.

A little after 7 p.m., after a journey of about an hour and twenty minutes, the ambulance rolled up to the Blackfan Street entrance of Children's Hospital, the vehicle's rotating emergency light announcing the arrival of tiny Patrick Bouvier Kennedy.

Crowds had congregated at points all around the hospital, uncertain where the ambulance would finally stop with the Kennedy baby: at the Emergency platform or at one of the entrances. Boston police, the Secret Service, and the hospital's private security agents worked to keep back the throng. Security also was tight inside the building. Four men had taken up position in the lobby, and two Secret Service agents were in position upstairs on Patrick's floor.

After his seventy-mile journey Patrick, lying in his incubator, was lifted out of the ambulance, placed onto a gurney, and wheeled through the lobby to the elevator. Dr. Drorbaugh, two state police officers, and Secret Service agent Landis accompanied the baby to the fifth floor. Several minutes earlier nurses had circulated along the corridor instructing parents and their children to remain in their rooms. As the president's son rolled past in his plexiglass box, eyes full of curiosity peered from the doorways.

Outside Room 2534, eight doctors—senior staff at Children's and specialists from Boston Lying-in—awaited the patient and followed the incubator inside. James Hughes, the chief pediatric resident, had a quick look at baby Patrick. "He didn't look like a healthy bouncing baby boy," Hughes recalled in an interview. "But he didn't look like a baby in extremis." Patrick's coloring gave Hughes a hint of optimism: to his eye, the baby's skin wasn't tinted blue but rather a hopeful pink.

Doctors immediately set to work: they removed the portable oxygen canister used inside the ambulance and connected the incubator to an external oxygen tank. Patrick was briefly removed for chest X-rays, which, as expected for a premature infant, revealed a haziness in the lungs. An IV line was inserted to keep him hydrated. Blood was drawn from his navel to evaluate his oxygen and carbon dioxide levels. A fairly large amount, about a cubic centimeter, was needed for an accurate reading on 1960s instruments; that is about ten times the amount needed for similar readings today. The sample was packed in ice and hurried to the blood gas machine at Boston Lying-in.

"We had to run it down in the elevator from the fifth floor at Children's, out onto the sidewalk, and across the street, to the lab at Boston Lying-in," Hughes explained. "Fortunately, there were a couple of hematology fellows who could run pretty well."

The lab tests showed that Patrick had too little oxygen in his blood and too much carbon dioxide. Dr. Drorbaugh boosted the oxygen flow into the incubator in hopes of spurring improvement.

Doctors and nurses would continue to monitor Patrick's vitals and keep him as comfortable as possible. "There wasn't all that much once we got him into the room that we could do," Hughes lamented. The finest medical minds in the nation had no modern neonatal devices or treatments to lift the tiny baby's chances of survival. The most doctors could do in Patrick's case was to chart his course: Was he improving or deteriorating? Slight adjustments could be made in oxygen flow or the warmth of the incubator, but no one could predict with any certainty the impact of those actions. The medical team served essentially as observers looking on as Patrick, just hours old, waged his own solitary battle for life.

At the Otis air base hospital, President Kennedy and his sister Jean Kennedy Smith climbed into a white convertible and rode to the house on Squaw Island. He let the kids know that their mother was doing well but their new baby brother had a little trouble breathing, so he was taken to see doctors at Children's Hospital in Boston.

While Jack was with Caroline and John Jr., nurse Luella Hennessey arrived at the hospital to look after Jackie. Hennessey had been assisting Ethel Kennedy at Hickory Hill since she had given birth in July. When she heard about Jackie's emergency delivery on Cape Cod, she jumped into the car and raced to Otis. Mary Gallagher was relieved to see the experienced, fifty-seven-year-old nurse and family friend. Her presence was, in Gallagher's view, "the very best start . . . for Jackie's recuperation."

Jack briefly visited Jackie again at Otis before leaving for Boston. Arriving at Logan Airport, he was greeted by a small but vocal crowd, apparently unaware of Patrick's frailty. "They screamed and jumped up and down like campaign crowds," recounted *The Washington Evening Star*'s Mary McGrory. The president, "unsmiling" and "somber-faced" at first, "seemed faintly cheered by their enthusiasm and waved a bit." He crossed the tarmac in a blaze of flashbulbs and climbed into the cruiser of Boston Police commander Edmund McNamara.

His motorcade screamed away from the airport with lights flashing and headed toward the Sumner Tunnel. At the Longwood Avenue hospital entrance, a throng awaited the president. "As he stepped out of the car," *The Boston Globe* reported, the anguished father looked "very pale." Someone called out "Good luck!" and Kennedy, expressionless, turned toward the voice.

At the door, the president was greeted by the hospital's acting director, Lendon Snedeker. The men disappeared inside and hurried up to the fifth floor. As the president walked quickly toward his son's room, he was eyed by three young pajama-clad patients crouching in a doorway.

Before entering the room, the president pulled on a white gown and mask. Inside, a team of specialists hovered around Patrick's isolette.

Doctors had deployed all the measures at their disposal: the IV line was in, oxygen was flowing into the incubator from an external tank, and a monitor was tracking the baby's heart rate.

Jack listened intently as doctors laid out the uncertainties of Patrick's fate. Dr. Drorbaugh warned that Patrick was still in serious condition. His breathing was labored. His heart was under strain, and his blood oxygen level was precarious. William Bernhard, a pioneering pediatric heart surgeon at Children's who was called in for consultation, said the president was "very congenial," though obviously careworn by his son's predicament. "Just like all parents, he was very concerned," Bernhard remembered. "He was a good parent and a wonderful father, and you could tell that."

After a long day, the president left Patrick in the hands of the specialists and headed for the Ritz-Carlton hotel. Stopping at a newspaper kiosk at the corner of Huntington and Massachusetts Avenues, Jack leaned out of the limo's back window and bought the evening papers from a surprised vendor. At the Ritz-Carlton, the staff had hurriedly prepared for the president's unexpected arrival. Its finest suite awaited him outfitted with newly installed direct telephone lines to Washington.

For the Kennedy clan, the Ritz-Carlton was a familiar comfort: the family had kept a suite of rooms there for years. Patriarch Joe Kennedy first lodged at the hotel soon after it opened in 1927. John Kennedy began visiting the place as a Harvard undergraduate in the 1930s. "He used to come over here from Cambridge and get his hair cut in the hotel barber shop," recalled a longtime employee, pointing to the very spot where the clipping took place. "He was a nice young man too."

⁂

Shortly after 10 p.m., press secretary Salinger stepped before reporters in a makeshift pressroom at the Statler Hotel. For the first time he acknowledged that Patrick had a breathing ailment, identifying it the way doctors did, as "idiopathic respiratory distress syndrome." Playing down the seriousness, he explained that the condition was not uncommon in premature infants. But he acknowledged it was "a cause for concern." He told reporters it would be four days before doctors could "make a final diagnosis."

A reporter pressed Salinger on the outlook for the baby: "Is it on the danger list?"

"I would not say that," Salinger replied.

"Would anybody else?" the reporter ventured.

"Well," Salinger snapped, "nobody that I talked to has."

He then revealed that Patrick was baptized soon after birth, prompting a reporter to ask why so quickly.

"I would rather not comment on that," Salinger answered.

In his suite at the Ritz-Carlton, Jack called Jackie twice around midnight. Wishing to keep her spirits up, he tilted his words toward the positive. "The President assured Mrs. Kennedy," the United Press International reported, "that everything was all right."

His calls had the intended effect. Jackie's mother, Janet Auchincloss, arrived at the hospital late in the evening and visited Jackie around midnight. She told a reporter that her daughter was in "remarkably good condition" and "awfully happy that everything was going well."

⸻

During the night, an enterprising photographer with a telephoto lens sneaked upstairs in a building opposite Children's and found a window in line with Patrick's room. While chief resident James Hughes hovered over the incubator, the photographer clicked off a series of shots.

Days later a grainy black-and-white image dominated the cover of

Life magazine under the headline: "Hospital Vigil over the Kennedy Baby." The photograph through the cross panes of Patrick's window showed an unnamed doctor—Hughes—in scrubs and a white mask, head bowed, looking down at what was the baby's incubator, though all that was visible on the cover was a fuzzy black smear in the lower-right corner. Standing beside Hughes was a nurse, her starched white cap perched high on her head, her face an indistinct blur.

A four-photo spread inside the magazine was blurrier than the image on the front: doctors and nurses moving about, their heads dark splotches against a gray-lighted background.

The magazine's report featured one more image, a particularly intrusive one. A *Life* photographer had managed to shove his way into a Children's Hospital elevator with President Kennedy for a candid, close-up shot that filled a full page. In the photo the beleaguered president is pinned against the elevator's back wall, shoulders hunched, arms crossed, eyes staring downward. The headline read ". . . A Worried Father Visits His Stricken Son."

Neither Hughes nor the nurse had any idea they were under press surveillance while looking after Patrick. Hughes learned of his anonymous fame only after the edition hit newsstands: "Somebody called us and said you're on the cover of *Life* magazine." Hughes embraced his anonymity. He had no wish to go public. "There was nothing magical about the moment," he explained. "It isn't as if I held up a newborn baby for the world to see. I was there attending as best we could as this kid struggled for breath."

Through the night, the crowds outside the hospital dwindled. Very late, a few onlookers drove up and scanned the entrance until police shooed them away. Inside, on the fifth floor, two Secret Service agents kept watch outside Patrick's room. It was mostly quiet on the floor as nurses and medical staff attended to the other young patients.

Telephone callers from across the nation and the world lighted up the hospital's switchboard until about midnight, asking after the president's baby and offering medical advice.

At daybreak Patrick's battle for life burst into a full-blown national sensation. News photographers had staked out both hospitals, on Cape Cod and in Boston. Television cameras and newspaper photographers had captured the incubator being placed into the ambulance at Otis and being unloaded in front of a crowd at Children's. Photographers competed intensely to snap a prized image of the baby himself, but none ever appeared.

Lendon Snedeker got an early peek at Patrick and told the press: "He's a loveable little monkey." Speaking of the boy's light brown hair, he added: "I wish I could say it has a touch of Irish red in it but it hasn't."

Asked how doctors were treating Patrick's breathing issues, Snedeker said the newborn was getting "tender, loving care, medication, oxygen and everything else we can do to correct these symptoms."

In Boston, the *Globe* and *Herald* blanketed the streets with frenzied coverage. "BABY SPED TO HOSPITAL," screamed the *Globe* across its front page. The paper, relying on Salinger's timeline, laid out the dire prospects: "4 Days Will Decide Infant's Chances." While Patrick's plight was disheartening, one *Globe* headline was a cry of confidence: "He's a Kennedy—He'll Make It."

Wire services and newspaper correspondents sent Patrick's tale ricocheting from coast to coast and around the world. "He is only 4 pounds 10½ ounces, but Wednesday he held the heartstrings of the world in his little red fists," wrote the *Globe*'s Gloria Negri. "In Washington, Bonn, Squaw Island, Hyannis Port, Rome, Paris and in the Kremlin, heads of state waited upon his every move along with the peasant in the field and the man on the street."

Morning in Boston was already afternoon in Europe, where news kiosks announced the First Family's woes. Parisians adored Jackie. In Paris, editors of *France-Soir* declared over seven columns: "Anguish of the Kennedys." *Paris Jour* supplied a brief biographical portrait of the first lady, raving that she had "the prettiest smile in the United States." In London, the *Daily Express* announced in a headline two inches high: "Jackie's Boy Ill." The *Daily Mirror* told the story: "Jackie Has a Boy—Ambulance Dash to Save Him." The *Daily Herald* summed up the crisis in three words: "Kennedy Baby Drama." In Frankfurt, the front page of *Abendpost* proclaimed: "A Son for the Kennedys—But the Baby Is Sick." Newspapers in Soviet-occupied East Berlin ignored the story.

Some foreign papers pointed out Jackie's history of troubled pregnancies and caesarean births. Swedish commentators took it upon themselves to provide medical enlightenment to the first lady, advising that "an abortion might have been recommended rather than a third surgical birth." *Le Monde* sympathized with Jackie, whose maternal tribulations were now worldwide public fodder: "The White House must be a glass house."

The president and first lady's exalted position, glamour, and wealth were of no matter now: they were just Jack and Jackie, the same as any parents confronting an illness of a child. Traumas like these, the *Buffalo Evening News* wrote, were "the great leveler."

In church and at home, Americans kept the Kennedy family in their thoughts. A "prayerful watch" had erupted, one paper said. It was not just Americans, but everyone everywhere, *The New York Times* reported: "The world shares President Kennedy's vigil at the cribside of his new son." As the *Times* observed, matters of state yielded to the sacred mission of a father. "What price the cold war, the posturings of General de Gaulle, the threat of a rail strike or slow motion in Congress, when measured against the value of this tiny life?" the paper wrote. "All Americans and countless millions across the seas are united in prayer that the youngest of the Kennedys will soon be well."

⸻

When Dr. Walsh told the president that his son had a fifty-fifty chance of surviving, he in fact had no idea. No one did. It was a convenient assurance but also left an equal measure of dread.

What the coin's-flip chance told the president was that no one was going to commit to a prognosis in one direction or the other.

For good reason. For newborns in Patrick's condition—born six weeks early with similar lung weakness—it was impossible to predict which baby would succumb and which would be hardy enough to beat the terrible odds. Treatments were so primitive that medical intervention scarcely worked into the equation.

If any device could improve prospects, even slightly, it was located far from Children's Hospital. Two doctor-scientists, Mildred Stahlman at Vanderbilt University in Nashville, Tennessee, and Maria Delivoria-Papadopoulos at the Hospital for Sick Children in Toronto, Canada, were experimenting with ventilators for premature infants. The women were recording very modest success using modified adult respirators or jury-rigged iron-lung machines on struggling newborns.

Both doctors received calls asking them to bring their ventilators to Boston. Each was eager to help. But too many hurdles existed, not the least of which were the doctors' own patients. Patrick would have to come either to Nashville or Toronto for treatment. But that was out of the question, explained journalist Sarah DiGregorio in her book *Early*, a history of premature birth inspired by her own experience: "His condition was too tenuous for him to be moved." As for the doctors coming to Children's with their ventilators, DiGregorio wrote, "both had essentially the same answer*: I can't leave my patients, because without me, they'll die.*"

Fifty-four years later, Stahlman was still emotional over her tough decision. "We were busy, busy, busy," she told DiGregorio. "Whose baby is more important than anyone else's? Is the Kennedy baby more important than your baby? Not in my book."

The absence of ventilator experimentation at Children's highlighted the difference between the work being done there and at other institutions. Children's was renowned for its particular advances. But the development of ventilators was too experimental and hazardous for Children's specialists to risk. "You would think the Kennedys would have the best of everything, and indeed, Boston Children's, affiliated with Harvard, was on the forefront of pediatric care," observed DiGregorio. "But mechanical ventilation at the time was still considered entirely unproven, more likely to cause a burst lung than to be an effective treatment. . . . Boston Children's had an evidence-based, gold-plated reputation to protect. Mechanical ventilation for babies was just too out there for them at that time."

ELEVEN

Prayers for Patrick

On the second day of Patrick's life, his father took his breakfast in his rooms at the Ritz-Carlton and addressed a few pressing White House matters. On this day, the president was to send a draft of his prized nuclear weapons test ban treaty to the Senate. In Washington, representatives from twenty-six countries without nuclear weapons were to sign the agreement at the State Department in individual, back-to-back, fifteen-minute ceremonies beginning at 8:45 a.m. So far, fifty-six nations had indicated their intention to commit to Kennedy's vision. Additional signings were to take place in London and Moscow.

On Monday, four days away, formal Senate hearings on the treaty were to kick off with testimony from Secretary of State Dean Rusk followed by prominent opponent Edward Teller, the "father of the H-bomb."

Expecting a contentious debate over ratification, Kennedy spent the early morning going over a personal message he intended to send to the Senate along with the treaty. The wording was crucial: he wanted to impress upon senators the urgency and necessity of ratification. Shortly after eight a.m., he conferred by phone with his wordsmith Ted Sorensen to work out the language.

The message as delivered implored senators to "move swiftly" on what Kennedy described as "a first step toward limiting the nuclear arms race." A failure to ratify the test ban would be a dangerous act of shortsightedness, the president asserted, warning the chamber: "It is rarely possible to recapture missed opportunities to achieve a more secure and peaceful world."

By 9:30 a.m. President Kennedy was speeding toward Children's Hospital in a motorcade of four police cruisers and a press bus. Traffic cops at every intersection cleared the roadway.

Shortly before the president arrived, police stopped a man in the stairwell between the hospital's fourth and fifth floors who explained, "I just wanted to see the baby." He was escorted out of the building.

When the motorcade pulled up, the windows on the hospital's upper floors filled with faces straining for a look. Outside, a boisterous crowd waiting in the steamy, overcast morning greeted the president "ghoulishly with applause and cheers," wrote *Washington Star* columnist Mary McGrory. "If they honored his anguish, they gave no sign." An elderly woman who had arrived to drive a friend home—a friend whose son was in the hospital with meningitis—stood in the lobby behind a rope holding back the public. She was aghast at the crowd cheering outside. "He has troubles enough, God knows, without them gawking at him," she told McGrory. "You would think that they would leave him alone at a time like this."

As the president rushed through the lobby to see his son, a tearful mother wondered if he would visit any of the other little patients. She felt bad for the president, but her own son was likely to have a shortened life. "He's got leukemia," she said. Her boy was asking if the president would come see him. "My son's had seven years," the woman said philosophically, "his had two days, how do you choose?"

Inside Room 2534, Kennedy gazed into the plexiglass incubator as Dr. Drorbaugh described Patrick's experience through the long night. The infant continued to breathe rapidly, his chest caved in with each inhale, and with each exhale he grunted; his nostrils flared over the exertion. He wasn't drawing enough oxygen into his bloodstream: the telltale sign being his blue-tinted skin. His tiny body was under significant stress. But, as the night progressed, Drorbaugh noted a hint of optimism: Patrick didn't worsen, he was not in a downward spiral, he was suffering but was stable. And he was fighting hard. If he didn't weaken further, there was a chance he could struggle his way through the next few days and hold on long enough for his lungs to begin functioning normally.

Patrick's birth was now a fast-moving news story, making the pressroom at the Statler Hotel about three miles from the hospital an impractical site for several briefings a day. So, a second pressroom was set up inside Children's with sixteen phone lines hastily installed.

At the morning briefing, Salinger delivered a sliver of optimism but also sowed confusion. He cautioned that the baby's condition was "still serious"—an assessment that took journalists by surprise. Mary McGrory observed that it struck "an ominous note since nobody had heard the word serious before, even if circumstances had argued it steadily."

Trying to explain, Salinger said doctors had been prepared for Patrick to decline overnight. "It is the normal pattern for conditions such as the baby's to get worse before they get better," he said. But Patrick held on—no downward slide. "The situation remains exactly as it was

Wednesday night," he said. "This is a source of some encouragement to doctors."

⁂

The president rushed out of the hospital after a twenty-minute visit, eager to bring the positive news to Jackie. He smiled wanly at the crowd outside before climbing into police commander McNamara's cruiser and speeding off. Less than fifteen minutes later, his motorcade pulled into a vast park, the Fens, and stopped on a dusty baseball diamond described as "the grubby little Fens Stadium." Some two hundred spectators, held back by a cordon of twenty police officers, had gathered to catch a peek at the president.

Minutes earlier, four helicopters had touched down on the field. The president's Marine chopper was waiting at second base. The whirling blades kicked dust a hundred feet into the air, forcing police, firemen, and reporters to scramble for cover.

When Kennedy, in his gray suit, left the car and strode toward the helicopter, the crowd cheered. Some hollered encouragement and the president turned, grim-faced but appreciative, and waved. White House staffers and Secret Service agents tumbled out of their cars and hurried aboard two helicopters. Journalists, however, were stranded. The third chopper assigned to the press failed to lift off due to a mechanical problem. Reporters scrambled to their cars, raced to Logan Airport, and chartered a plane to the Cape.

At 10:17 a.m., the president was airborne, beginning a period of frenetic shuttling between Boston and Cape Cod. Newspapers published a chronology of the president's movements in almost minute-by-minute increments. *The Miami News* devoted nearly an entire page to photos of the president getting on and off airplanes; speeding in open-air limousines past spectators holding up placards reading "It's a Boy!"; Salinger delivering news briefings; and the president with his sister Jean Smith riding together on the Cape to see Caroline and John Jr. Above the tick-by-tick timeline was the headline: "Daddy's in a Whirl."

The president's fluid plans kept his assistants scrambling. Constant motion and sudden schedule changes called for nimble reactions. Advanced planning dissolved into immediate action. Robert Manning, the assistant secretary for public affairs, couldn't recall a time "when we have done so much sudden moving around." Since the president left the White House abruptly less than twenty-four hours earlier, his schedule was "so helter-skelter, it was difficult to make any preparations."

By 10:44 a.m., President Kennedy was on the ground at Otis Air Force Base. Dr. Walsh had good news, as he told reporters: Mrs. Kennedy had "a very good night and is in good spirits. Her post-operative condition is good and she's taking fluids nicely."

During his visit, Jack delivered his positive update from Children's, lifting Jackie's hopes, and Jack himself showed a flash of his usual buoyancy. Now, for the moment, they had modest good news to celebrate together. As *The Boston Globe* reported, "The hospital visit with his wife obviously cheered the President for he was smiling at his departure."

After Jack's visit, Jackie was feeling so upbeat she began looking past Patrick's crisis. She had turned her attention to planning White House dinners for King Mohammad Zahir Shah of Afghanistan on September 5 and Haile Selassie, the emperor of Ethiopia, on October 1.

She asked Mary Gallagher to arrange a hair appointment the following week with her stylist Kenneth Battelle, known as Mr. Kenneth.

She also sent her personal secretary out shopping. "She wanted me to pick up Revlon lipsticks," Gallagher recalled, "Nearly Peach, Strawberry White Pale."

The president planned to return to the Otis hospital to see Jackie again at 4 p.m., then head to Boston at six to check on Patrick. First, he and Jackie's mother, Janet Auchincloss, helicoptered to the house on Squaw Island for lunch with Caroline and John Jr.

But after less than an hour with the children, Jack's plans abruptly changed.

Dr. Drorbaugh at Children's phoned him with disconcerting news: Patrick's condition had worsened, and doctors were considering extreme measures to save the baby's life.

A grim Pierre Salinger burst into the press headquarters on Squaw Island a little after 1 p.m. and delivered a terse announcement: "After consulting with the doctors, the President is returning to Boston immediately."

The newsmen rushed to the telephones.

White House staff—some had only just made it to the Cape—scrambled back to their vehicles. Jackie's press secretary Pam Turnure was instructed to withhold the seriousness of the situation from the first lady. With Jackie's mood and strength improving, the president and her doctors didn't want to disrupt her rest. She was napping and expected to see Jack again at four. Dr. Walsh, who was fielding Jackie's calls, would give her the news of the president's departure, using his intuitive tact and discretion.

⸻

In the era of Patrick's birth, doctors were only just beginning to understand what caused the breathing difficulties so common in premature newborns. In 1959, researchers at Harvard University discovered that these babies suffered from an insufficient amount of a fluid in the lungs called surfactant, short for surface active agent. But it would be years before medical scientists were able to transform this knowledge into a viable treatment.

Surfactant lubricates the tiny elastic air sacs in the lungs called alveoli that expand like balloons with each breath to capture necessary oxygen from inhaled air. Surfactant is crucial to the act of breathing in newborns and adults, paving the way for a lifetime of smooth inhales and exhales.

The substance is produced only in the last few weeks of a baby's development in the womb, leaving premature infants at particular risk. When a newborn lacks enough surfactant, a glassy membrane forms and smothers the alveoli, hindering breathing and causing the lungs to become stiff and rigid.

Patrick's shallow, rapid breaths, his bluish skin, his unusual "singing," or grunting, all pointed to an insufficient coating of this vital substance on the lungs. The resulting condition is called hyaline membrane disease: hyaline from the Greek *hyalos*, meaning glassy. It is also known as respiratory distress syndrome.

Judging by Patrick's symptoms and his decline, the specialists at Children's Hospital were beginning to suspect that it was hyaline membrane disease that was ravaging the lungs of the president's son.

Just the previous month, seven doctors at Buffalo Children's Hospital had published a study in a medical journal that showed hyaline membrane disease, or HMD, was "the most common single cause of death among the newborn."

The Boston Globe summed up the frustrations of parents and doctors confronting this all-too-common killer, writing on the day Patrick's condition worsened: "No action can be taken to prevent hyaline membrane disease, except what physicians call 'supportive' measures which include oxygen, temperature control of the Isolette and mist to facilitate breathing."

In the absence of transformative medical solutions, Cardinal Richard Cushing of the Boston Roman Catholic archdiocese, a close friend of the Kennedys, issued a call for "the prayers of all citizens for the speedy recovery of the child."

⸻

By 2:15 p.m., the president was back at Boston's Fens Stadium, his helicopter touching down again just four hours after it had lifted off. He climbed into a waiting police cruiser and sped to the hospital. Upstairs in Room 2534, he found Dr. Drorbaugh consulting with top specialists from Children's and other institutions. Patrick's latest lab results, the president learned, presented a grim picture: the oxygen level in his blood was deteriorating while the amount of carbon dioxide was spiking. The baby's outward appearance—flared nostrils, rapid breathing at a rate of more than a hundred gulps per minute, and a deeper bluing of the skin—pointed in only one direction: the First Couple's son was on a perilous descent.

With no lifesaving treatments available, the conversation turned to radical approaches. Desperate circumstances, the thinking went, called for desperate measures. Everyone saw Patrick's sapped body and the light of life flickering, and "they . . . wanted to try everything possible," recalled Dr. William Bernhard, a pioneering pediatric heart surgeon. "Everyone was trying so hard to save this baby." It was, after all, the president's son. The medical team felt intense pressure to do something—anything—"because of the situation and the high-profile nature of the case," Bernhard said.

What emerged was an historic decision: the doctors—and the

president—agreed to rush into untested and unproven territory on the slim hope of saving Patrick's life. The risk was extreme and the outcome wholly unknown. The gamble underscored the depth of desperation. In a first for premature infant research, Patrick Bouvier Kennedy, the son of the president, was to become a tiny human subject in a medical experiment.

At the center of the dramatic decision was a monstrous, submarine-shaped, steel structure thirty-one feet long and eight feet wide outfitted with air vents, pressurized doors, and a window. The president had consented to placing his newborn son into this hyperbaric oxygen chamber located in the basement of Children's Hospital. The contraption, which flooded oxygen into a pressurized environment, was built in 1928 to train submarine crews and to treat deep-sea divers suffering decompression sickness. It fell out of service for years until the late 1950s when trailblazing doctors began climbing inside to perform corrective heart surgery on babies with low blood oxygen levels. The chamber's pressurized environment temporarily raised the saturation of blood oxygen in the babies' bodies, improving the chances of surviving surgery.

Some of the consulting specialists believed that Patrick might benefit from oxygen bombardment in the pressurized conditions of the chamber. The proposal sounded reasonable: Patrick wasn't getting enough oxygen into his bloodstream. But his weakened lungs may not have had the ability to safely absorb the intensified oxygen flow. Exposure to too much oxygen could injure many of his organs. "It will injure the eyes, it will injure the brain, it will injure the kidneys, it will injure the liver," Dr. Donald Null, a neonatologist and emeritus professor at the University of Utah School of Medicine, explained in an interview for this book. Powerful blasts of oxygen also posed the risk of damaging Patrick's fragile lungs, causing further impairment and possibly death.

During the consultation, the president "remained pretty cool and calm throughout, asking appropriate questions as any concerned parent would," Hughes recalled.

But at one point, he raised an issue much on his mind. Patrick already was suffering from hypoxia, or oxygen deprivation, a condition common among premature infants with underdeveloped lungs. The president wanted to know whether, if Patrick pulled through, his son would have mental disabilities, a known outcome of hypoxia. Jack already had personal family experience: his sister Rosemary was deemed intellectually challenged from birth and, in 1941, when she was twenty-three, Joseph Kennedy secretly subjected her to a catastrophic prefrontal lobotomy that left her unable to speak clearly or care for herself.

Dr. Alexander Nadas, the founder of the Children's cardiology program, was explaining the workings of the hyperbaric chamber when the president interrupted him. "If the baby survives," he asked pointedly, using the era's common term, "will there be mental retardation?"

The president's suspicion was warranted. Hour after hour during his brief life, Patrick was unable to take in enough desperately needed oxygen to maintain the health of his brain. "The longer a baby is hypoxic, the more likely the baby will have profound injury," Null explained. "If Patrick had survived, there was a good chance he would have been brain-injured."

When Nadas told the president he couldn't say for sure what Patrick's mental condition might be in the end, should he survive, the president kept at it—probing repeatedly for an answer. Nadas finally cut off the inquiries: "Mr. President," he said sternly, "we are trying to save the baby's life."

Whether the hyperbaric chamber was the best path remained far from certain. Dr. Bernhard, who had the most experience inside the chamber, was skeptical. He had studied Patrick in his incubator and quickly deduced that he was "in rough shape, working really hard to breathe. . . . He was in significant respiratory distress."

Under the best scenario, Patrick's exposure to the oxygen in the pressurized tank could help stabilize him long enough for his body to begin producing sufficient amounts of surfactant on its own to heal his lungs. But Bernhard believed that was a long shot. He had performed heart surgery inside the tank on about a hundred children, most with excellent results. But none of his patients had a lung condition: they were tested and screened to make sure their lungs were healthy. Under Bernhard's watch, no child had gone into the tank with pulmonary disease.

Putting an infant in Patrick's condition into the hyperbaric chamber, Bernhard said later, was "something I would have not done." Under the circumstances, however, he had to go along. "I couldn't possibly refuse not to get involved."

But this straight-talking doctor felt an obligation to be honest with the president. And what he had to tell him was not reassuring. Powering up the oxygen chamber in hopes of saving his son was a last-ditch measure: "I told him the baby was probably going to die."

⸻

Fifteen minutes after the president had disappeared inside the hospital for his consultation, press secretary Salinger issued a brief statement to reporters. "The president's new son is encountering increasing new difficulties," he explained, adding that doctors were awaiting results from blood tests assessing Patrick's "oxygen problem." Asked if the baby was in serious danger, Salinger admitted: "The condition of the child is worse than this morning."

The afternoon newspapers sounded the alarm. *The Boston Globe* pasted a foreboding headline across its front page: "BABY PAT HAS

BAD TURN—JFK Quits Wife's Side, Flies Back to Hub—Goes at Once to Hospital Where Son Fights for Life."

⁂

As the pensive president crossed the hospital lobby on his way out, a girl in a wheelchair was saddened he didn't stop to greet her. "You mustn't blame him," her mother consoled her, "he's worried about his son, you know."

Inside the gift shop, kids were lined up to buy get-well cards for Patrick. A best-seller, costing a nickel, read: "This comes with more wishes / Than any words can tell / That you are feeling better / And soon completely well." A dime bought a larger card featuring a drawing of a child with an uncanny resemblance to Caroline pushing her baby brother in a carriage.

The president stopped at the lobby newsstand to buy magazines and newspapers from starstruck vendor Eva Needle. He asked for *Esquire, Fortune, Holiday, Town & Country*, and four newspapers. When he tried to pay, Needle wished him and his family all the best and declared grandly: "It's on the house, Mr. President."

Back at the Ritz-Carlton, the president decided to consult another medical expert. Though the doctors at Children's were some of the nation's brightest practitioners of pediatric and neonatal care, the voraciously curious Kennedy typically sought a range of views—whether on nuclear disarmament, civil rights, or steel prices. On a matter as dear as the health of his son, he had the same instinct: he was open to all opinions.

Jackie's sister, Lee, now married to her second husband, Prince Stanislaw Radziwill, had gotten word to the president that Samuel Levine, a prominent pediatrician in New York, had steered her premature daughter Tina to health. Intrigued, the president picked up his hotel phone and found Levine at his Manhattan apartment at Sixty-Ninth Street and First Avenue.

"I want you to try to save my baby Patrick," he told him.

Later in the day, the doctor's wife, Bella, returned home from a shopping trip and was greeted by the building's distraught doorman: "Mrs. Levine, I don't know what happened but the police just came—put Dr. Levine in the back seat of the police car and went down the street—the wrong way with sirens going full blast."

Bella was alarmed. But once she got upstairs, her housekeeper filled her in with the surprising news: President Kennedy had called at about 3:30 p.m. to summon Dr. Levine to Boston.

Dr. Hughes later learned that the president tasked an Air Force officer with getting Levine from his home in New York to Children's Hospital in Boston, and the officer relied on standard military protocol for mobilizing aircraft in an emergency situation. In Hughes's telling, the officer called out: "Scramble! And they scrambled a jet." Dr. Levine was soon aboard an Air Force jet heading to Boston.

The president had something else on his mind.

Evelyn Lincoln was resting in her room at the Ritz-Carlton when the president telephoned.

"Where are you?" he wanted to know.

"In my room, down the hall from you."

He asked her to bring him some of his personal stationery.

When valet George Thomas opened the suite door to her, Lincoln found the president sitting on the bed without his suit jacket on.

"He was just staring into space," Lincoln recalled. "I thought to myself, this man is really suffering."

She asked how the baby was, and he said there was probably a fifty-fifty chance he'd pull through. Hoping to hearten him, Lincoln reminded him: Patrick was a Kennedy, all he needed was a fifty-fifty chance.

The president asked her to stick around for minute while he wrote a note. In poor handwriting, he scrawled: "Please find enclosed a contribution to the O'Leary fund. I hope it is a success."

He then signed a check for $250, inserted it into an envelope, and asked Lincoln to have the Secret Service deliver it.

James O'Leary was a Boston police officer who had chased a liquor store robber through the city's dark streets the previous Friday until the thief shot him twice in the chest, then climbed into his getaway car. The officer died, leaving behind a wife and three kids.

Several weeks later, the president's bank raised some concern over the check: the terrible handwriting didn't look like Kennedy's. When Lincoln fielded the call, she remembered the president's troubled state of mind at the time: while he was suffering his own heartache, he still wanted to help support the officer's family. She advised the caller: "Tell the bank that the check and signature are authentic."

TWELVE

"Chances of His Survival Are Very, Very Slim"

Dr. Bernhard led the small team accompanying Patrick into the chamber: Dr. Drorbaugh, anesthesiologist Robert Smith, technician James Carr, and a nurse. Tests were conducted on the tank's components: the valves, the wiring, the compressors, the door and window seals. "The air in that basement was pungent and musty," neonatal pediatric specialist Michael Ryan wrote in his book, *Patrick Bouvier Kennedy: A Brief Life That Changed the History of Newborn Care*. "The massive iron tank resembled a wartime vehicle, and its odorous smell, its electrical components, and the lather of grease combined to create an atmosphere that seemed the antithesis of a healing environment, but it was Patrick's last chance."

At 4:41 p.m., on August 8, less than twenty-eight hours after his birth, Patrick Bouvier Kennedy in his incubator was carried into the chamber.

The doors were closed and locked, and the medical team, in white gowns and masks, went to work. As the tank was powered up, a panel flashed colored lights. The compressor motor accelerated and fell into a high-pitched whir. The infant wore a monitor on his chest that captured his heart and breathing rates. Dr. Drorbaugh watched the readings from his position inside the tank, and the numbers were transmitted to another doctor seated outside the chamber. An intercom system facilitated communication between staff inside and outside the steel monster.

After ten minutes in the oxygen bath, Patrick raised everyone's hopes.

From inside, Drorbaugh cried out: "His EKG looks better!"

Bernhard took note: the oxygen level in Patrick's bloodstream had improved slightly and his heart was benefiting. But, he observed, the baby "was still very short of breath."

On Cape Cod, Jackie woke from a long nap expecting to see her husband. But instead Dr. Walsh was there to inform her that Jack had to rush back to Children's Hospital. Hard as everyone tried to protect Jackie, the reality of her son's condition came crashing through. Dr. Walsh's tender bedside manner could not disguise the unsettling trend: Patrick was in distress. Jackie's spirits plunged. Instead of another hopeful visit from Jack, she was suddenly grappling with anguish over Patrick's decline.

Then her phone rang.

It was Jack calling from his suite at the Ritz-Carlton. He knew Jackie would be agitated by Patrick's sudden downturn and by his departure to Boston. Now he was able to soften the blow. He wanted to immediately pass along the news that doctors had just given him: in his first few minutes inside the chamber Patrick had a tiny rebound. Their son's condition, he was pleased to tell her, had "slightly improved."

Jackie's plunging emotions caromed in the other direction.

As *The Washington Post* reported: the president's call "brought a glow to her face."

Jackie's mother, who had returned to the Cape, wanted the press to know she was encouraged by the news about Patrick, telling reporters: "He's doing very well." But Frank Falacci of *The Boston Globe* was skeptical she believed her own words. Patrick was, after all, in dire condition. "Although maintaining her poise," Falacci wrote, "Mrs. Auchincloss appeared somewhat distressed."

⸻

Dr. Samuel Levine walked into the basement of Children's Hospital around 5 p.m. His Air Force jet had deposited him at the Boston airport where he climbed aboard a Marine helicopter for the flight to Fens Stadium, and there he found a police cruiser waiting to speed him to Children's.

The New York pediatrician received at best a lukewarm reception from the Boston physicians and medical staff at work in the basement. Levine had traipsed in after the renowned Children's specialists had studied Patrick's situation, analyzed his prospects, performed medical tests, and decided on a last-ditch Hail Mary to save his life. Underlying the tensions was a touch of Boston–New York rivalry and local pride. The hyperbaric chamber, now the center of attention, belonged to the Harvard School of Public Health; it was leased to Children's for Dr. Bernhard's groundbreaking surgeries and clinical experiments. Levine was an outsider and a Johnny-come-lately, forced upon the team by Mrs. Kennedy's sister.

In his own right, however, Levine was a distinguished sixty-eight-year-old pediatrician and something of a competitor: he was not affiliated with Harvard and Children's but was trained at Cornell University

Medical College and was a Cornell emeritus professor of pediatrics and former chief pediatrician at New York Hospital–Cornell Medical Center. New York Hospital, which moved into the forefront of preterm baby care when it established its Premature Unit in 1948, had honored Levine by naming its pediatric ward after him.

Years later, Bernhard put Levine's arrival in perspective. "He showed up at a time when the baby . . . began to show some signs of fleeting hope," Bernhard recalled, and as a luminary in the field and a Kennedy family doctor he began "putting pressure on the other pediatricians, increasing their stress level."

Buoyed by Patrick's slight rebound, the president was in good spirits when he returned to the hospital at 5:45 for his third visit of the day. He was glad to see the newest member of Patrick's medical team. Levine told the president he was astonished by the coordination of police and the military in conveying him rapidly from New York to the basement of Children's.

"I'm very impressed with the efficiency of the government," he said dryly.

The president, displaying his easy rapport with Levine, ribbed him over the American Medical Association's resistance to government intervention in the profession. Yes, the president countered with a laugh, the government was efficient: "It's about time you doctors learned that."

Shortly after 6 p.m., Salinger summoned the White House press corps to a briefing at the hospital. "I have quite a bit to tell you," he began. "In late afternoon, there was a halt in the downward trend of the baby's condition."

He explained that Patrick was placed in a high-pressure chamber "to force oxygen into the baby's lungs." He added: "This is the only tank of its kind in the United States."

A reporter interrupted: "The only one here, Pierre?"

He affirmed it was, then continued: "Placing the baby in the chamber has had an immediate reaction. The respiration rate has gone down, the baby is breathing with less effort and other laboratory tests . . . have shown improvement."

Salinger cautioned reporters not to overplay Patrick's improvement. "The condition of the baby is still serious, as I described it this morning. However, since entering the chamber," he repeated, "the condition of the baby has improved some."

⁂

Salinger's call for restraint did little to stop newspaper editors from splashing their front pages with overly optimistic headlines. Newsstands in New York burst with copies of the *Daily News* screaming: "BABY RALLIES AFTER CRISIS." Flipping to page three, readers came upon standard tabloid exaggeration: "Son Past the Crisis, Kennedy Tells Wife."

President Kennedy left the hospital at 6:40, returning to the Ritz-Carlton for dinner served in his suite. He called Jackie again. Patrick's tiny rebound gave Jack and Jackie a moment of guarded hope.

The first lady's press secretary Pamela Turnure fed upbeat reports to the press, telling reporters the way Jackie bore up to "the double strain" of her surgery and Patrick's health crisis was "simply fantastic." Turnure, social secretary Nancy Tuckerman, and private nurse Hennessey brightened up Jackie's room with displays of pink sweet peas they found flowering in the sandy soil alongside the former barracks. Plants and bouquets from well-wishers dotted the room.

The first lady was "cool and calm," according to *The Boston Globe*'s Gloria Negri, as she awaited updates on Patrick from her husband. "If she is dispirited," Negri wrote, "she tries hard to conceal it."

Jack and Jackie's lavish September 1953 wedding reception for 1,200 guests at Hammersmith Farm, her stepfather's estate in Newport, Rhode Island, prompted comparisons to Queen Elizabeth's recent coronation. The fairy tale soon darkened as Jack's infidelities strained the marriage.
Toni Frissell Collection/Library of Congress

After three ill-fated pregnancies, Jackie gave birth on November 27, 1957, to Caroline Bouvier Kennedy, who was christened in New York at St. Patrick's Cathedral by Boston's Archbishop Richard Cushing. Jack, who had been wary of marriage and even warier of having kids, was smitten by his baby girl. "I don't think he really knew what loving someone was like until he had Caroline," a family friend recalled.
AP Images/Tony Camerano

Moments after his inauguration on January 20, 1961, Jack and Jackie were captured in a private moment in the Capitol Rotunda. During their first two years in the White House, the First Couple confronted persistent marital tensions.
AP Images/Henry Burroughs

On Easter Sunday 1963, the First Family attended Mass at the Palm Beach estate of patriarch Joseph Kennedy. The next day the White House announced Jackie's pregnancy. The prospect of a third child brought Jack and Jackie closer than ever before.
Cecil Stoughton, White House/John F. Kennedy Presidential Library and Museum

During the summer of 1963, Jack visited Jackie and the kids almost every weekend on Cape Cod. In late July, a relaxed JFK enjoyed a cruise aboard the presidential yacht the *Honey Fitz* with five-year-old Caroline.
Cecil Stoughton, White House/John F. Kennedy Presidential Library and Museum

Doctors designated the nearby hospital at Otis Air Force Base on the Cape as a backup in case Jackie had a pregnancy emergency before her expected September delivery at Walter Reed Army Hospital in Washington. Otis's VIP wing—a barracks-like building on a dusty terrain—presented a stark contrast to the Truman-Eisenhower Suite awaiting Jackie at stately Walter Reed.
US Air Force Photograph/John F. Kennedy Presidential Library and Museum

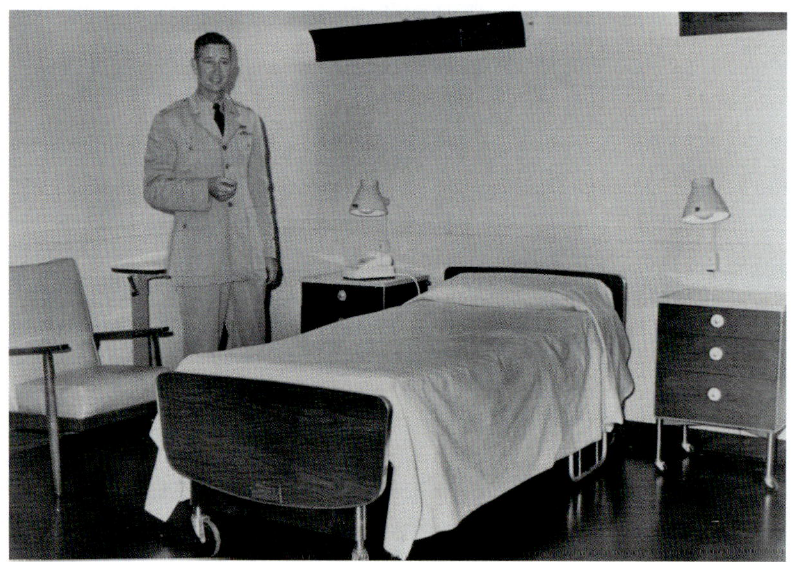

A brouhaha erupted when the Air Force spent a considerable sum upgrading the Otis hospital VIP suite for Jackie, risking a political backlash. The president fumed when military brass allowed news photographers inside the suite. "See that fellow's picture by the bed?" Kennedy railed, only half-jokingly ordering that the "silly bastard" get transferred to a new post in Alaska.
Bettmann/GettyImages

With Jack at the wheel, a buoyant Jackie went for a spin on the Cape in late July. Taking in the sun in the backseat were the Kennedys' friend Chuck Spalding and Jackie's brother-in-law Prince Stanislaw Radziwill of Poland.
Cecil Stoughton, White House/John F. Kennedy Presidential Library and Museum

In early August, Jackie joined family and friends for a cruise off Hyannis Port aboard the *Honey Fitz*. Her pregnancy was smooth until August 7, when she went into premature labor and delivered Patrick in an emergency caesarean operation six weeks early.
© CORBIS/Corbis via GettyImages

An ambulance raced the ailing newborn from Cape Cod to Children's Hospital in Boston. Throngs filled sidewalks and overpasses as baby Patrick, escorted by police cruisers and motorcycle cops, flew past.
Boston Herald/John F. Kennedy Presidential Library and Museum

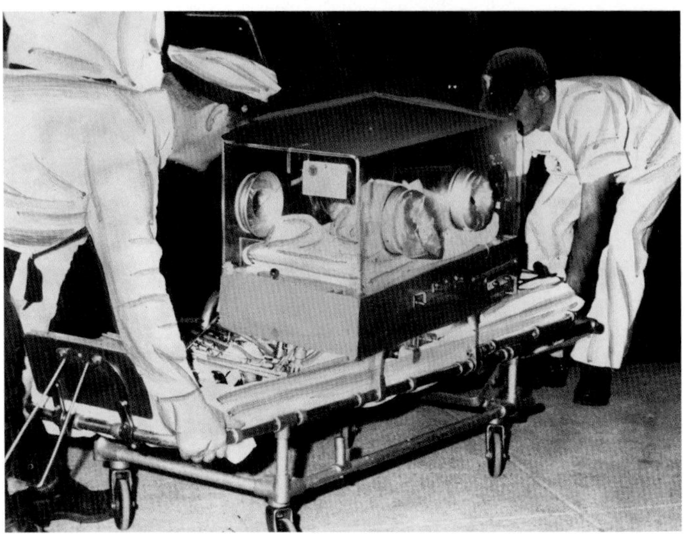

Patrick in his plexiglass isolette was placed on a gurney and wheeled into the hospital a little after 7 p.m. As he was rolled along the corridor, young patients and their parents watched from their rooms.
Calvin Campbell/Boston Herald/John F. Kennedy Presidential Library and Museum

Patrick was whisked into the hospital to begin a harrowing journey into a medical world lacking today's modern lifesaving treatments for premature infants. Outside, gawkers surged forward for a peek into the ambulance.
Calvin Campbell/Boston Herald/John F. Kennedy Presidential Library and Museum

Having sped from Cape Cod to Boston, a pensive President Kennedy headed to his son's room accompanied by Children's Hospital acting director Lendon Snedeker, at left, and Jerry Behn, head of JFK's Secret Service detail, at right.
Bob Dean/The Boston Globe via GettyImages

From August 7 to August 9, the president shuttled between the Cape and Boston, comforting Jackie and keeping close to Patrick. The Kennedy baby had become a national sensation. Prayer vigils sprung up across the country.
Dan Sheehan/The Boston Globe via GettyImages

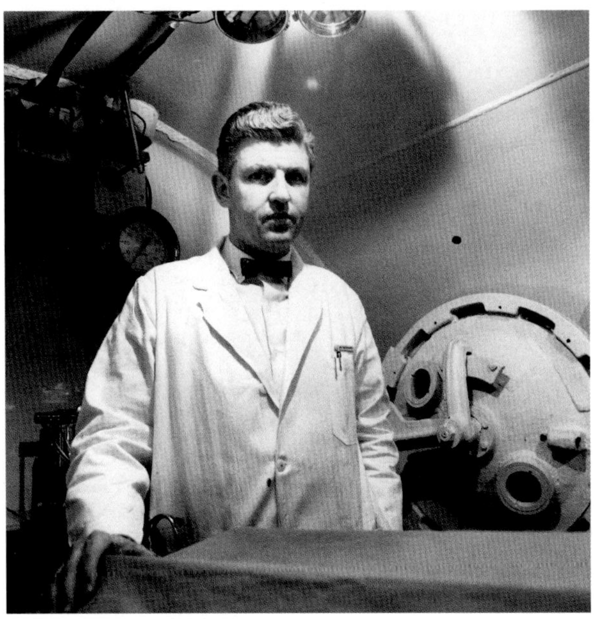

When Patrick took a turn for the worse, he was placed in a steel, submarine-like hyperbaric chamber in a risky, last-ditch gamble to save his life. Dr. William Bernhard and four others joined Patrick inside. At first, the baby improved slightly from bombardment of oxygen into his lungs, but hopes soon faded. Patrick died at 4:40 a.m. on August 9, thirty-nine hours after he was born.
Photograph by Irene Shwachman/ Boston Children's Hospital Archives, Boston, Massachusetts

In the morning, Jack flew to the Cape and entered the VIP suite at Otis Air Force Base as Secret Service agent Clint Hill held the door. In Jackie's room, they wept in each other's arms.
AP Images

A little after 8 p.m., Jack's brother Attorney General Robert Kennedy and close friend and adviser Dave Powers swept past reporters clustered at the Children's Hospital entrance. Bobby muttered, "I just wanted to be near my brother."

The president showed up a short time later in a silent police escort, for his fourth visit of the day. From then on, he ordered, "it would be more appropriate if the cavalcade moved about the city without the screaming sirens." When he passed the crowd waiting outside, the *Boston Herald* observed, "a trace of a smile masked the agonies known to every father of a desperately sick child."

The president went down to the basement to join his brother and Dave Powers beside the hyperbaric chamber. For a short while, Jack and his two fiercest champions took turns peering through a porthole of the hissing mechanical monster at the ailing infant inside. From his perch, Dr. Bernhard kept a close eye on Patrick. Though it was the president's baby under his care, he proceeded as usual. "Everything was quiet and businesslike," he said. "This was a routine pressurization inside the hyperbaric."

Bernhard was a Republican who voted against Kennedy, but the two men had some shared experiences: both were naval officers in World War II serving in the South Pacific.

"Both of us were dads, too," he said.

Bernhard admired Kennedy's remarkable poise throughout the crisis. "He was a diligent, caring parent," he said. "He kept his emotions to himself, made very intelligent inquiries, and was just the nicest person."

From inside, Bernhard gave the president realistic updates over the intercom. "You gave him the straight stuff, he got it, and that was it," he recalled. "He wanted the best for his child, but he knew from the beginning [the prognosis] was very bad."

Through four hours in the tank, Patrick had registered modest progress, or at least stability. But he was working very hard to breathe, and his expended energy was destined to exhaust him. "We were giving him some glucose and water by vein," Bernhard recounted, "but he could not make up for the caloric loss he was sustaining."

If Patrick kept laboring at his current rate he would tire out, and anesthesiologist Robert Smith would have to assist his breathing by inserting a tube into his trachea. Smith would then squeeze an oval-shaped, rubber ball called an Ambu bag attached to the tube and inflate Patrick's lungs to sustain respiration. This process of ventilating was called "bagging." If Patrick reached that point, Bernhard informed the president, "the chances of his survival are very, very slim."

As the night wore on, Patrick's fate darkened while the president watched through a porthole. Bernhard and the president had a number of chats over the intercom, and Bernhard sugarcoated nothing. "He understood with one look at the baby what the problem was," Bernhard said, "and . . . he knew we were not accomplishing anything." Bernhard told the president: "I think we're not going to be able to provide help for the little boy."

Accepting the inevitable but still clinging to hope, Kennedy stayed near his son through the night. A room normally used by a medical resident was readied for him on the fourth floor of Farley Building. A bed was moved in, and two phones were installed: one, a red hotline connected to the Strategic Air Command headquarters in Omaha. A cot was brought in so Dave Powers could bunk with his buddy.

For a few hours Jack and Bobby and Powers kept a vigil in the basement, their noses against the porthole. Now and then, they broke away, pacing the cement floor to the noisy industrial huffing of the chamber. Patrick's tortured breaths kept coming, his will to live prevailing over his weakened body. If the end was near, it was impossible to know when it would come.

At around 11 p.m. Jack and Powers went up to the room, and Bobby headed to the Ritz-Carlton for the night. The president was distraught and exhausted, in need of a brief doze.

But first he needed to pray.

Powers was often by Jack's side at night, particularly during the summer when Jackie and the children were on the Cape. During the week, Ken O'Donnell recounted, "the President faced solitary confinement in Washington." Powers would stick around, eat broiled chicken with Jack in the second-floor residence, watch television, and join him on the Truman Balcony until bedtime.

"Dave would watch him kneel beside his bed and say his prayers," O'Donnell said. Then he would put out the light and drive home.

Now, in the cramped hospital room, Jack got down on his knees in front of Powers. After two long, excruciating days he prayed for his son. Then he climbed into bed and immediately fell asleep. Powers stayed with him, resting on the cot.

At 11:30 p.m. Salinger announced the hospital sleepover, telling reporters that the president planned to confer with doctors the following morning at eight o'clock. He informed a crowd of stubborn spectators outside the hospital that they would not see the president again tonight. The gawkers groaned in protest.

In the basement Patrick fought on—his will fighting off the inexorable sapping of his strength. But Bernhard, keeping close watch, couldn't ignore the grim signs. "Sometime during the night," he recalled, "I got the feeling the baby was about ready to stop breathing."

Patrick had already had apneic periods: interludes when he stopped breathing and then started up again. Bernhard worried that he might not revive after his next pause. It was time, he concluded, to take the final drastic action: he conferred with anesthesiologist Smith, who agreed "things were not looking very good, so he popped a tube in the trachea, taped it up and 'bagged' him."

Patrick calmed as oxygen was pumped straight into his lungs: he no longer had to fight for every breath. It was, however, a palliative measure, not a mark of improvement. "As soon as [Smith] 'bagged' him, the baby stopped struggling," Bernhard explained. "The baby looked absolutely peaceful because the anesthesiologist's hand was doing the work, rather than this infant."

⸻

On Cape Cod, Jackie was having an uneasy night.

Outside her room, Agent Wells of the children's detail had taken over for Agent Hill, who had been on constant duty for almost two days. Through the night, Wells watched as Lieutenant Nancy Lumsden, the night duty nurse, went in and out of the room.

"Each time she came out," Wells said, "I'd ask, 'How is she doing?' And every time the answer was the same. She'd say, 'Mrs. Kennedy is really having a tough time tonight. She's been so restless . . . just tossing and turning. She just can't seem to get to sleep.'"

⸻

At 2:10 a.m. agent Jerry Behn, head of the president's Secret Service detail, notified Dave Powers that Patrick was slipping away. Powers woke Jack. A call was placed to Bobby at the Ritz-Carlton. As Bobby rushed to the hospital, the president set off for the basement, passing ailing children in their rooms along the fourth-floor corridor. While waiting for the elevator, he paced restlessly.

His eye wandered into a nearby room, falling on a badly burned little girl who lay unconscious in an oxygen tent. The president summoned the night nurse and asked about the child and her parents. He wanted to know how the accident happened and how often the mother visited. The mother, he learned, sat with her two-year-old daughter, Sandra Cramb, every day.

He asked the nurse, "Could you tell me the mother's name?"

Taking a slip of paper and a pen from Powers, he scrawled a note: "Dear Mrs. Cramb, We saw your daughter. I hope she is better soon. She looks sweet. John F. Kennedy."

Powers later recounted: "There he was, with his own baby dying downstairs, but he had to take the time to write a note to that poor woman, asking her to keep her courage up."

Years later, after her daughter had recovered, Mrs. Cramb told *Ladies' Home Journal* that when she got the president's note she "began to feel, for the first time, that my baby would be better soon, and a few weeks later she regained consciousness."

Down in the basement, the president and his brother and his friend began a sad vigil, watching little Patrick slowly surrender. Inside the chamber, anesthesiologist Smith was helping the baby breathe by hand-pumping the Ambu bag.

After nearly forty hours of life, Patrick was slowly departing.

"His tiny arms and legs were losing muscle tone and taking on a floppy appearance, an indication that his oxygen-deprived brain was no longer able to send signals to contract his muscles," explained author

Michael Ryan, whose interest in Patrick grew out of his work as a registered respiratory therapist and neonatal pediatric specialist.

After an hour, the president had cast aside any illusion of his son's recovery: Patrick's descent was irreversible. Restless and broken, Jack needed to be alone. He walked off, returning to his room upstairs.

Bernhard, keeping close watch on Patrick, soon acknowledged "there wasn't enough functioning lung to sustain life."

At 3:40 a.m., less than a half-hour after the president fled the heartbreak in the basement, he was summoned back. Over the intercom, Bernhard notified him that Patrick's death was imminent. Bernhard later recounted that he needed the boy's father to know "we were losing . . . so he was prepared. It was important there were no shocks to anybody."

At 4:04 a.m., Patrick's overtaxed lungs gave out. His heart stopped.

Jack and Jackie's third child had lived for thirty-nine hours and twelve minutes. He died inside a colossal steel contraption while his father peered in at him through a porthole.

"He put up quite a fight," Jack murmured. "He was a beautiful baby."

Press secretary Salinger, who was in the basement along with Bobby and Powers, recalled that the president "walked away from us and through a door into the hospital boiler room." Out of sight, "he wept for ten minutes."

When he came back, Bobby wrapped his arm around his brother's shoulder.

Doctors began the process of decompressing the chamber. Dr. Bernhard and his team would have to wait several hours before coming out. Patrick's body was confined inside along with them.

The president fled upstairs to his room. Powers followed him.

Jack sat on the edge of the bed and asked Powers to go do him a favor. Powers understood immediately: he took his orders, got up, and left, closing the door behind him. In the corridor he heard what few outside a very close circle ever heard: Jack Kennedy sobbing. "He didn't want anybody to see him crying," Powers explained. "So he asked me to go outside and telephone Teddy."

⟡

At the Otis base hospital, Jackie was unable to settle down. Nurse Lumsden kept coming and going, trying to calm her. Jackie knew nothing of the tragedy unfolding in the basement of Children's. Nobody on the Cape knew anything about it.

At 4 a.m., about the time Patrick's heart stopped, Lumsden emerged from Jackie's room. "She's finally gone to sleep," she told Agent Wells. "Just now. She just fell asleep."

A few minutes later, the phone rang at the Secret Service post down the corridor. A voice on the other end delivered the news from Children's.

⟡

At 4:26 a.m., Salinger stepped to the microphones inside a dining room at the hospital. Reporters, domestic and foreign, some slumbering at the Statler-Hilton in Boston, others maintaining a vigil at Children's, raced to the briefing at Salinger's sudden summons.

The press secretary came right to the point:

"Patrick Kennedy died at 4:04 a.m."

The press corps let out a collective groan.

"Ohhh boy," someone said mournfully.

Another voice called out: "Say it again."

It was Friday, August 9. Patrick was born just a day and a half earlier.

Salinger plowed on somberly: "The struggle of the baby boy to keep breathing was too much for his heart."

He gave only the bare details.

The president had been called down to the chamber at 2:10 a.m.

"From that time until the baby's death the path of the baby's health was downward," Salinger said.

The president was in the basement when the baby died, he told reporters. Robert Kennedy and the president's friend Dave Powers were with him.

Salinger said he didn't have a lot of information.

Reporters volleyed questions at him anyway, shouting over each other.

Was a clergyman present?

No.

Can you give a final cause of death?

He would defer to the hospital for that announcement.

Did Patrick remain in the chamber until the last minute?

Yes. He died in the chamber.

Reporters were peppering him in such a noisy, chaotic barrage, the press secretary couldn't hear what was being asked.

"I can just take one question at a time," he pleaded.

One pertinent inquiry caught his ear: "Has Mrs. Kennedy been notified, Pierre?"

"Not yet," he said, shaking his head. The president, he said, intended to fly to the Otis hospital at 9:15 a.m. to see his wife.

Someone asked again: "Has Mrs. Kennedy been notified?"

Salinger repeated: "She has not yet."

"Do you know when and how she will be notified?"

"I do not. I will try to gather that information."

"Do you know if Mrs. Kennedy will be told before the President gets there?"

"I couldn't tell you that."

A final question concerned how the president took the loss of his child.

"Was there any reaction from the President you can tell us about, Pierre?"

"No."

For Dr. Hughes, what began as a possible hoax—a voice on the phone requesting a transfer to Children's for the son of the president—ended with a formality that proved beyond a doubt this tragedy was no prank.

As physician of record, Hughes was called upon to fill out the death certificate. He conferred with Dr. Leonard Cronkhite, the hospital's director, and members of Patrick's medical team, to arrive at a final diagnosis and cause of death: prematurity and hyaline membrane disease. Hughes then scratched his signature on the document.

At Otis, Jackie slept undisturbed—unaware of what had befallen her. Reporters, meanwhile, were telling the world. Street-corner kiosks in Europe shouted the headlines. The *Evening News* in London: "Jackie's Baby Dies." *Paese Sera* in Rome: "The Third Child of Kennedy Is Dead."

⸻

At 6:25 a.m., her obstetrician John Walsh entered Jackie's room: the dreadful task of informing her had fallen to him. After her rough night, she had slept only about two hours. Less than two days earlier she had undergone an emergency caesarean requiring two blood transfusions. Physically she was regaining her strength. But each tremor from Boston—Patrick's decline, his improvement, and the endless uncertainty—had unnerved her.

Walsh woke her gently. Initially he had shielded her from the details of her son's predicament. Now he had to deliver a truth that not even the most graceful bedside manner could soften. Jackie had already lost three children—her sorrow over the past was always with her. And now here she was again. The news of Patrick left her bereft. To benumb the heartbreak, Dr. Walsh sedated her, and she fell back asleep.

When she awoke, a sympathetic squad of women was there to look after her. Joining the hospital nurses were family nurse Luella Hennessey and personal aides Nancy Tuckerman, Pamela Turnure, and Mary Gallagher. Showered with kindnesses, the grieving mother still couldn't stop herself from writhing through bouts of despair.

When Agent Hill checked on her, he witnessed the depths of her sorrow. "She was devastated. It was heartbreaking to see her in such emotional pain," he recalled. "There was nothing I could do, nothing anyone could do to protect her from the pain."

THIRTEEN

"No Privacy in Their Grief"

That morning of August 9, the mood on the base was a "tense stillness," in the words of United Press International. Flags flew at half-staff. The only relief in the "solemn atmosphere," according to UPI, "was a tiger-striped kitten who scampered carefree over the lawn near the hospital."

Kennedy family members streamed into the Otis VIP suite and sat gloomily in the lounges. Jamie Auchincloss, the first lady's sixteen-year-old half-brother, kept asking his father, Hugh Auchincloss, "why such a terrible thing had to happen to Jackie." The elder Auchincloss had no words to comfort his son. "It was obvious," Mary Gallagher realized, "that Jamie was simply voicing the question that everyone pondered: *Why* did it have to happen?"

The president, having slept only a couple hours, pulled up to the suite in the late morning. In joyful times, he was happy to tool around on the Cape in his open-air convertible. But now, the Associated Press reported, he "rode concealed beneath the car's top." The president got out and went swiftly inside, his red eyes and lined face a measure of his grief.

For her part, Jackie wanted to look her best for Jack. Nurse Hennessey and private secretary Gallagher teamed up, primping her and brushing her hair. "She had been crying but, with some freshening up and some encouraging words, she was propped up comfortably with pillows and looked as presentable as possible under such trying circumstances," Gallagher recounted in her memoir.

When Jack and Jackie saw each other for the first time, they were each on the verge of emotional collapse. Alone with her, Jack described the agonizing final hours of their son's life until the telling became too much for him. In a decade of marriage, Jack had cried twice in front of Jackie, and each time he shed quiet tears. His earliest bout, in 1954, came after his near-fatal back surgery and prolonged convalescence: "just out of sheer discouragement," Jackie said, "he wouldn't weep but some tears would fill his eyes and roll down his cheeks." The next jag struck after the disastrous Bay of Pigs invasion in 1961: "He came back over to the White House to his bedroom and he started to cry, just with me," she remembered, "just put his head in his hands and sort of wept."

But this time, after Patrick, his cataract of tears was on a whole new scale.

He dropped onto his knees beside her bed and let himself go—"just sobbed and put his arms around me," as Jackie later told historian and Kennedy special assistant Arthur Schlesinger. His fragility "stunned" her, recalled friend Betty Spalding: Jackie had "never seen anything like that in him."

Jackie, too, was in a vulnerable state that morning. Having lost Patrick, she fell into a panic. Who else might suddenly be taken from her? And then she blurted out to Jack: "There's just one thing I couldn't stand, if I ever lost you."

The president pulled himself together before setting off for his next duty: to deliver the sad news to Caroline and John Jr. at Brambletyde. On his way out of the suite, Jack bumped into the chief of surgery, Charles Sanislow. "He was going in one direction and I was coming in the other," Sanislow recalled. "So we were suddenly face-to-face." The doctor detected no vestige of Jack's emotional outburst. "He looked as he always did, very handsome and very much in control."

When Sanislow offered his condolences, the president expressed his gratitude to him and the entire hospital staff. "Thank you very much," Kennedy told the doctor, "for all that you folks did to help the family."

Kennedy's graciousness still moved Sansilow sixty years later. "I truly have feelings about the whole period," the doctor recalled in an interview for this book, "but that particular moment is the one thing that has stuck with me more than anything." At one of the saddest periods of his life, the president didn't choose to brood over his own tribulations. But rather, Sanislow remembered, he recognized others for their contributions to his baby's care: "That bespeaks the man he was."

When Jack arrived at Brambletyde, the kids' excitement over seeing their father was tempered by the look on his face. Caroline and John Jr. both sensed something wasn't right. "Because we had told the children they were going to have a brother or a sister," nanny Shaw recalled, "they had to be told their brother was not coming home." Their father kept it simple, explaining that their baby brother "had been sick and he had gone to heaven." The president's handling of this delicate moment, and his tenderness with the children, sharpened Shaw's appreciation of the man, as she said in a 1965 oral history interview for the Kennedy Library: "He proved himself a wonderful father."

While John Jr. didn't quite understand, his big sister took everything in. "Caroline was very concerned about it all," Shaw recalled. "The news brought tears to Caroline's eyes." Her father kept her close and consoled her. His compassion throughout the crisis, Shaw said, "was really astounding to me." Shaw, too, sought to comfort the children: "That night, the three of us knelt and said a special prayer for Patrick and for Mummy and Daddy."

⁂

Speaking to reporters in Hyannis Port, Salinger outlined plans for Patrick's funeral the following day.

"There will be a private Mass in the private chapel of Cardinal Cushing in Boston at 10:00 a.m. which will be attended only by members of the immediate family," Salinger said.

"This is absolutely family only?"

"Immediate family only."

"What do you mean by immediate family?"

"Sisters, brothers-in-law, and so on. No friends of the family are coming."

"Children?"

"I don't know if any children will come."

Salinger moved on to the burial, informing reporters that the baby would be interred at the Holyhood Cemetery in Brookline, Massachusetts.

"Is that where the president was born?"

"That is right."

"Is that a family plot?"

"That is a family plot," Salinger replied, adding: "There are no other members of the family buried there."

"This will be the first burial in the plot?"

"That is right."

Then came the matter of primary interest to reporters: press coverage. The family insisted on absolute privacy, Salinger said, so there would be no coverage of the funeral or burial. He agreed to allow a small team of pool reporters to be nearby, only because the president would be in the vicinity. But he underlined that no reporter would be admitted to the Mass or burial. Just in case someone wasn't listening, he reiterated: "There will be no pictures and no coverage."

America awoke to impassioned headlines announcing the death of Patrick Bouvier Kennedy. *The Boston Globe* spread three words in giant type across the entire front page: "PRESIDENT'S BABY DIES." Just below that story was another charting the president's heartbreaking journey under the headline: "Helpless As Any Father . . ." *The Tampa Times* pointed to the poignancy of a mother kept in the dark: "Mrs. Kennedy Unaware."

The New York Times, perhaps crushed by a tight printing-press deadline, didn't lead its front page with the baby's death. That news was tucked into a secondary position between two stories about a Securities and Exchange Commission report on high-pressure mutual fund sales to hapless victims.

Condolences poured in from presidents, prime ministers, kings, queens, the secretary-general of the United Nations, the pope, and everyday folk. Among them were Winston Churchill, former president Eisenhower, former vice president and political rival Richard Nixon, Lyndon and Lady Bird Johnson, and figures as disparate as Martin Luther King Jr. and George Wallace, Charles de Gaulle and Francisco

Franco. Senators, members of Congress, governors, mayors, union leaders, academics, and journalists sent telegrams, cards, and letters.

Words of sympathy spilled from the typewriters of editorial page writers as if Patrick's was a death in the family. *The Boston Globe*, hometown paper of the Kennedy clan, wrote: "For Bostonians there is a special poignancy, as if the loss were to one of their own."

The *Buffalo Evening News* grieved with Jack and Jackie as though their mansion at 1600 Pennsylvania Avenue was in the neighborhood: "So closely do we all identify with the personal joys and sorrows of the family occupying the White House that its loss calls forth, not just sympathy, but a nationwide sense of sharing in the bereavement. To the President and First Lady go . . . the special understanding of everyone who has ever experienced the anxiety of becoming a parent."

Such an outpouring ensured that the Kennedys' mourning over Patrick would not be a private affair. Patrick, Americans proclaimed, belonged not just to his parents but to the nation—he was everyone's baby. By this compact, the president and first lady were obligated to stagger through their sorrow in the public spotlight. "Theirs is the added burden of having no privacy in their grief," *The New York Times* sympathized, "for they must endure their family tragedy before the eyes of all the world."

It was a comfortless fact that four other presidents had suffered the loss of a child while in office: John Adams, Thomas Jefferson, Abraham Lincoln, and Calvin Coolidge. All of them, like Jack, suffered profound grief. Coolidge's sixteen-year-old son Calvin died of blood poisoning in 1924. "When he went," Coolidge wrote in his autobiography, "the power and the glory of the Presidency went with him."

At Brambletyde, Jack and Dave Powers tried to create a sense of normalcy for Caroline and John Jr. The men spent the morning playing with the kids and watching them swim in the private cove behind the house.

After lunch with Jackie's mother and stepfather and their two teenage children, Jack grabbed a couple of hours to catch up on lost sleep. He woke in the afternoon, eager to be with his wife. He asked Powers to come along, but under one condition: "You can't let Jackie see you in that horrible suit."

Jackie was in a fragile condition and Jack was feeling overly protective. But he hoped to lighten the mood by bringing along Powers, who was always good for a laugh in tough circumstances. But that suit of his, the same one Powers had slept in on the cot at Children's, was such a rumpled mess that Jack only half-jokingly begged his friend to grab something from his closet: "Pick out one of mine."

At Otis, Powers impishly put on a fashion show for Jackie in an expensive suit tailored for a president. He pirouetted around her room, stopping to pose with his hands on his hips.

Jackie clapped and laughed.

His show over, Powers departed, and Jack and Jackie spent an hour and twenty minutes together commiserating over Patrick. Jackie's good humor with Dave Powers, it seemed, was faked: her emotional state, Jack swiftly deduced with growing alarm, was poor and deteriorating. Her downward spiral would intensify in coming weeks, prompting historian Barbara Leaming to conclude: "the child's death sent Jackie into a deep depression."

The public, however, was led to believe something entirely different. Family and friends told the press that Jackie was gliding through her grief. The reports had a certain consistency: "One person who visited her briefly said 'she is magnificent.'" In another account family members insisted, "she was taking the death of the child 'very well.'"

Dr. Joyce Brothers, a star newspaper columnist and television psychologist, was distressed by reports that Jacqueline Kennedy was taking it all "well." Such depictions of a mother who just lost an infant child were a disservice to women everywhere.

Brothers, who had a PhD in psychology from Columbia University, cast herself as a mother, wife, and psychologist who discussed women's subjects that until then lay largely in the shadows: love, marriage, sexual satisfaction, menopause, and childrearing. In the early 1960s, a newspaper writer drew a snappy portrait of the Joyce Brothers phenomenon in these words: "She looks like Loretta Young, walks like Marilyn Monroe, and talks like Sigmund Freud."

Brothers took issue with the suggestion that any mother felt "magnificent" after losing a baby. "I doubt it, and I fervently hope not," she wrote in a column published a week after Patrick died in an era when people typically kept tragic personal losses to themselves.

Brothers, who was just two years older than Jackie and a mother herself, devoted the column to the dangers of masking the sadness that grief demanded. "There are certain human situations where it is normal, natural, and necessary to submit to the ravages of overwhelming grief," she wrote. "The death of a new baby is possibly the most biologically basic and undeniable of all griefs."

She explained that the mother often felt crippling guilt over a baby's loss. "She feels as though the burden of responsibility is hers alone," Brothers said. "The intensity of her unjustified, but almost inevitable self-blame, combined with her excruciating physiological disappointment, make her a likely candidate for severe pathologic depression, and other mental ailments."

Speaking directly to women who might have taken Jackie's publicly reported toughness as a model, Brothers warned: "If a mourning mother doesn't cry, if she doesn't rage, if she insists on assuming a stoical pose then she's almost certainly courting prolonged turmoil. . . . She can fool her friends, her husband, and perhaps even her own conscious intelligence, but she can never fool her unconscious into believing she's 'taking it well.'"

⸻

Shortly after 9 a.m. on August 10, the president lifted off from Squaw Island in a procession of three Marine helicopters for the funeral and burial of his son Patrick. Thirty-seven minutes later, the choppers landed on a ballfield of Saint John's Seminary in Brighton. It was here on this hundred-acre expanse of greenery that Cardinal Richard Cushing had his home and a private chapel. A press helicopter touched down soon afterward, and the pool reporters on board would remain stranded on the field throughout the ceremonies. *The Boston Globe* published the family's plea for privacy in its morning edition, begging the public "to stay away . . . and leave the President and his family to themselves." A few hundred spectators nonetheless had gathered outside the locked seminary gates. Boston police and firefighters were on hand to keep order.

A somber procession of family members descended from the helicopters. One fireman so eager for a souvenir whipped out a camera and snapped a photo when the president crossed the field toward his limousine. Secret Service agents pounced on him and confiscated the film.

The small funeral party included Robert Kennedy; Ted Kennedy; Eunice Kennedy Shriver and her husband, Sargent; Jean Kennedy Smith and her husband, Stephen; Patricia Kennedy Lawford; and Jackie's mother, Janet Lee Auchincloss, her husband, Hugh, with two of their teenage children, Janet and Jamie. Jackie's sister, Lee Radziwill, who had been sailing the Aegean with her lover Aristotle Onassis when Patrick died, flew in the previous night to attend the ceremonies.

Absent were Ethel Kennedy and Joan Kennedy, who stayed at the

Kennedy Compound in Hyannis Port to look after their own young children and Caroline and John Jr. Also missing was Peter Lawford, who was with disabled patriarch Joe Kennedy in Hyannis Port, and Rose Kennedy, who was vacationing in France. Jack had phoned her in Paris on the morning of Patrick's death and persuaded her that she need not rush back for the funeral and burial.

The most prominent absence was the baby's mother. For the second time, Jackie was unable to attend the burial of her own newborn: first, Arabella, in 1956, and now, in the same month seven years later, Patrick. Dr. Walsh insisted that Jackie have a quiet day. She was not only in a delicate emotional state but had hardly stood up since her caesarean surgery three days earlier. Walsh reported that her physical condition was "excellent" but she still was consuming only fluids and a little toast. Throughout the Mass and burial, Jackie would spend her time in private prayer and resting, with Dr. Walsh by her side.

At the seminary, five black Cadillac limousines carried the mourners about three hundred yards through a wooded grove to the cardinal's chapel. The sanctuary was so tiny it accommodated only eighteen worshippers. The president led the family down a red-carpeted aisle, stopping to pray on a walnut kneeler near the marble altar. He then moved into a right pew and sat alone.

Cardinal Cushing had decorated the altar in white blossoms: carnations, gladioli, and snapdragons. Behind the altar stood a gold-leaf screen, and on either side was a statue of St. Joseph and the Virgin Mary.

Patrick's closed, small, white-and-gold coffin was draped in white carnations, at the request of his mother. The infant lay inside adorned in a white gown. A stained-glass window shone high on the wall overhead.

Joining the family were Cardinal Francis Spellman, the archbishop of New York, and the only friend in attendance, Judge Francis X. Morrissey, who helped arrange the funeral.

Once the mourners were seated, Cardinal Cushing entered behind the cross-bearer, Right Reverend Francis Rossiter, chancellor of the archdiocese. At the president's request, the cardinal would celebrate a Mass of the Angels for Patrick. Unlike the requiem for adults, this was a Mass of praise: joyful and optimistic, not one of sorrow. It was permissible for Patrick because he had been baptized shortly after his birth and, according to Catholic belief, after his death he immediately entered into heaven sinless. It was the cardinal's first Mass of the Angels, and he was robed in white vestments to celebrate innocence and purity and to welcome the baby into the company of angels.

The cardinal sprinkled Patrick's closed casket with holy water. "Blessed be the name of the Lord," he said, "now and forever." He accentuated the theme of the Mass in a prayer he composed for the occasion. "O God, the Author of life . . . to Thee we return this little child, Patrick Bouvier Kennedy, whom momentarily Thou didst loan to us. . . . Help, O Lord, the parents of this child to realize that begetting him was not in vain. Remind them, when they think of him, that they have been very near to a little saint who is now serving before the heavenly throng and praying for them. . . . Farewell to you, little child of God, Patrick Bouvier Kennedy. God hath given. God hath taken. Blessed be the name of the Lord."

The words brought Francis Morrissey to tears. "It was a beautiful day," he said. "The sun was out, everything in white, the Cardinal in white." The cardinal, he recalled, offered "one of the most touching talks ever given . . . about that little baby. He had an understanding of the tragedy and what it meant for a mother to lose a baby."

The family filed out of the chapel. But the president couldn't bring himself to leave Patrick. He went up to the little coffin. In his hand was a St. Christopher medal Jackie had given him as a wedding gift. He placed the medal inside the casket with Patrick as a symbol of love from his mother and father. Jack then collapsed onto the coffin. "He literally put his arm around that casket," recalled Cardinal Cushing, who had lingered. "He wouldn't take his hands off that little coffin. I was afraid he'd carry it right out with him." Slumped over the white-and-gold box, Jack shed "copious tears," the cardinal remembered. Jack wouldn't get up, he wouldn't leave his son. He had to be prodded. "Come on, Jack," the cardinal told him. "Let's go. God is good."

Jack's emotion stunned Morrissey, a friend of nearly twenty years who also had stayed behind. "One of the few times in my experience I saw the President cry," he said. It was "one of the most moving and touching scenes that I ever witnessed."

Though Jack's sorrow ran deep, Cardinal Cushing believed the funeral celebration gave him some solace. "He is very tired," he told the *Boston Herald* afterward, "but the Mass seemed to help him. There is a spiritual uplift in the realization the child is in Heaven."

After the thirty-minute Mass, the Kennedy cortege set off for Holyhood Cemetery about two miles away. A Secret Service sedan led the procession, followed by a car carrying the cardinal and the chancellor and vice chancellor of the archdiocese. Next came the hearse followed by the president, his brother Bobby, and his mother-in-law in a black limousine. At the end of the short motorcade was a police cruiser. The convoy traveled along Commonwealth Avenue and turned at St. Ignatius Church on Lake Street just as a wedding party spilled out the doors.

Outside the cemetery, a cluster of courteous spectators awaited: women in light summer dresses and sunglasses holding the hands of their young children, and men in shirtsleeves. "Their mien," the *Herald* reported, "was sober and sympathetic."

No one waved or applauded as the president rode by. A few caught a glimpse of him through the limousine windows, his face "rigid, frozen in sorrow," wrote the *Globe*. "He stared forward, and those who watched seemed in their silence to share his grief. Only the scores of police who lined the route gestured—they raised their right hands to cap visors in a salute of respect."

At the family plot, the mourners climbed a slight slope to the gravesite under a large canopy. Patrick's open grave was four feet long and two feet wide. Beside it sat his baby-sized coffin.

The service was brief, just seven minutes. The cardinal asked God to comfort those in grief. "Bow down Your ear in pity to Your servants, upon whom You have laid the heavy burden of sorrow," he prayed. "Grant that they may not languish in fruitless and unavailable grief, nor sorrow as those who have no hope, but through their tears look meekly up to You, the God of all consolation."

During the ceremony, presidential Secret Service agent Andy Berger stood behind the president and saw "his shoulders rise and fall because he was sobbing so hard." At the close of the prayers, Jack broke away from the tiny assembly and went to his son. He laid his hand on the coffin and whispered a brief prayer, then turned and went down the steps alone to his limousine.

The motorcade retraced its journey to the cardinal's residence. Patrick's emotional farewell, the Mass and burial together, took little more than an hour from the moment the three helicopters first touched down on the seminary ballfield. When the Kennedy family lifted off again, kids outside the gates pedaled their bicycles hard to chase the choppers overhead.

The flight plan toward Cape Cod took the funeral party back over Holyhood Cemetery. Glancing down, Jack saw workmen shoveling dirt into Patrick's grave. As the *Herald* put it: "From high in the sky, his grieving father could catch a last lingering look."

From that day until his death, Jack held Patrick near in his thoughts. Francis Morrissey remembered Jack telephoning "to tell me how much he loved that baby." Jack's flood of tears over Patrick's coffin, Morrissey believed, flowed from "great love . . . the love and feeling he had as a father."

Just as Jack was different after the birth of Caroline, more emotional and more engaged, he was different after the death of Patrick, more reflective, more affectionate, more somber. The arc of his life had brought him through the joys and sorrows of fatherhood, into Cardinal Cushing's chapel for his infant's Mass of the Angels, then up the slope at Holyhood Cemetery. His aides, his friends and family, and his wife all noted that after the brief burial prayers for his sinless son, Jack walked away down the slope into a new phase of his life. "From that sad summer day forward," concluded biographer Donald Spoto, "John Kennedy was, by every account, a changed man."

FOURTEEN

Lifting Jackie's Spirits

After Patrick's Mass and burial, Jack raced back to Jackie, arriving at Otis air base before noon. He visited with her for nearly an hour, recounting the beauty of the Mass, the loveliness of the white flowers she wanted covering the coffin, and re-creating the burial scene at Holyhood Cemetery.

The couple cried together. Jack gave in to an easy flow of tears, weeping not only for himself but also for Jackie and the kids. Unwilling to grieve with Jackie over Arabella, he now embraced their shared sorrow over Patrick. "The degree of compassion and concern which he experienced when the little boy died . . . surprised everybody," said Jack's friend and journalist Alastair Granville Forbes, "and I think surprised his wife not least."

Through his children, his abundant love, and his grief, something in Jack's heart had opened to Jackie: there was in him an empathy that earlier had been lacking. "Their parenthood bound and bonded them,"

Spoto observed. They were joined together in "their nurturing of those who lived and their sorrow for those they lost."

Jack rarely spoke of Patrick's death outside a very small circle. But he did express a profound sadness for Jackie, who, after six pregnancies, had only two surviving children. "It is so hard for Jackie," he told his friend Paul Fay. "She wanted to have another child. Then after all the difficulties she has in bearing a child, to lose him is doubly hard."

After Patrick, Jack answered a need in himself to draw ever closer to Jackie and their kids. "This man," Spoto perceived, "was never more attentive to his wife and children than during . . . the last three months of his life."

Though Jack and Jackie never got to know Patrick—his character, quirks, ambitions—they shared in the dream of his life: first in the secret of her pregnancy, then through the lazy summer days of anticipation, and finally through the traumatic hours of the brief life their boy had been granted. Patrick came and went too quickly, but he was fully realized in his parents' hearts.

"Pregnancy is the waiting time," reflected an editorial writer at the Richmond, Virginia, *News Leader* the day after Patrick's death. "The wait is made endurable—even fun—in the anticipation of the child in being. Boy or girl? Blue eyes or brown? The infant turns in the womb, and it becomes a matter for tender teasing. 'How's young Pat tonight?' Every man and woman who ever shared in the experience of pregnancy will know that Patrick Bouvier Kennedy did indeed have a life of his own, none the less real because it existed prospectively, in the minds and imaginations of his parents."

Deep in his own sorrow, Jack grieved for others—all whose lives were touched by Patrick and scarred by his loss. For Caroline and John Jr., who missed out on growing up with their little brother and growing old with him. For Patrick's many cousins and his grandparents, and for those who would never know Patrick as a friend. He grieved for Jackie and the lifelong sorrow that would trail her. He grieved for his own crushing loss. He grieved for the little boy himself, Patrick, who fought so hard and would miss out on all life held for him.

"I am convinced this was one of the hardest blows the President ever experienced," said Evelyn Lincoln. "He looked at this little boy and wished with all his heart there was some way to give him a chance to live." Jack grieved "for a potential that would never be realized."

The same day as Patrick's funeral, Secret Service agent Andy Berger was jolted by a middle-of-the-night phone call from home: his wife, Dolly, had gone into premature labor with their child who was due in September. She delivered a son on August 10 suffering from the same lung ailment that had killed Patrick.

Berger phoned presidential aide Ken O'Donnell, who informed the president, who immediately ordered a private jet for Berger to fly to New York. A police escort would be waiting at the airport to speed Berger to the hospital. By the time he arrived, his son, Andrew Paul Berger, had been baptized and was in his incubator battling hyaline membrane disease. Andrew was one of the lucky ones: he beat the disease.

Sometime later, President Kennedy called Agent Berger into the Oval Office to present him with an etching of the White House inscribed to Berger's new son and signed by the president and first lady. The health of his agent's premature boy was something to celebrate, as Jack told him: "My son didn't make it, but your son did."

At his afternoon press conference in Hyannis Port on Saturday, August 10, Pierre Salinger said nothing about the Mass or the burial or the president's visit with Jackie.

Instead, he diverted reporters to two bits of official White House news: the president's statement on the death of Tennessee senator and 1956 vice presidential candidate Estes Kefauver; and a telephone conference scheduled for Sunday and a meeting on Monday with Secretary of State Dean Rusk, who attended the signing of the nuclear test ban treaty in Moscow.

Reporters then flipped the session back to Patrick, and the president and first lady. One correspondent wanted to know how Jackie bore up to the burial of her son in Brookline that morning from her hospital room at Otis.

"Was there anyone with Mrs. Kennedy?"

"Dr. Walsh was with her," Salinger replied.

"No one from the family?"

"That is correct."

A reporter said: "I understand she was sitting up today."

"I believe she has sat up briefly," Salinger confirmed. "Yesterday and today."

A reporter pressed Salinger for details on Jack and Jackie's private time together.

"Would you give us a fill-in on what happened?"

"No."

"You don't know?"

"No," Salinger said.

⟡

On Sunday morning, Jack had a surprise for Jackie.

First, he attended the 10 a.m. Mass at St. Francis Xavier Church in Hyannis Port, arriving and departing to the applause of onlookers. From the pulpit, Monsignor Leonard Daley offered his sympathies to the president, then urged the twelve hundred congregants packed into the pews, and others standing in the aisles, and swarming outside, to respect the privacy of the Kennedy family. In a not-so-subtle plea, he called upon the vast assembly to "offer prayers that God may grant [the Kennedy family] solitude in their great sorrow."

The pastor's appeal went unheeded.

Before his final blessing, a crowd swarmed out of their seats to take up viewing positions outside the church. When the president walked by, there was a moment of pandemonium as gawkers in the back cried out: "Down in front." A cigar-smoking man in Bermuda shorts aimed his camera at the grieving father, and a policeman on the scene grumbled: "They don't know how to behave—people."

After church, Jack went to Brambletyde to fetch his surprise for his wife: their nearly six-year-old, ponytailed daughter outfitted in a blue-and-white beach shift and blue sneakers. The president and Caroline climbed aboard a helicopter at the summer house and lifted off for Otis hospital. His companion, Jack hoped, would be a burst of youthful sunshine to brighten his wife's day. "The President was very concerned about her," recalled special assistant Arthur Schlesinger. "He tried to think of ways to cheer her up."

Jackie's convalescence was progressing well, with hopes she would leave the hospital within days. That morning, before the arrival of her visitors, Dr. Walsh had her out of bed for a brief stroll in the corridor.

Outside the hospital suite, father and daughter walked hand in hand past spectators, newsmen, and photographers. In Caroline's fist was a colorful bouquet of wildflowers she had picked herself from the gardens around Brambletyde: larkspur, black-eyed susans, and pink trumpet lilies. Before stepping inside, Caroline brought her father's hand to her face and kissed it to the rapid clicking of camera shutters.

Caroline's love peck, along with a stream of recent family photos, struck one journalist as proof of Jack's special relationship with his children. "It is clear from merely looking at the pictures which have been appearing in the papers that his two children adore him and that he and his wife somehow have managed, despite their position, to make them normal, well-brought-up kids," wrote Victor O. Jones columnist and executive editor of *The Boston Globe*. "It will be a long time before any photographer snaps a better picture than the one showing [Caroline] with her do-it-yourself bouquet kissing her father's hand as the two walk into the hospital."

Inside, mother and daughter had a tender reunion after four days apart. Jackie felt strong enough to walk to a lounge, where Jack showed her condolence notes and telegrams from the pope, French president Charles de Gaulle, and other heads of state and friends. He told her Soviet premier Nikita Khrushchev sent his sympathies through Dean Rusk before the secretary of state departed from Moscow.

Nearly an hour later, father and daughter walked out of the hospital wearing faint smiles.

Associate press secretary Andrew Hatcher, filling in for Salinger, presided over a briefing on the mother-daughter get-together. He revealed nothing except that Mrs. Kennedy "was greatly cheered by Caroline's visit." He made no mention of a second surprise Jack had for Jackie, saying only: "the President will return early this evening to visit his wife."

"With Caroline?" a reporter wondered.

"I said the President," Hatcher repeated.

The president, balancing grief and governing, took his scheduled phone call in the afternoon with Rusk to discuss the treaty signing in Moscow. After the call, Kennedy, who had worn a dark blue suit to see Jackie in the morning, put on casual white slacks and a gray sweater for his return visit. He arrived a little after 6 p.m. bearing Jackie's second surprise of the day: her almost-three-year-old son, John Jr.

For John, the thrill of seeing his mother was surpassed only by climbing aboard a Marine helicopter on Squaw Island for the twelve-minute flight to Otis. On the brief drive to the hospital, John Jr. amused himself by standing up on the backseat of the president's white convertible Continental. Walking toward the VIP wing holding his father's hand, he scratched the back of his head and wondered out loud: "Where's mummy?" As he passed a phalanx of reporters and photographers, he whispered loud enough for everyone to hear: "I betcha they're taking our pictures." His boyish nonchalance prompted his grieving father to smile.

The following day, Monday, Jackie got a double-dose of kids: Caroline and John Jr.—and their father—piled into the backseat of the Continental, the top in place, along with Caroline's Welsh terrier, Charlie. With a Secret Service agent at the wheel, the foursome rolled up to the barracks-like hospital looking a little cramped: John Jr. propped on his father's lap, Caroline peering out the window, and Charlie up on all fours between them.

Caroline and John Jr. were good medicine during their nearly hour-long visit. Afterward, Jackie began eating solid food and taking walks along the corridor. Her private secretary Mary Gallagher noted in her diary: "JBK pulling herself together. Thinking of an anniversary present for JFK."

Their tenth wedding anniversary was a month away, and Jackie had decided on at least one meaningful gift for her husband: a St. Christopher medal to replace the one Jack had laid in Patrick's coffin. She wanted the medal on a money clip, Gallagher noted in her diary, "about the size of a silver dollar, gold-dipped, with a plain back for engraving." Jackie told her private secretary: "Get in touch with Tiffany's. If they don't have it, either Cartier or Charles Ernest."

⁂

Jack visited Jackie one more time in the afternoon on Sunday before flying back to Washington for the start of Senate hearings on the nuclear test ban treaty on Monday. Rusk was to appear before the Senate Foreign Relations Committee, kicking off the administration's campaign to win ratification. Other officials, including Defense Secretary Robert McNamara, were testifying later in the week. Early Monday evening, the president met with his State Department and foreign affairs advisers in the Oval Office ahead of his return to Cape Cod the following day.

Monday night, after his Oval Office meeting, Jack asked Mimi Beardsley to join him in the White House residence. Her liaisons with the president were winding down, and Beardsley was getting serious about marriage. She had her "first real boyfriend," who was about to propose. In her memoir, she was vague about whether her visit with the president that night was platonic. But it was emotional. "He invited me upstairs, and we sat outside on the balcony in the soft summer evening air," she recalled. "There was a stack of condolence letters on the floor next to his chair, and he picked each one up and read it aloud to me. Some were from friends, others from strangers, but they were all heartfelt and deeply moving. Occasionally, tears rolling down his cheeks, he would write something on one of the letters, probably notes for a reply. But mostly he just read them and cried. I did too."

On Tuesday, the president attended a routine breakfast with Democratic congressional leaders, then prepared to take off for Cape Cod to see Jackie. And he wasn't coming alone: he had with him another surprise.

On his visit to Ireland in June, the president was given a cocker spaniel puppy by cousins who lived in the Kennedys' ancestral hometown of New Ross, County Wexford. The dog was subjected to several weeks of tests before arriving at the White House. When Jack laid eyes on the nine-week-old, long-eared, blue roan with black patches on a white mottled coat, he turned to personal secretary Evelyn Lincoln and said: "Gad, he's sad-looking, don't you think?"

It was raining that Tuesday night when Jack and his buddy Dave Powers brought Jackie's gift to Otis. Powers wrapped the puppy in a towel and carried him across the tarmac snuggled against his raincoat. A photo on page one of the *Globe* the following morning showed the little cocker spaniel in Powers's arms, with soggy fur mussing its snout. The headline announced: "Very Important Puppy." Jack presented his "VIP" gift to Jackie in hopes of buoying her spirits, and, it was reported, she "just adored" it.

FIFTEEN

"Like a Couple of School Kids"

The next day, Wednesday, August 14, one week after Patrick's birth, Jackie got up at 8:30. She slipped into a bright pink, sleeveless Oleg Cassini shift and stepped into white, low-heeled pumps. The previous night she had her hair washed and then set it herself.

A flutter of anticipation ran through the hospital staff. The president was coming to take his wife back to the comforts of their summer home on Squaw Island. Dr. Walsh had given his approval: Jackie was now well enough to end her hospital confinement.

But Walsh had noticed something that concerned him. He summoned Captain Charles Sanislow, chief of surgery at the air base, and pointed to a small mole on Jackie's left foot. He wanted it removed.

"The first thing she said to me is, 'I don't know why I have to have this done now,'" Sanislow recalled in an interview for this book. "'Can't my podiatrist do this when I get back to Washington?'"

Walsh was adamant. The mole, he said, was pigmented, in some cases a sign of melanoma, and he didn't want his patient going home with it.

Years later, Sanislow applauded Walsh's decision. "Malignant melanomas appear on the foot and go elsewhere on the body," he explained. "It was good medicine."

Sanislow removed the mole and covered the wound with a Band-Aid. It would take a keen eye to detect a sliver of the bandage poking out from Jackie's pump. But one of her assistants was alarmed. "Do you have to have that Band-Aid on it," the staffer said, "because surely the press is going to notice it and they will be asking all kinds of questions."

The first lady's social secretary Nancy Tuckerman and press secretary Pamela Turnure were already worried about the press scrutiny that would bombard Jackie the moment she stepped outside the hospital. Nosy reporters, they believed, posed a threat to her still-frail health. They debated whether the first lady should confront the press at all. In their view, just walking down the front steps would be an act of courage. For a moment, Jackie considered sneaking out the back. "If she had said, 'I cannot go through with it,' then it would have been done some other way," Turnure recalled. "But she said, 'Yes, I can do it.'"

Shortly before 11 a.m. Jack pulled up to the entrance of Building 3703 in his father's blue Chrysler limousine. His first matter of business was to settle Jackie's modest hospital bill. As commander in chief, he was charged a military rate for her stay: $1.75 a day. The cost for seven days, including delivery of the baby, drugs, and round-the-clock nursing care, came to $12.25 ($125 in today's dollars).

Separately, the president paid for Jackie's food and medicine and for food and shelter in the VIP suite for Dr. Walsh, White House aides, and Secret Service agents. He wrote a personal check to the Air Force for $174.25 to cover those costs.

In gratitude for the attentive care she received, Jackie gave doctors and nurses a signed, gold-framed lithograph of the White House inscribed: "With deep appreciation, Jacqueline Kennedy, August 1963."

The first lady spoke to the assembled medical team in a whispery voice laced with lighthearted optimism: "You've been so wonderful to me that I'm coming back here next year to have another baby," she joked. "So, you better be ready for me."

⁂

Jack and Jackie stepped out of the suite together into the bright sunshine. Jackie, without her customary dark sunglasses, started slowly down the steps.

"Just to do that took a lot of effort," Secret Service agent Clint Hill recalled in an interview for this book. "She was really weak."

Jack was at her side aiding her. "Careful," he whispered.

Something extraordinary grabbed everyone's attention: she and Jack were holding hands "like a couple of school kids," as one photographer marveled.

Friends and aides, and the press, were transfixed by this moment of tenderness. "It was a small gesture, but quite significant to those of us who were around them all the time," Hill remembered. "Prior to this, they were much more restrained and less willing to express their close, loving relationship while out in public. The loss of Patrick seemed to be the catalyst to change all that."

Martha Bartlett, a close friend of both Jack and Jackie and godmother to John Jr., was astounded. "It was the first time I noticed he held her hand in public, which was a wonderful thing," she said in an interview for this book. "For him to come out of the hospital holding her hand was really quite something . . . quite unbelievable."

To Bartlett, it was all the more startling because most couples of that era—and particularly Jack and Jackie—adhered to a code of conduct that discouraged such displays of affection. "It was just good manners," Bartlett said. "Your personal life and your personal manners should be private."

But here were Jack and Jackie breaking from cultural constraints and from their own guarded behavior. "Holding hands is quite affectionate," Bartlett said. "I don't know what you do in public, but I would say that was quite affectionate."

Jack guided Jackie to the Chrysler, their fingers interlaced all the way, and he eased her into the backseat for the brief trip to the Otis helicopter pad. After the air journey of just several minutes, Jackie came down the chopper's airstairs outside Brambletyde with Jack at her side. She carefully negotiated the five steps, his arm around her waist, stabilizing her. They descended together at a slow, synchronized pace, their heads down, watching their feet to prevent any stumbles.

If journalists were distracted by the First Couple's new affection, they were still careful to scrutinize Jackie from head to toe. "By golly," chief of surgery Sanislow recalled, "she went out the door, and one of the first things, one of the people from the press asked: 'What's wrong with Mrs. Kennedy's foot? Why does she have a bandage on it?'"

⁂

Home for Jackie meant children, relaxation, and privacy. She rested on the porch upstairs for most of the afternoon, coming downstairs once to sit in the sunshine on the terrace. Still dressed in her pink shift, she was surrounded by Jack, and John Jr., and Caroline, and six dogs. Her son, his arm wrapped around Shannon, the new cocker spaniel, dangled his bright red sneakers off the edge of his mother's lounge chair, one untied shoelace drooping down. Caroline sat on the ground cuddling Charlie the Welsh terrier. The president looked on from behind, wearing tortoiseshell sunglasses, a blue polo shirt, and a rare, relaxed smile.

It was a portrait of a family hoping to recover joy.

"For the children and myself," recalled nanny Maud Shaw, "life went on much as usual. We went swimming, played on the sand, had cookouts, and went for walks." The kids showered their mother with their happy spirits, but Mrs. Kennedy needed peace, too. So, Shaw said, "I did try to keep them a little quieter near the house."

About an hour after Jackie returned to Brambletyde, Salinger stood before reporters in Hyannis Port to outline the days and weeks ahead. First, he said, the president was returning to Washington that evening. He would come back to Squaw Island two days later, on Friday, to be with Jackie and the kids for the weekend. Reporters wanted to know more about Jackie, but Salinger was under strict orders to say as little as possible. He diverted attention to global and national affairs, announcing a few inconsequential presidential actions and the U.S. bid to hold the 1968 Winter Olympics at Lake Placid.

Salinger then turned to Jackie.

"Dr. Walsh has asked me to make the following statement."

"Is this his statement?" a reporter asked.

"No, this is my statement on the basis of information given to me by Dr. Walsh." Salinger read: "Mrs. Kennedy has made a very satisfactory recovery. However, in order to insure her complete rehabilitation and continuing good health, it will be necessary for her to curtail all of her activities and not undertake an official schedule until after the first of the year."

"Is that the end of the statement?"

"That is right," Salinger said.

A reporter asked: "What about her immediate plans, Pierre?"

"To remain at home on Squaw Island," the press secretary said. "The President and Mrs. Kennedy have a lease on that home until September 15th. I think it is likely, if not probable, that she will remain there until the lease expires."

With Jackie at home, Jack began a period of intensive shuttling between Washington and wherever she convalesced: first on Squaw Island, later at her family's estate in Rhode Island. From early July to the end of August, he spent every weekend on the Cape with Jackie and the kids, often visiting during the week, too. Between August 14 and September 24, he spent more than half his time with her. Jackie would return to the White House in late September.

"The President's only concern at this time was the welfare of Mrs. Kennedy," recalled Evelyn Lincoln, who watched him come and go. "Each time he wanted to take her something that would let her know he had been thinking about her."

He wanted to share with her something from his life in Washington. Often, he would arrive on the Cape with a bouquet of flowers collected from the White House gardens.

Jack's behavior throughout the crisis earned him plaudits from the press. "To the natural feeling of sympathy which went out to President Kennedy," wrote *The Boston Globe*'s Victor O. Jones, "I sense was added a widespread reappraisal of his character, his public image, to use a currently popular term. The image is of a man more warm-hearted, more considerate, more kind."

That Jack raced to and fro to be with Jackie left a lasting impression. "The President's demeanor and his devoted attendance at his wife's bedside," Jones noted, "have gained him the respect and admiration of all his fellow-citizens."

Unseen in public, however, was the private grief that still overwhelmed Jack. He was disinclined to speak about it, even to close friends. His under secretary of the navy and confidant Paul Fay remembered Jack as "a happy man" who allowed only "occasional moments when the depths of his feelings were revealed suddenly and briefly." Fay recalled a rare instance after Patrick's death when Jack acknowledged the cloud of sorrow that had enveloped him and his wife. After describing Jackie's anguish, Jack's voice trailed off, as if he were peering into the lost future of their expanded family: his girl Caroline (or Buttons), little John, and baby Patrick. "It has been so much fun with 'Buttons' and John," he said somberly, "it would have been nice to have another son."

SIXTEEN

A President's Pledge to Save Newborns

In the days after Patrick died, President Kennedy channeled his grief into action. He instructed his longtime personal aide T. J. Reardon Jr. to quickly get him a memo on the status of research into hyaline membrane disease. Kennedy intended to deploy the full power of his office to inspire research, innovation, and life-saving treatments. He wanted to vastly reduce, even eliminate, the death of the 25,000 babies who were lost each year to the dreaded lung disease that killed his son.

Reardon took the president's urgent request to Boisfeuillet Jones, a special assistant to the secretary of health, education, and welfare, who rushed it into the hands of top officials at the National Institutes of Health. On August 20, eleven days after the president lost his son, a four-page interim NIH report landed on his desk. Thumbing through it, the president saw in abbreviated form what U.S. researchers knew about hyaline membrane disease, what treatments were available, and what studies were underway to better understand the affliction. Reardon added a breakdown of the government money already devoted to pertinent research at U.S. universities and medical centers.

Much of what the president read in the memo he already knew: that hyaline membrane disease was associated with premature birth; that male premature babies had a higher incidence of death than female premature newborns; that the disease was more common in premature caesarean births than in deliveries through the birth canal; that if an infant survived seventy-two hours it had an excellent chance of living; and, as he experienced himself with sad precision, that for children who showed no substantial improvement "death comes most often at about 40 hours after birth."

Medical researchers regarded hyaline membrane disease as something of a mystery, as the memo noted: "Little is known about the cause of the disease." Efforts to understand it had proved fruitless so far, and the development of groundbreaking treatments, as the president knew all too well, were largely at a standstill. Though studies conducted in recent years had proposed many theories on the cause of hyaline membrane disease, the memo said, "none of them [were] proved." It mentioned a couple of the unconfirmed theories, then underscored the disappointing state of affairs: "This, at the moment, is the extent of medical knowledge of the disease."

The president was understandably impatient over the limitations of U.S. medical science. But he was not alone. Patrick's death had ignited a groundswell of interest in driving research forward to revolutionize care for premature infants. Doctors and medical staff who tried to save Patrick were left saddened and frustrated. Many set themselves a personal goal of pioneering new treatments. Some devoted their careers to the task.

Nonmedical outsiders also were awakening to the need for swift and substantial progress. On the day of Patrick's death, Alfred A. Benesch, a lawyer in Cleveland and a Harvard alum, wrote to press secretary Salinger, informing him that some of his college buddies had suggested establishing "a fund for the study of the ailment that caused the tragic death of Patrick Bouvier Kennedy." Benesch wondered if any similar nongovernment action had been undertaken and whether such a foundation seemed warranted.

Salinger sought the opinion of newly appointed chief White House physician George Burkley, who deemed the fund "a good project." The proposal then landed on the desk of Dr. James Drorbaugh at Children's Hospital, who did more than just approve of the idea. After noting that Benesch's effort "sounds like a good one to me," he explained: "I do not know of any foundation that is exclusively interested in the problems of the newborn." Drorbaugh outlined specific areas where the money could be most helpful: he pointed to the need for innovative studies of sick premature newborns, research into new therapies for respiratory disease, and programs to get hospitals to work together. Each hospital had only its own cases of premature infants, providing a limited range of data. "If different hospitals could be encouraged to collaborate, necessary answers could be found in a much shorter time," Drorbaugh explained. He concluded that if the foundation came to pass, it should be regarded "as 'a fund for furthering neonatal research' since the problems of hyaline membrane disease are really the problems of a newborn premature infant."

Recognizing Kennedy's dissatisfaction with the state of research, Jones had attached a brief cover note to the preliminary memo, showing that some early steps were already in the works. His note highlighted potential advances promised by an NIH institute focusing on children that was established the previous year. "Prematurity has been selected as a major area of concern of the new Institute of Child Health and Human Development," Jones indicated. "Undoubtedly, this will lead to a considerable increase in research activity pertinent to this disease."

Eight days after the president received the preliminary memo, Jones delivered a final, twelve-page document. It included the preliminary findings and added detail on government funding, particularly the projected budget growth in 1964 for the new National Institute of Child Health and Human Development. Under the 1964 funding expansion, "two program areas are planned for special emphasis, namely, mental retardation and prematurity," Jones noted. Future research, the memo instructed, must reflect the "solid conviction" that hyaline membrane disease arises from premature birth and that to understand the disease, there must be "a definitive inquiry" into the causes of prematurity.

Before Patrick's birth, the dangers of premature birth rarely made news. After his death, press coverage spurred a new wave of public discourse on the subject. The headlines brought the issues to kitchen tables across the country: "Baby Disease Baffling in Cause and Effects," "Premature Infants Subject to HMD," "Disease That Killed Kennedy Baby Is Biggest Danger in Premature Birth."

The public conversation served as the leading edge of a coming surge in neonatal research, as the Tulare, California, *Advance Register* informed its readers: "The death of infant Patrick Bouvier Kennedy will stimulate further interest in the major health problems of premature births."

Thousands of American parents recognized their own grief in Jack and Jackie's suffering and took to their pens to let the First Couple know: "We had a similar experience when our second little boy lived only one day," wrote Robin Brown, a mortgage broker in Fort Lauderdale. "So we know well your sorrows."

The letters poured in. A Vassar classmate of Jackie's passed along her own "identical" misfortune. Others divulged that they, too, had lost newborns to hyaline membrane disease. Among them: WTOP TV anchorman Tony Sylvester and his wife; ambassador to Poland John Cabot; co-winner of the 1951 Nobel Prize in Chemistry and Kennedy's chairman of the Atomic Energy Commission Glenn Seaborg.

Long Island six-term Republican representative Steven Derounian divulged that he and his wife lost four premature newborns. Syd Herlong, a ten-term Democratic representative from Florida, told Jack and Jackie that his granddaughter survived a bout of hyaline membrane disease and was left severely brain-damaged. Herlong, offering tone-deaf consolation to the First Family, added: "Death is not the worst thing that can happen."

Herb Klotz of McLean, Virginia, revealed his own sad experience, which had touching, even eerie, similarities to Jack and Jackie's. "As the father of a son who died under similar circumstances as your Patrick I have shared your agony and your prayers in a very special way," Klotz wrote. "I remember only too well a father's pain when his gladness and his pride and his hopes turn first to concern, then to worry and apprehension, only to be snuffed out in the finality of the grim realization that all is over. And I know something also of the anguish and despair of a mother who is deprived of her baby without being allowed even once the satisfaction of holding it in her arms and spoiling it with her love. . . . May you find new strength in the knowledge that in your hour of grief the hearts of an entire nation beat as one in their loyalty and sympathy to their president."

For many Americans, Patrick's loss stirred memories of their own deceased children who died of other causes: leukemia, umbilical cord distress, accidents.

Some letter writers empathized with the Kennedys' lack of privacy during their time of grief. Writing to his friend Jackie, Random House senior editor Joe Fox noted: "It's a terrible thing for anybody to endure under ordinary circumstances, but to have to be in the public eye at a moment when you just want to run away and hide is unbearably cruel." Supreme Court Justice Arthur Goldberg, whom Kennedy appointed to the court in 1962, commiserated over "the double ache of having one's grief also so publicly reported."

Parents expressed their bewilderment over the untimely death of a child. James Reston of *The New York Times* admitted in his note to the Kennedys: "I don't like to argue with the Lord but sometimes I think that even *He* hasn't figured everything out." Cecil Sanders, an attorney in Lancaster, Kentucky, ruminated: "I find that as I get older, my knowledge and understanding of this thing called 'life' grows less and less." Birch Bayh, Democratic senator from Indiana, echoed the helplessness of many in the face of a child's death: "It certainly is beyond my wisdom to comprehend the justice in such events."

If adults were confounded by Patrick's fate, some children—such as those of Walt and Elspeth Rostow—quieted their questions in prayer. As Rostow, a Kennedy special adviser, wrote to Jack and Jackie: "If there is any comfort, it may lie in the unexpected and uncoaxed way the children prayed for Patrick last night, and it must have been like that all over the world."

People across the seas closely followed the news and were driven to share their sympathy. Bob Eunson of the Associated Press was in Korea at the time and sent a note to press secretary Salinger: "I don't know the President, but like every other American I am very sad about the tough luck he and his wife had with their little baby boy. I hope he knows that even in Korea, we were all sweating it out with him and felt sick at the end. They are too nice to have such a bad run of luck."

Goro Nakajima, navigation officer of the *Amigiri*, the Japanese destroyer that rammed and sank Lieutenant John Kennedy's PT boat in World War II, wrote to the president to express his "very sincere sympathy in the sad loss of your son. I daily listened to the radio bulletin hoping for your son's recovery." He noted: "I am at present in New Zealand and can tell you that here as in Japan people are expressing very kindly thoughts to you and Mrs. Kennedy."

In Israel, deputy prime minister Abba Eban had special empathy for the Kennedys' "pain and anguish." As he wrote to them: "My wife and I had a similarly tragic experience with our first daughter who passed away in the second week of life."

The doctors and nurses at both hospitals, Otis and Children's, had developed a special attachment to Patrick and the First Couple. Dr. Peter Liebert, a twenty-seven-year-old pediatric resident in surgery at Children's, was entrusted to monitor Patrick's heart rate and oxygen level from a station outside the hyperbaric chamber. He, like others on the medical staff, was saddened and frustrated the Kennedys' son didn't make it. "We tried our best," he said in an interview for this book. "But it didn't work." Liebert was the father of a young son of his own, Peter Jr., at the time. "I was grateful for the health of my infant," he recalled. "He was not premature, and he was not anything but healthy."

Immediately after Patrick's death, Liebert sat down at his desk to convey his sympathies to the Kennedys: "I had to write the note because I was stricken by the outcome." In his brief letter, he offered "the most sincere sympathies" of the resident staff at Children's. "Although only a few of us were involved in his care," he added, "we were all pulling for him."

Several days later, Liebert was thrilled to see in his mailbox an envelope with the return address: the White House. The president's typed reply on White House stationery read: "You and the resident staff were kind indeed to think of us at this very difficult time. Your message was a comfort to me and my family and we are very grateful to you." The president signed the note in his own hand and scrawled a personal message at the bottom: "Many thanks for all that you did."

Carol Timothy, an attending nurse at Children's, did her best to enlist divine intervention on Patrick's behalf. When doctors embarked on their last-ditch effort to save him, nurse Timothy placed her own medal of the Blessed Mother in the hyperbaric chamber with him. Timothy later sent the medal to Mrs. Kennedy along with her sympathies and received a note and a photo of the first lady from Nancy Tuckerman. "It will mean a great deal to Mrs. Kennedy to have this medal," Tuckerman said, "and she appreciates so much your sacrifice and thoughtfulness in wanting her to have this."

David Reinsberg, a first-grader in Highland Park, Illinois, and his sister Sharon, a fourth-grader, loved their neighborhood library. What better way to commemorate the life of Patrick Bouvier Kennedy than by donating a book in his name? So, David and Sharon scrambled to raise money. Less than a week after Patrick died, the Reinsberg kids approached the Highland Park children's librarian, Inger Boye.

David handed her two one-dollar bills.

"These are for you to buy a book in memory of the Kennedys' baby," he told the librarian. "I sold some of my guinea pigs and Sharon did some babysitting."

Boye, who had emigrated from Oslo, Norway, in 1928, made sure the president of the United States knew of the kindheartedness of her two young patrons. "Mr. President," she wrote in mid-August, "last Saturday a small boy stopped by my desk. In his hand he had two one dollar bills."

She then informed the president why the boy thrust the dollar bills at her. "Very soon," she explained, "there will be in our library a book inscribed: 'In memory of Patrick Bouvier Kennedy.' Mr. President, I thought you might like to know the feeling of sympathy that goes out to you and Mrs. Kennedy from even the youngest of us."

A couple of weeks later, an envelope from the White House arrived at the library. Inside were two letters: the first thanked Boye for letting the president and Mrs. Kennedy know about "the kindness of David Reinsberg and Sharon Reinsberg," and it asked her to pass along the enclosed note to the children.

"Dear David and Sharon," the president wrote. "Mrs. Kennedy and I have learned of your kindness in asking that a book in memory of our son be placed in your local library. Your thoughtfulness means much to us, and we are deeply grateful to both of you."

Boye included details of the Reinsberg kids' endeavor in her report of August activity in the Children's Department. She noted that "a book of David's choice was ordered." But she didn't mention the title. It's unknown what book once sat on a shelf at the Highland Park library in honor of Patrick. Julia Johnas, who retired as the library's director of adult services in 2018 but still looks after its local history archive, sighed: "There's no record of it."

⸻

While Jackie rested, read, went through mail, painted, sat in the sunshine, and was said to be "feeling great," Jack dashed between Washington and the Cape, absent from his family for barely a day or two at a time. The president ran the government from both Washington and Squaw Island, addressing a range of international and domestic issues: rising turmoil in Vietnam, foreign aid battles in Congress, civil rights tensions in the South. In late August, he was growing increasingly alarmed that violence might erupt when an expected one hundred thousand people congregated on the Washington Mall for the March on Washington for Jobs and Freedom.

While the president was fully engaged in White House urgencies, the First Family was still stumbling through its grief over Patrick. Caroline was out of sorts, feeling the loss in her five-year-old way. Family friend Bill Walton remembered one weekend at Brambletyde when "Caroline was being a very bad girl, acting up a lot."

Between taking calls from his aides and reading international cables, the president spent his time comforting his troubled daughter: "Jack was the only one who could quiet her down."

Though they tried to project an image of life as normal, close friends who joined them at Brambletyde couldn't help noticing the reality. "The house was full of sadness," Walton recalled.

Jack pored over condolence notes that were piling up at the summer house. "We were sitting in his office," Walton recalled, "and he was going through the papers on his desk, mostly condolences from the leaders of the world. He'd read them and pass them over to me to look at, and he'd say, 'Look at what the pope said,' or, 'How am I going to answer that one?'"

During his stay, Walton saw Jack and Jackie openly relying on each other for support: "She hung onto him, and he held her in his arms—something nobody ever saw at any other time because they were very private people."

⁂

With the loss of Patrick, Jack now drew Caroline and John Jr. close. "I noticed that he was paying more and more attention to the children than ever before," said agent Clint Hill. Jack took John Jr. over to the Kennedy Compound for visits with patriarch Joe. He went with Caroline to her riding lesson out at the stables in Osterville, and brought her little brother along. He made a point of bringing Caroline to St. Francis Xavier Church in Hyannis Port with him on Sundays. He had Caroline and John Jr. fly with him in the helicopter to the Otis air base when he was heading back to Washington.

"This was all new," Hill explained.

As the family spent time together on the Cape, Jack became uncharacteristically vocal about Jackie's unique hold on him. On one occasion, he turned ruminative while he and his friend Red Fay were floating in the swimming pool at Joe Kennedy's house. "As if looking back over his adult years," Fay recounted, "he said, 'I'd known a lot of attractive women in my lifetime before I got married, but of all of them there was only one I could have married—and I married her.'"

Father Joseph Leonard, Jackie's confidant, believed Patrick's loss would have a profound impact on Jack as a father and husband. Jackie maintained a fourteen-year correspondence with the Irish priest from their first meeting in the 1950s to his death in 1964. On the day of Patrick's funeral, Father Leonard, then eighty-six years old, sat down at his desk and composed a letter of condolence. In near-illegible handwriting, he scrawled: "My dearest Jacqueline, I hope that yourself and his [*sic*] President will allow me to join in your grief of the death of your little son, who is enjoying the glories of now eternal life." He called on St. Paul for his words of comfort: "Father of Mercies, the God of all consolation, console you in your tribulations."

Father Leonard perhaps offered his greatest consolation when he predicted that Patrick's death would steer Jack toward meaningful personal change. "I can't refrain from adding," he wrote, "that I believe Patrick Bouvier will do more for his father and . . . for his spirituality [and] transforming than if he had lived to be a very old man like I am."

SEVENTEEN

They Had Weathered It All

Though still in mourning, Jack and Jackie had something important to celebrate. On September 12, they hosted twelve family members and close friends at Hammersmith Farm, in Newport, Rhode Island, for festivities marking their tenth wedding anniversary. They arrived separately, Jackie showing up first with the kids. Jack came later with Ben Bradlee and his wife, Tony, and Rhode Island senator Claiborne Pell, who were among the few guests invited for a long weekend of boating, golfing, swimming, and bursts of merriment.

When the helicopter touched down on the lawn at the family estate, Bradlee was taken by Jack and Jackie's ease with each other. "This was the first time we had seen Jackie since the death of little Patrick," he said, "and she greeted JFK with by far the most affectionate embrace we had ever seen them give each other."

Their physical comfort with each other, even in public, was becoming ever more pronounced. "It was only after the death that they really let their hair down in public," Agent Hill recalled. He glimpsed them holding hands, embracing, just enjoying their time together—the old rules no longer applied. "They didn't care."

Hammersmith, the site of the couple's glamorous wedding reception, was an ideal setting for a weekend of celebration and reminiscence. The partygoers had cocktails in what the Auchinclosses called the Deck Room overlooking Narragansett Bay. Recalling the event, Jackie's mother, Janet Auchincloss, ruminated on the many trials Jack and Jackie had confronted together. "They'd certainly been through as much as people can go through together in ten years: tragedy and joy," she said. She noted the births and deaths of their children, Jackie's caesarean operations, Jack's illnesses, the campaigning for office, and the highs and lows of life in the highest seat of power—they had weathered it all.

Janet sensed the promise of their invigorated relationship. "All their strains and stresses, which any sensitive people have in a marriage, had eased to a point where . . . they were very, very, very close to each other and understood each other wonderfully," she said. "He appreciated her gifts and she worshiped him and appreciated his humor and his kindness, and they really had fun together."

With touches of lighthearted humor, Jack and Jackie presented their gifts to each other over cocktails before dinner—gifts that were so elaborate and idiosyncratic it was apparent they each had put considerable thought and time into the planning and selection. The three artbook-style scrapbooks Jackie had envisioned back in July clearly pleased Jack. The books chronicling the three years of his administration captured the history of the White House, the Kennedy-era reimagining of its gardens, and crucial presidential moments during his term. One scrapbook displayed a photo of the Rose Garden on a given day along with a copy of the president's schedule. On each page Jackie had written in her own hand a quote from a Joe Alsop column on gardening. The president's delight filled the room when he "read all the quotations aloud, pausing to admire Joe's ornate prose," Bradlee recalled. The garden book brimmed with historical photos dug up in White House archives as well as family images such as "a sweet one of John sniffing tulips and wearing a red jacket," recalled White House usher J. B. West, who assisted Jackie on the project. Among photos in the book on presidential moments was one of Jack ordering out the National Guard at the University of Mississippi to quell racist riots sparked by the admission of the school's first Black student.

For his presentation, Jack had arranged for Jackie's personal maid Providencia "Provi" Paredes to march into the room with an array of boxes sent from the New York antiquities dealer J. J. Klejman. Inside were extraordinary—and expensive—pieces: an Etruscan artifact from the second century BC, an Egyptian head, necklaces, bracelets. If Jackie wasn't in the mood for antiquities, Jack was able to play to her taste in fine drawings: the Manhattan art gallery Wildenstein & Company had sent works by French Impressionist Edgar Degas and the eighteenth-century artist Jean Honoré Fragonard.

Jack told Jackie she could have any piece she wanted—but only one. He then read a letter from Klejman describing each antiquity. He didn't mention the prices, except when he came to a particularly expensive piece and he whispered loud enough for all to hear: "Got to steer her away from that one."

One of the pieces was a gold Egyptian bracelet shaped like a coiled serpent. "I could see the present he wanted me to choose the most was this Alexandrian bracelet," Jackie recalled. "It was the simplest thing of all and I could just see how he loved it. He'd just hold it in his hand." Her mind was made up. "That was a special present," she surmised, "so I chose it."

The most meaningful, and personal, gifts were yet to come, and these Jack and Jackie presented to each other in private. After studying a range of options, Jackie decided on a St. Christopher medal to replace the one Jack sent to heaven with Patrick: a Tiffany's gold-plated money clip and medal.

Jack also honored Patrick with his gift. The idea arose, according to biographer Barbara Leaming, on that tearful morning with Jackie at the Otis hospital immediately after Patrick's death. "As he knelt beside her bed and told her about the little boy he had come to love," Leaming recounted, "she had begged him that Patrick not be forgotten, and asked him then to give her something that would be their private reminder, not of Patrick's loss, but of his life."

The gift Jack presented to her at Hammersmith was a slender gold ring with emerald chips. The green emerald, historian Thurston Clarke observed, symbolized "that their son had fought like an Irishman to live."

Over the four-day weekend, Jack and Jackie and their friends kept up a vigorous pace of activity. It was clear that Jackie was ahead of schedule in her recovery. She felt well enough to join in a round of golf with Jack and the Bradlees at the Newport Country Club. "It was the first and only time I ever saw Mrs. Kennedy swing a golf club," said agent Paul Landis, who shadowed the foursome. "She was a little awkward but didn't do too badly." Good-natured ribbing flew in all directions and everyone laughed a lot. "It was obvious," Landis observed, "that the First Lady was feeling better."

Agent Hill, who also was keeping a close eye on Jackie, was pleased by what he saw. "Mrs. Kennedy seemed to be slowly coming out of the depressed state she had been in," he said. "It was wonderful to see her renewed spirit and happy expression return."

As the weekend wound down, Jackie reflected on her decade with Jack. Writing to their good friend Charley Bartlett, she said she couldn't imagine a life without him. "Jack—or really any man—could have had a worthwhile life without being happily married," she said. "But I couldn't have. It would have been a wasteland, and I would have known it every step of the way." She thanked Bartlett and his wife, Martha, for their wisdom in bringing her and Jack together. "Lots of people match-make by chance—or by whim," she wrote. "But you did it with lots of thought and apprehension—because you cared about us both."

She confided to Bartlett that she now felt she could truly celebrate her marriage. "At your tenth anniversary you rather take stock of things," she explained. "It could have been the most incredibly happy time—almost more than people have a right to—with the new longed for, most beautiful child—But we don't have him." She turned philosophical: "So it could have been a tragic time—but it isn't because of Jack—and all he has done to reattach me to life and to thinking of all the lucky things we have."

EIGHTEEN

Jackie's Aegean Adventure

With the summer officially over, Jack and Jackie returned to the White House on September 23. Back in June, when expectations of a new child were running high, White House chief usher J. B. West constructed a low-key, blue-and-white nursery in the upstairs residence. Working to Jackie's specifications, he had outfitted the room with crisp white curtains, a soft white rug, and John Jr.'s white crib.

But then on August 9, at 4:04 a.m., everything changed. As soon as word reached the White House, West knew what he had to do: that baby's room had to go—it had to disappear without a trace. "Immediately I called the carpenter shop," he recalled, launching his men on a mission to return the room to its original state. "Get the rug up, the crib back in storage, the curtains off the windows."

When the first lady surveyed the upstairs residence on her return, everything looked exactly the way it was before she left. West recalled: "Nothing was said about the nursery."

The day after their return home, President Kennedy headed out for a five-day swing through eleven Western states to "honor the cause of conservation," as Ben Bradlee described the trip. The nation's mountains and fields and forests were gaining in importance but were not an issue close to the president's heart. "Except for his love of the sea, John Fitzgerald Kennedy was about the most urban—and urbane—man I have ever met," Bradlee observed. "An outdoorsman he was not."

The Western expedition was an opportunity for a first test run of the 1964 campaign. Kennedy dutifully set off but he couldn't disguise his discomfort expounding on the country's bountiful natural heritage. He looked rather "ill-at-ease," the press noted, and delivered "sometimes rambling speeches."

While out West, the president was heartened to learn the Senate ratified his limited nuclear test ban treaty by a large margin, eighty senators in favor and just nineteen opposed. A few weeks earlier, the treaty had won a moral boost from famed humanitarian Albert Schweitzer. The Nobel Peace Prize winner wrote to Kennedy to thank him for "the foresight and courage to inaugurate a world policy toward peace." Schweitzer deemed the treaty "one of the greatest events, perhaps the greatest in the history of the world." The agreement, the distinguished philosopher and theologian declared, "gives us the hope that war with atomic weapons between East and West can be avoided."

Kennedy welcomed this culmination of a long, hard-fought battle to turn down the temperature on a possible nuclear confrontation. "No other single accomplishment in the White House," recalled aide Ted Sorensen, "ever gave him greater satisfaction." The president regarded the treaty "as his greatest accomplishment," Ken O'Donnell and Dave Powers said.

The news allowed Kennedy to set aside his less-favored speeches on conservation and shift to elevated rhetoric on world peace. But would voters in these conservative states welcome the president's determination to slow nuclear weapons proliferation? In 1960, Kennedy had won only three states in the West: Nevada, New Mexico, and Hawaii. Now he worried that mentioning the treaty might get him booed.

But Americans living in the West had apparently warmed to the president over the past three years. Before he uttered a word at the Mormon Tabernacle in Salt Lake City, Utah, the crowd gave him a rousing, five-minute standing ovation. He then spoke at length on America's role in preserving peace in the nuclear age. Graphically illustrating his point, he mentioned he had flown over the battlefield of Little Big Horn the previous day. It was there, he said, that General Custer was killed along with four or five hundred men. He then compared those casualties to the multitude of deaths from a nuclear holocaust: "We are talking about three hundred million men and women in twenty-four hours. I think it is wise to take a first step to lessen the possibility of that happening." The crowd was back on its feet again, cheering. As author and journalist Richard Reeves observed in his biography of Kennedy: "For the first time, he felt sure that he was going to be reelected." Salinger, speaking to reporters, took note of the crowd's enthusiasm: "We've found that peace is an issue."

⸻

Before heading West, the president had made a stop in Milford, Pennsylvania, at the childhood summer estate of Mary Pinchot Meyer. By this time, Jack by most appearances had backed away from her as a mistress. Meyer and her sister Tony Bradlee accompanied the president on this first leg of his Western jaunt. The Pinchots' 1886 French-château-style mansion, Grey Towers, on more than a hundred acres was touted as a fitting stopover. The family had recently donated the estate to the U.S. Forest Service to advance conservation efforts. At the site, the president accepted the gift and dedicated the Pinchot Institute of Conservation Studies. The ceremony was by no means necessary but rather an excuse, as Ben Bradlee speculated: "A chance to see where his friends the Pinchot sisters had grown up was apparently irresistible."

The president then pushed off on his cross-country speaking tour, leaving Meyer and her sister behind. Tony, for her part, picked up on nothing that suggested anything other than friendship between her sister and Jack. As she told biographer Sally Bedell Smith, "There was no sexual thing evident."

Mimi Beardsley also was aboard for the trip out West and traveled with the president to all eleven states. She had stayed on at the White House after the summer to finish her work in the press office and, she thought, to end her relationship with the president. "What I didn't realize at the time," she explained in her memoir, "was that I didn't need to finish up with the President. In his sly and graceful way, he was finishing up with me." She didn't specify exactly when their affair ended, noting only: "The President and I had stopped being sexual partners at the end of the summer."

She was now engaged to be married and appreciated the new tenor of her friendship with the president. He gave her an engagement present and affectionately signed a photo of himself for her. "It's a testament to how much more I valued being in his presence—being *around him* rather than *with him*—that it had escaped me that he no longer needed me for sex," she recounted. On the road, Jack maintained his sexual distance from Beardsley. "When I was on the five-day trip out west in September," she wrote, "I didn't spend the night with him."

After Patrick's death, Beardsley observed, the president devoted himself to Jackie and the kids with renewed intensity. "The tragic death of his son," she speculated, "must have filled him not only with grief but with an aggrieved sense of responsibility to his wife and family. Even an irrepressible Don Juan like him might think it unseemly to continue his philandering ways when his family needed him so much." It was clear to her "that he was obeying some private code that trumped his reckless desire for sex—at least with me."

On a later trip to New England, he again asked her to come along but kept to his narrow path. "When I was in Boston in October," she said, "I slept in my own bed at the hotel."

Jack didn't like the idea at all.

But Jackie was adamant. Her sister Lee had invited her to Greece for a two-week cruise on the Aegean Sea aboard the magnificent 325-foot yacht of Lee's lover, the Greek shipping tycoon Aristotle Onassis. It seemed the perfect tonic for a mother in grief.

Jack would begrudge Jackie nothing to heal her sorrows—but he reviled Aristotle Onassis. He regarded him as little more than a publicity-seeking rogue and shady businessman. Onassis's philandering was public and boastful. He had paraded around with his lover opera singer Maria Callas, prompting his first wife to divorce him. His affair with Lee aroused suspicion. Columnist Drew Pearson speculated in *The Washington Post* that Onassis's ambition was to become President Kennedy's brother-in-law. Why not indulge the president's wife aboard his yacht, the *Christina*, regarded by some as the most luxurious floating extravagance in the world? That Jackie would consider convalescing anywhere near this schemer exasperated Jack. His personal secretary

Evelyn Lincoln heard him let loose at times. "Kennedy said to me," Lincoln told biographer Laurence Leamer, "'Onassis is a pirate. He's a crook.' He didn't want any part of him. And he didn't like Jackie going off with Onassis on his yacht. He didn't like it at all."

The president did everything he could to change Jackie's mind. "Jack went down on one knee, begging Jackie not to go," their mutual friend Martha Bartlett told biographer Sally Bedell Smith. "Neither of them was giving in. When she wanted to do something, she did it."

Both the first lady's aides and the president's were sympathetic to Jackie's need to get away but advised against the Aegean cruise. Jackie's press secretary Pamela Turnure raised her concern with social secretary Nancy Tuckerman, Kennedy political aide Ken O'Donnell, and press secretary Salinger, all of whom agreed the Onassis adventure "should be rediscussed before the plans were definitely decided upon."

When Turnure had trouble rounding up everyone to discuss the issue with the president, she headed over to the Oval Office on her own. "The door was open as usual, and the President looked up and said, 'Pam, do you have something for me?'" she recalled. She was about to begin her "little speech," as she called it, when Salinger and O'Donnell walked in. She laid out her view to the president and was surprised to discover he had already had a change of heart: "The President looked up and said, 'Well, I think it will be good for Jackie, and that's what counts. I think it will be beneficial for her.'" O'Donnell spoke up: "You know, you have an election year coming up, and it may not look right to have this sort of trip."

The president shrugged off the concern: "We will cross that bridge when we come to it, and that's final. I want her to go on the trip. It will be good for her, and she has been looking forward to it."

Turnure regarded Jack's decision as an act of compassion. What took precedence, in his judgment, was Jackie's state of mind and her need to get away and spend some time with her sister. "He felt the most important thing to him was his wife's wellbeing and return to good health," Turnure said. "Therefore he felt capable of coping with whatever the consequences might be."

In a 1964 interview, Jackie said Jack's decision reflected his concern over her weakened psychological state. "He sent me to Greece, which was, you know, for a sad reason," she told Kennedy aide Arthur Schlesinger. "He thought I was getting depressed after losing Patrick." In the interview, Jackie didn't mention the tensions the cruise caused nor Jack's opinion of Onassis.

But the president was so uneasy about Jackie cavorting with Onassis that the White House scrubbed any mention of her host in the initial press release announcing her Greek trip. The news, buried on page twenty of *The New York Times* and page eleven of *The Boston Globe*, attracted little attention. "Mrs. Jacqueline Kennedy," the reports said, "is going to spend the first two weeks of October in Greece, vacationing and convalescing." The papers emphasized Jackie's continued recuperation from the birth and death of Patrick, indicating only that she planned to stay with her sister, Lee, and her second husband Prince Stanislaw Radziwill in their rented house in Athens. "White House sources said the trip to Greece was planned because it is felt a change of scenery would do Mrs. Kennedy good," the Associated Press reported.

The truth leaked out in a dispatch from Paris a week later, revealing that Jackie would be "the guest of Greek shipowner Aristotle Socrates Onassis" aboard his yacht *Christina*.

⸻

Jackie had six seats on her TWA flight reserved in first class. Four were configured into a bed so she could sleep during the journey. She brought a tiny entourage: just her personal maid Provi, tasked mostly with looking after her clothes, and her two Secret Service agents, Hill and Landis.

While Hill and Provi were seated with Jackie in first class, Landis was stationed just outside the luxury cabin in the first row of economy. "While they flew in comfort," he recalled, "I catnapped and prevented anyone from entering their private space."

On a one-hour stopover at Leonardo da Vinci Airport in Rome, Jackie was greeted by the U.S. ambassador and his wife and a representative of Italy's protocol office, their arms filled with bouquets of flowers. During the last leg of her journey—one and a half hours to Athens—the first lady became fatigued and needed oxygen from a portable tank while the plane cruised at 29,000 feet.

But when she came off the plane at Athens "she was smiling broadly," the Associated Press reported, "and kissed her sister." Eager to embrace her freedom, she asked Agent Hill with a smile: "Are you ready to have some fun? I sure am."

Throughout her *Christina* cruise Jackie and her sister, Lee, had ample time for swimming in the Aegean, sunbathing, laughing, and teasing. The two women were often happily cloistered together. Jackie was a woman accustomed to luxury, but even to her, the *Christina* exceeded all measures of extravagance. Her lavish stateroom was like a palace with gold bathroom fixtures and dolphin-shaped faucets.

Agents Hill and Landis were housed in a cramped room below deck with the yacht's crew. It had a sink, a closet, and bunk beds. Landis was pleased he and Hill at least had their own toilet and shower.

Jackie's adventure was under a near-total news blackout, but bits and pieces filtered out mostly as bland descriptions of her movements among the islands, her shopping trips, her tea with the queen of Greece. Unofficial reports managed to dribble back to the States. Days after her arrival, paparazzi captured Jackie and her sister in their bathing suits riding in a speedboat off Athens after a swim in the bay waters. *The Boston Globe* splashed the photo on page one.

Some Americans, ignoring Jackie's sorrow, chafed at her privilege. "Most women have to plunge right back into housekeeping, baby nursing, and husband-cajoling after delivery, to say nothing of their own convalescence," a reader wrote to her newspaper. Referring to Jackie's "convalescence" in Greece, the letter writer groused: "Sure is a nice way to get out of her official duties."

Newspapers across the country piled on. *The Detroit News* opined: "Mrs. Kennedy should not have touched the yacht of Aristotle Socrates Onassis, the Greek tycoon, with a 10-foot pole. . . . It was no place for a president's wife." Columnist Drew Pearson took aim at Jackie and Onassis in a "Washington Merry-Go-Round" piece headlined: "First Lady's Cruise Causes Stir."

Jackie tried to stay in touch with her husband by phone, but the time zone difference and faulty communications gear proved a challenge. "She would wait three hours and then learn from the little local switchboard that they had 'lost the connection,'" reported author William Manchester. One time, a White House operator accidentally reached the wrong Mrs. Kennedy in Athens. At midnight in Greece, Mrs. Moorhead Kennedy Jr., the wife of a U.S. consular official, picked up the phone and heard: "This is Washington. We want Mrs. Kennedy."

On his own in Washington, Jack took on full father duties. During the day, in the evenings, and on weekends he seemed to need Caroline and John Jr. around him as much as they needed him.

With Jackie, the enforcer of kid conduct somewhere on the Aegean, the pattern of life in the White House shifted. In their mother's absence, "both children . . . had special leeway to drop in on father in his working wing," recalled journalist Laura Bergquist. Caroline and John Jr., adept at exploiting their father's leniency, turned the Oval Office into their own carpeted playground.

On one occasion, the president was conferring with Randolph Churchill, son of Winston Churchill, who was delivering the secret news that British prime minister Harold Macmillan was on the verge of resigning. Churchill had come to the White House with Kay Halle, a journalist, heiress, and Kennedy family friend. When she entered the Oval Office immediately after the two men had concluded their meeting, she was surprised to see John Jr. pop his head out of what he called the "secret door" in the president's oak Resolute Desk.

"He held out pieces of gum and paper that he was trying to give me," Halle recalled. "The President leaned over and said to him, 'I'm a great wolf and I'm going to eat you up in one big bite.' At which little John laughed his head off."

Then Caroline strolled into the Oval Office, and the president explained to Halle: "You know, I've been taking care of the children because Jackie is away, and I'm having the most marvelous time."

Important presidential business was conducted during the two weeks Jackie was vacationing, and John Jr. managed to insert himself into a variety of meetings like a tiny member of his father's cabinet. One day, he attended a breakfast briefing where aides prepared the president for that evening's press conference. After shaking hands with each staff member, the toddler seated himself in the chair reserved for Under Secretary of State George Ball. When the meeting began, John Jr., still in Ball's seat, listened carefully as his father opened the discussion asking: "What have we got today?"

John Jr. piped up: "I've got a glass of ice water."

Little John was in the Oval Office when his uncle Bobby came in for a meeting: before getting down to business, Bobby twirled the giddy boy round and round in the air. On another occasion, John Jr. met Prime Minister Cyrille Adoula of the Democratic Republic of the Congo. And he was there when top advisers discussed the latest crisis with the Soviet Union: the interception of U.S. convoys heading to West Berlin. The men stood in a tight circle around the president, listening, their eyes fixed on him in a moment of rising tension, everyone ignoring the cheerful tyke grinning at them as he climbed out of the secret door in his father's desk. While the president addressed the five men, looking thoughtful, arms folded in a steely pose, there lying on the carpet between his feet was one of his son's discarded shoes.

John Jr. became accustomed to being welcome in his father's inner sanctum at all times, and he did not take quietly to exclusion. He once howled his displeasure when he was blocked from entering the Oval Office during a delicate session the president held with Soviet foreign minister Andrei Gromyko. The disgruntled boy planted himself outside the door and, by one person's estimation, in a voice loud enough to be heard on Pennsylvania Avenue, chanted: "G'omyko! G'omyko! G'omyko!"

Caroline and John Jr. popped over to the Oval Office together a few times each day, showing up for a final visit in the early evening in their pajamas and bathrobes ready "to romp with their daddy before he went to the pool," Evelyn Lincoln remembered.

The kids wanted a final roll across the carpet or a clamber on the furniture. If the Oval Office door was closed, they would wait outside, banging on Lincoln's typewriter or messing around with stuff on her desk until their father came out. "He always acted very surprised," Lincoln said, "but he couldn't help knowing they were out there with the squeaks and giggles they let out."

To John, he would say: "Hello there, Sam, how are you?"

"I'm not Sam, I'm John. Daddy, I'm John."

To Caroline, he would say: "Hello, there, Mary."

"No," she replied, correcting him severely: "My name's Caroline."

When that silly welcoming ceremony was completed, Jack would return to the Oval Office and sit in his rocking chair while his son and daughter climbed on him.

Look magazine photographer Stanley Tretick was taken by the deep affection he saw one evening when John Jr. sat on the floor goofing with his father. "The President was looking down and talking to him. And then he just kind of reached for him—he reached for the boy and pulled his pajama up—you know, bathrobe and pajama—and he kind of rubbed his bare skin right above his rear end. He wanted to touch him," Tretick recalled. The quiet intimacy soothed his son. "It was a genuine thing between the two of them. The boy also sensed his father."

After messing around with the kids in the Oval Office, the president would challenge them to a race to the pool. But it was no match. Their father would stand frozen watching the kids dart away. Evelyn Lincoln recalled: "Their little legs would start running before he even moved a muscle."

On October 7, in the solemn setting of the White House Treaty Room, President Kennedy signed the Limited Test Ban Treaty. On the wall hung a portrait of President William McKinley looking on as officials agreed to the peace protocols ending the Spanish-American War. Kennedy sat at an antique table and put his signature to four leather-bound copies of the document using sixteen pens, one given to each of the men around the table who had played a significant role in seeing the project through.

After handing out all the pens, he realized, "I haven't got one for myself."

So, he grabbed an extra pen and slipped it into his breast pocket and later passed it on to Jackie as a gift.

The president told his close aides the treaty was the most gratifying action he had taken in his three years in the White House. He was hopeful that it would spare the world's entire population—not least, its youngest inhabitants—from the horror of nuclear annihilation. "He believed," historian Thurston Clarke explained, "that the treaty made it less likely that millions of innocent children would perish in a nuclear war."

A week after Jackie departed for Greece, Stanley Tretick came to the White House camera-laden and ready for a photo session. His much-delayed project, in the works for a year and a half, was finally taking off. He had written to Kennedy in June 1962 proposing a photo story titled "The President and His Son." It would be a chance, the pitch went, for the president to properly introduce his lively son to the public.

In the early years of the Kennedy term, Caroline had been the leading young star of the White House. John Jr. popped up on newspaper and magazine pages only rarely, running to his father's helicopter or showing off his small-boy shaggy haircut. "He was still an unknown Kennedy, a mystery," observed Laura Bergquist, who was to write the accompanying story for the magazine. The timing was right. By now, October 1963, John Jr. was nearly three years old and bursting with his own unpredictable character. He was an amusing contrast to his popular big sister.

From the moment it was proposed, the president liked the photo project. He thought it "was one of the 'best ideas' he'd heard in a long time," Bergquist recalled. But one thing or another had intervened.

Tretick wrote to the president several times over the ensuing months and in return heard encouraging words from Evelyn Lincoln: "He's going to do it, he's going to do it," she said.

But the delays kept coming without explanation.

One likely hurdle, Tretick knew, was the most formidable one: the young boy's mother. Jackie made no secret of her opposition to thrusting her children into the public spotlight.

Then came a possible breakthrough. When Tretick read "a small news item" announcing Jackie's trip to Greece, he phoned Lincoln. Without spilling any details, Lincoln hinted that a window for the photo shoot could very well be opening.

If Jackie was "going out of town," Tretick thought, "you know, maybe she's been the stumbling block all along."

His suspicion proved right.

"As soon as she snuck out," Tretick said, "I snuck in."

And now, on the morning of October 9, here he was at the Oval Office, eager to start capturing the president and his boy. Jack was candid about the pressures on the project. "Now you know we better get this out of the way pretty quick," he told Tretick. "Things get kind of sticky when Jackie's around."

But then came another delay. Kennedy wanted the writer Bergquist on the scene, but she was tied up for hours on something else. With the instincts of an editor, Jack expected the piece would be richer if the writer observed John Jr. in action during the shoot. "If she's not here . . . how is she going to get the mood of the boy?" he wanted to know.

So, Tretick waited for his colleague, and the president passed the day attending to the nation's business.

Finally, with Bergquist looking on, Tretrick started clicking his shutter at 7:10 p.m. when John Jr. padded into the Oval Office in his pajamas.

"How do you like him?" the president called out. "Isn't he a charge?"

John Jr. had discovered as he grew up that "a father can be quite as interesting and necessary as a mother," Bergquist explained, and now between father and son there was "an open mutual admiration society." When the infant John Jr. became a toddler, Jack craved the boy's company as "a real male kin spirit," she observed. Ben Bradlee also saw the special interaction between father and son during his visits to the White House. "John-John and JFK quite simply break each other up," he noticed. "Kennedy likes to laugh and likes to make people laugh, and his son is the perfect foil for him."

But between the two of them something more was at play than the usual father-son tomfoolery. Jack now poured double doses of affection into John Jr. and held him particularly close to help salve the wound he suffered only weeks earlier. In better circumstances, two sons would have shared their father's attention. Here in Jack's overflowing love for John Jr. was the presence of the missing son. Here in Jack's joy was a father coping. "He felt the loss of the baby in the house as much as I did. He never said so, but I know he wanted another boy," Jackie recalled in 1964. "John was such pure joy for him."

At 7:50 p.m., the president called the session to an end when he said to his son, "Let's go see grandaddy."

Jack and John Jr. set off to entertain the patriarch, who was staying the night in the White House. After they left the Oval Office, Tretick snapped the pair from behind in a soft-focus image, the boy in his robe and pajamas, his father in his suit, holding hands as they walked along an outdoor corridor toward the living quarters, John Jr. barely as tall as his father's hip.

Over four days at the White House and Camp David, John Jr. was a wild, wriggling, darting, smiling imp who dominated Tretick's camera lens, in graceful composition with his father. In the photos, the boy was full of confidence, had no fear of strangers, willingly greeted any dignitary who passed through the Oval Office even though he didn't have a clue who any of them were.

If someone told the boy he was a big man, he'd flex a bicep and declare: "Yeah, and I've got big muscles, too." If someone told him he was cute, he would run around yelling: "I'm cute, I'm cute!"

The photos for the article captured the joy of a boy and his dad. Love gleamed in their eyes and in the rapt attention they gave each other: John Jr. whispering secrets to the most important man in his world, flashing his little boy smile, and delighting in a father's hug and back rub.

Before the images ran in the magazine, Tretick presented the president with his own set of pictures. Jack was delighted. "He ran all over the White House with them, showing people," Tretick recalled. "It was like . . . a father showing a wallet full of pictures—this is my boy, how do you like him?" When Jack showed the photos privately to Jackie after her return from Greece, she, too, was pleased. "She wasn't mad about it at all," Tretick said. "She couldn't wait for the magazine to come out."

A week before the First Couple set off on their fateful trip to Texas, Tretick gave the president a preview copy of the magazine bearing the headline: "THE PRESIDENT AND HIS SON: an exclusive picture story." Jack and John Jr. dominated the cover: the toddler standing on a bench in brilliant sunshine with his hand on the shoulder of his seated father, the Kennedy males smiling, on the point of laughing, fully absorbed in each other. "I got him a copy before he died," Tretick said. "He did see it."

The December 3, 1963, edition of *Look* hit newsstands four days before the president's motorcade rolled into Dealey Plaza. Newspapers across the country published one photo that became iconic: John Jr.

peeking out of his "secret door" while the president was working, seemingly oblivious to his playful son.

After she lost Jack, Jackie was grateful Tretick and the president conspired to sneak in the photo session. She felt blessed to have these final images of father and son. Bergquist recalled Jackie treasuring their creation as an "act of God."

Jack's friend Paul Fay had closely observed the intimacy of John Jr. and his father in many settings, much as their frolicking was depicted in the *Look* article. Once, after Jack and his son had tumbled around playfully together on the Cape during their last summer together, Fay noticed a wistful look cross his friend's face. It was as though Jack was pondering the ever-so-brief childhood of a young boy. "I felt that the father realized more vividly than most of us," Fay explained, "that the process of growing up would soon bring to an end the wonderful honest charm of a boy discovering the world around him."

Late in Jackie's Aegean adventure, the president urged her to cut the trip short. Instead, she added another stop, a hastily arranged jaunt to Marrakesh to see King Hassan II of Morocco. In March, the president had hosted a state dinner for the thirty-four-year-old Hassan, known as the playboy prince before his ascension to the throne in 1961. After his visit, Jackie sent a five-page letter in French to the young king and later begged Jack that "more than anything in the world" she would like to see Morocco.

The president acceded to Jackie's wish, though the timing was inopportune, not only because of the negative publicity already surrounding her trip but also because Morocco was engaged in border clashes with neighboring Algeria. While the Secret Service was scrambling to arrange the journey, Jackie had already worked out some details herself without notifying anyone. She informed Agent Hill, "King Hassan is sending his personal plane to pick us up in Athens and take us straight to Marrakesh. So you see, it won't be any problem at all."

Jackie happened to arrive in Morocco during the celebration period for the birth of King Hassan's first son and future successor. The rejoicing traditionally began forty days after delivery when it was believed mother and baby were out of harm's way and destined for survival. The baby was born August 21, two weeks after Patrick.

Both Hill and Landis kept a close eye on Jackie, worried the ceremonies might dampen her apparent good spirits. "She showed no open signs of grief," Landis noted, while Hill saw in the first lady only "grace and dignity." If she was subdued by the festivities over the king's son, she kept a stoic face. "Isn't it wonderful, they are able to celebrate the life and hope for the future of their new son?" Jackie told Hill. "The president and I had similar hopes and dreams for Patrick."

⸻

On the two weekends his wife was away, Jack took the kids to Camp David in northwestern Maryland. The presidential retreat in the wooded Catoctin Mountains was an ideal getaway for the three Kennedys. There was stunning scenery, a heated swimming pool, a three-hole golf course, stables for Caroline's ponies, swings and other playground fun, a movie theater, bowling alley—and absolute privacy.

On Sundays, the president took the kids to Mass attended by Navy and Marine personnel in a recreation hall. No press, no photographs. Presidential aides doled out minimal details of the threesome's activities: dips in the pool, walks on wooded paths, Caroline's pony riding, John Jr.'s swinging on the jungle gym, their father's storytelling in the evenings.

On her overseas escapade, Jackie was often in a playful mood, grinning and teasing. "Mrs. Kennedy laughed and laughed and laughed. It was so wonderful to hear that laugh again," Agent Hill recounted in his book *Mrs. Kennedy and Me*. "It was music to my ears, and I knew everything was going to be okay."

At home, Jack swung between alternating moods: playfulness with the kids and lingering sorrow over Patrick. He was socializing very little, avoiding friends and the Washington glitterati, spending time instead with Caroline and John Jr. To those around him he seemed uncharacteristically gloomy. He had been enthusiastic about the *Look* article, Laura Bergquist recalled, but throughout their work on it she sensed that Patrick still preoccupied his thoughts. "It struck me very forcibly that he was different," she remembered. After the baby died, "he seemed very serious, very sober. There was . . . a somberness about him . . . an edge of sadness."

The photo shoot was the first time Bergquist had seen the president since he lost Patrick two months earlier. "He was heavier physically, he looked older, and he did have this vein of seriousness. Usually we had had a lot of fun and games, or a lot of bantering or, 'What have you read?' . . . 'Where have you been?' He had very, very little time for that." Other than his moments of doting over John Jr., Bergquist said, he "was very businesslike." For her, the sessions were unforgettable. "That was the last time I saw him," Bergquist said, noting that she detected in his dark mood "a streak . . . of fatalism."

On October 15, the president hosted a state dinner for Irish prime minister Seán Lemass in gratitude for his visit to Ireland in June. The evening had little political import: in some ways, it was meant more for the president than the prime minister. His four-day tour of Ireland was, he told the country's president, Eamon de Valera, "one of the most moving experiences of my life." Jack had visited his ancestral homeland as a young man: once during a stint as a journalist in 1945, and again as a first-term congressman in 1947 when his favorite sister, Kathleen, was living there. He and Kathleen drove to the site where the Kennedy clan began, a thatch-roofed stone house in the tiny hamlet of New Ross in Wexford County.

On his return trip in 1963, Jack was charmed by the wheat and barley fields and the stone walls of the countryside. He received an enthusiastic welcome and showed an uncharacteristic overflow of affection. On the doorstep of a modest whitewashed home, he kissed a distant relative and squeezed the hands of her daughters. He was proud of his heritage and his family's long climb to success. "When my great-grandfather came to America and my grandfather was growing up, the Irish-Americans had a song about the familiar sign which went: 'No Irish Need Apply,'" Kennedy told his assembled family members. "In 1960, the American people took the sign down from the last place it was still hanging—the door of the White House."

On his trip, "Jack Kennedy seemed to rediscover something in himself," observed Thomas Maier in his sweeping Irish Catholic history of the clan, *The Kennedys: America's Emerald Kings*. "In such a short time, Ireland had changed and so had Jack Kennedy himself."

Stirred by nostalgia, Jack wished Jackie was with him at the Ireland state dinner. But she was spending four days with King Hassan in Morocco. Jack's sister Jean Kennedy Smith took up hostess duties in Jackie's stead.

Other irritations still festered over Jackie's high life away from home. The president "was disturbed over the tittle-tattle, the acid-sweet whispers going around Washington about her Mediterranean merry-making," revealed Jack Anderson, substituting for his boss Drew Pearson, in the syndicated Washington Merry-Go-Round column. Anderson played down the tension between the president and first lady, in light of signs the couple was drawing closer. "Intimates recall too many tender little incidents, however, to believe there could be any serious trouble between the First Couple," he observed. "Their marriage may not have been sprinkled entirely with rose petals, say those who should know, but it has become firmly rooted."

Before the state dinner's official ceremonies, the president entertained Prime Minister Lemass and his wife, Kathleen, in the private residence. Caroline and John Jr. raced in for an introduction. "The little ones came in their pajamas, and like all children didn't want to go back to bed," Kathleen recounted. "Caroline sat on her daddy's lap."

Following the formal dinner, about a dozen friends and notable figures, such as the Lemasses and dance icon Gene Kelly, retreated to the residential quarters for a private party with the president. Soulful music streamed from a violin ensemble and the Bagpipe Band of the United States Air Force in their saffron kilts. "The Irish have their very happy songs and they also have their very sad and plaintive melodies," explained assistant secretary of the treasury James Reed, a longtime friend of the president's. The mood tilted toward the mournful. "I cried at every Irish tune," remembered Gene Kelly. "It was definitely a four-handkerchief evening."

To some, Jack seemed remote, lost in melancholy as he listened to his favorite ballads, "The Wearin' o' the Green" and "The Boys of Wexford." Reed recalled, "I think one of the most vivid recollections of him is how he looked that night. . . . He was standing by himself, leaning against the doorway." Of course, no one could know what he was thinking. But Reed remembered, "The President had the sweetest and saddest kind of look on his face."

NINETEEN

"He Seems So Alone Here"

On October 17, after fifteen days on the Aegean, and in Greece, Turkey, and Morocco, Jackie boarded King Hassan's private plane in Marrakesh. She was headed home. During a brief stop in Paris to catch a Pan Am flight to New York, she looked over a selection of Dior ties that the company had sent out to the airport. She bought a dozen for Jack and packed them away.

Her adventures seemed to have rejuvenated her. As they streaked over the Atlantic on the way home, Agent Hill recalled, "Mrs. Kennedy couldn't stop talking about the trip. She was in great spirits."

In New York, she transferred to the Kennedy family plane, the *Caroline*, for the flight to Washington. Despite the troubling photos and unflattering press coverage, her trip abroad had been pure escape. She was pampered at every turn and had ample opportunity for shopping, fine dining, and high times. "The party continued nonstop," biographer Donald Spoto observed. She came home with an abundance of antiques, gifts, and new additions to her wardrobe. "She seemed to have banished the summer's depression. But this she had achieved only by distractions, only by acquisitions, only by an almost total immersion in a world of luxurious indolence."

Did her escape overseas relieve her sorrow? Or was she, as Joyce Brothers would say, masking her lingering sadness, maintaining a "stoical pose" certain to prolong her period of mourning? Or had she, out of public view, cried and raged, had she pondered her guilty feelings over the baby's loss, as Brothers recommended? If, on her journey, she had turned to the serious business of grappling with the emotional depths of her grief, it was not apparent to biographer Spoto. "In a way," he concluded, "she had floated, somewhat dazed, through those two weeks."

Caroline, John Jr., and the president awaited Jackie's arrival on the tarmac at National Airport. Caroline had rehearsed ceaselessly to perfect a new French phrase to welcome her mother home: *Je suis contente de te revoir*. I'm happy to see you again. She also had made a gift: a clay bird's nest. When she and John Jr. climbed out of the limousine, Caroline calmly watched the planes overhead gliding down through the darkness, keeping an eye out for her mother's. Her brother toddled off toward Secret Service agent John O'Leary, ignoring his sister's motherly admonition: "Come, here, John. Now, come with me." John Jr. put a hand up toward O'Leary's hat, and the agent obligingly bent over so the frisky boy could snatch it, put it on his own head, and pull it down over his ears.

When the *Caroline* rolled to a stop and the stairs dropped down, Caroline raced up, her bird's nest in her hand. At the top, she threw herself into her mother's arms. John Jr., moving at his own pace, crawled up the stairs froglike on all fours. Jackie stooped to hug and kiss him. The president came up behind. When he reached his wife, she wrapped a white-gloved hand around his neck. He stepped aboard and was seen through the airplane door tilting his head to one side as if to position himself to kiss her. Jackie drew him inside the cabin for a moment out of sight.

When the family came back down the stairs, Caroline led the charge. But suddenly remembering the clay bird's nest still in her hand, she scampered back up past her brother, handed the nest off to her mother, then raced back down, gliding past John Jr., who was descending carefully step by step holding the handrail. Caroline had been so intent on reciting her perfect French phrase she had forgotten to present her gift.

Crossing the tarmac to their limo, the reunited family looked happy together. Jack was smiling, and glancing again and again at his beaming wife. Everyone disappeared into the car for the return to the White House, John Jr. riding on his mother's lap.

⊱◈⊰

It wasn't long before Jackie realized she had chosen a poor time to have deserted her husband. On their first evening together, she picked up on Jack's somberness that others had noticed in her absence. When Laura Bergquist told her later she had detected a bleak mood in the president, Jackie understood immediately and said: "Oh, you caught that?"

Jackie realized that she let Jack down by missing the signing ceremony for the nuclear weapons test ban treaty. "She was really sad to have missed it," Powers recalled. She regretted failing Jack, for she understood the significance of the treaty to him personally and to his presidency. "She felt it was the most important step he took for nuclear disarmament, that it was an important extension of peace to the Soviets," Powers said.

Though their marriage was stronger than it had been in years, it still needed constant tending from both sides. Powers remembered Jackie vowing: "I'll never be away again at such important moments of accomplishment. Everyone needs to have support and pride from those they love when they have accomplished something great."

She later admitted to her confidant Father Richard McSorley, a Jesuit priest and professor at Georgetown University, that she ought to have cut her overseas adventure short to be with Jack for the Ireland state dinner and the private party in the residence. She confessed to McSorley in 1964: "I was melancholy after the death of our baby and I stayed away . . . longer than I needed to."

After two days together at the White House, the president and first lady set off in opposite directions. Jack flew to Maine on Saturday morning to begin a two-day swing through New England, another warm-up for his looming reelection campaign in 1964. Jackie spent the weekend at Camp David with Caroline and John Jr.

At the University of Maine, the president delivered a major foreign policy speech, touting his successes in easing U.S.-Soviet tensions. "Americans should be satisfied in mind and heart," he said, that the United States is "doing everything possible to avoid the terrors of nuclear war."

The same day, New York's moderate Republican governor Nelson Rockefeller scalded his likely opponent for the 1964 Republican presidential nomination, right-wing Arizona senator Barry Goldwater, in a speech at the University of New Hampshire. Rockefeller warned that the staunch conservative intended to end all U.S. foreign economic assistance, which "would be catastrophic," and to withdraw the United States from membership in the United Nations. Sharply cutting back on America's role in the world, Rockefeller said, ensured that any Goldwater administration would be a "disaster."

Following his Maine speech, the president caused a stir when he showed up at Harvard Stadium to watch his alma mater battle Columbia. When Kennedy settled into his seat on the 45-yard line, the excitement he generated in the stands topped the action on the field. Two women seated in front of him blushed, smiled, and took a discreet look over their shoulders. When a member of the Harvard band spotted him, a rousing rendition of "Hail to the Chief" swept through the air. Heads turned. A roar went up. When Columbia chalked up a first down, Harvard spectators incongruously applauded with wild fervor. "But," as the *Globe* pointed out, "they were watching JFK, not the game." The newspaper ran a large photo of young women in the stands smiling broadly, their heads turned away from the field, the caption reading: "Co-eds at Harvard-Columbia game would rather watch president."

As halftime neared, Ken O'Donnell and Dave Powers, the president's two seatmates, noticed that their boss had fallen "unusually silent, as if his mind was far away from the game."

Since Patrick's death, Cardinal Cushing had been sending the president sketches for the baby's headstone. None had satisfied Jack. So, one day in the White House, the president had grabbed a piece of paper off of Evelyn Lincoln's desk and drew his own rendition. "Mrs. Lincoln, this is the kind of headstone I would like," he told her. He instructed her to send his sketch to Cardinal Cushing and ask him to use it to create Patrick's headstone—and he wanted it in place on the grave by the time of his trip to Boston.

During halftime, the president and his men watched the Harvard and Columbia bands perform. Then, O'Donnell recalled, the president "turned to me and said, 'I want to go to Patrick's grave, and I want to go there alone, with nobody from the newspapers following me.'"

Jack and his two buddies slipped out of the stands and moved quickly toward his car. Press secretary Salinger followed with a posse of reporters on his tail. O'Donnell instructed a Secret Service agent to ensure that the president got away without being followed. After the agent had a few words with the Boston police officer in charge of the parking lot, reporters found themselves hemmed in until the president had vanished.

When the president arrived at Holyhood Cemetery in Brookline, the headstone he designed was in place on Patrick's grave in the family plot, just as he had requested.

Something else awaited the president.

Behind the scenes over the past three months, a quiet flurry of activity drew together a group of boys from a small town in Italy, a local Italian parish priest, the U.S. consul in Milan, State Department officials in Washington, Kennedy's national security advisor, the president's personal secretary at the White House, and Cardinal Cushing in Brighton, Massachusetts. The endeavor had begun on August 11, two days after Patrick died, when twenty-two Catholic boys in the tiny town of Cura Carpignano about twenty miles south of Milan composed a letter to President Kennedy offering comfort for "the pain you carry in your heart" from the loss of "little Patrick." They asked the president to accept their "sincere condolences" and "simple homage." The boys had collected 10,000 lire for a "bouquet of white flowers" to be placed on "the resting place of Patrick Kennedy" (10,000 lire equaled $16.10 in 1963 and $162 in today's dollars).

But how to get the letter and a 10,000-lire money order to the president?

With help from their parish priest, Father Don Luigi, the boys sent the letter and the money not to the White House but to the U.S. consul general in Milan, Earl Crain. Their letter initiated a multistep undertaking to make good on the boys' request. First, Consul Crain cashed the 10,000-lire money order and wrote a personal check to the Department of State. He sent the check to Secretary of State Dean Rusk's executive secretary, Benjamin Read, with a full explanation. Executive secretary Read in turn prepared a memo for National Security Advisor McGeorge Bundy at the White House. In it, Read asked that the White House reply to Consul Crain in Milan, who would pass it on to Father Luigi and the boys. The national security advisor's assistant for Europe and Canada, David Klein, then wrote to Cardinal Cushing requesting his assistance in getting the flowers placed on Patrick's grave. Klein informed the cardinal: "The President just received a check for $16.10 from the Parish Boys' Group of the Church of San Tarcisio Martire in the little town of Cura Carpignano, Italy, for white flowers to be placed on the grave of the President's son, Patrick." He said the money had been raised by "twenty-two poor children" who also expressed "their profound sympathy" to the president and his family. A reply from Cardinal Cushing written by his secretary Joseph Maguire swiftly made its way to Klein at the White House. "You may be sure that in accordance with the request of President and Mrs. Kennedy His Eminence will arrange for flowers at the grave."

When the president mounted the slight slope to his son's resting place, he carried his own bouquet of yellow chrysanthemums. Also greeting him on the grave was a bouquet of white flowers, along with a card reading: "From the Parish Boys' Group of the Church of San Tarcisio in the little town of Cura Carpignano, Italy." A short time later, the boys received a note from the president's personal secretary. "Dear Boys," it read. "When the President visited little Patrick's grave on October 19, he found the lovely flowers that you had put there. He and Mrs. Kennedy were deeply touched by this expression of sympathy and asked that I thank all of you for your kindness. With the President's every good wish, Sincerely yours, Evelyn Lincoln."

On that afternoon in October, President Kennedy stared at his son's grave for a moment, then prayed. The simple arched headstone he had designed poked from the grass; etched into its stone face was: PATRICK BOUVIER KENNEDY and below it, two dates: AUGUST 7, 1963–AUGUST 9, 1963.

Behind the small marker loomed a massive, twenty-ton Vermont granite monument bearing the name KENNEDY. Joe Sr. had bought the plot at Holyhood fifteen years earlier as the final resting place for the Kennedy line. It was large enough for twenty-four graves—and until now not one had been used. Patrick's headstone was off to the right down the slope in the shadow of the gigantic monument. "The President looked at the simple headstone," O'Donnell recalled, "and said to Dave and me, 'He seems so alone here.'"

⸻

The president managed to brighten somewhat after his gravesite visit. He had a little time to himself before he was to speak at a fundraiser in the evening. So, he and his entourage took a nostalgic stroll along Boylston Street, popping in at Schrafft's restaurant. Back in the 1940s and 1950s, during his congressional and senatorial campaigns, Jack used to make nightly ice cream stops at his favorite soda fountain. When he showed up at the counter now as president, teenaged clerk Peter Pellegriti froze, calling out: "Look who's here! Look who's here!" When Pellegriti was unable to pull himself together, another clerk, Diane Batchelor, stepped forward to take the president's order: a butterscotch sundae. Moments later, when she placed his sundae down on the counter, the starstruck Batchelor stood staring at the president for so long an irritated customer snapped: "How about some service here?"

"Can't you see who I'm serving," she shot back. "You'll just have to wait."

The president settled onto a stool, with buddy Dave Powers beside him working his way through a frappe (a New England milkshake) and two Secret Service agents nearby, one sucking down a chocolate frappe, the other lifting a soft drink to his lips. Partway through his sundae, President Kennedy realized he would need another round of cheering up later. "Get me a chocolate frappe with vanilla ice cream to take out," he instructed Powers, "so I can have it later at the hotel."

The men left Schrafft's and strolled along Boylston, pitching the street into chaos. A crowd of gawkers trailed the president. Powers in a hat walked at Jack's side with a paper sack that hid his chocolate frappe inside. "The automobiles on Boylston Street were bumping into each other, because the drivers were staring at the President," Powers recalled, "and everybody I knew in Boston wanted to know later what I was carrying in the paper bag."

In the evening, the president spoke at a $100-a-plate fundraiser at the Boston Commonwealth Armory attended by 7,500 supporters. (The $750,000 raised during the evening equals $7.5 million in today's dollars.) The president's welcome was deafening, in the words of *The Boston Globe*, "a resounding cheer that must have been audible from the Charles River to the Potomac."

On Sunday, the president left Boston to spend the day with his father in Hyannis Port. As his helicopter settled on the grass inside the family compound, the stroke-impaired seventy-five-year-old sat on his porch watching from his wheelchair. Joe Kennedy had wanted nothing more in life than a son in the White House, and he took immense joy in the performance of his son the president arriving and departing in his chopper. Still ringing in the president's ears perhaps was his father's repeated injunction issued to all the Kennedy kids as they grew up: "We don't want any losers around here. In this family we want winners."

But Joe's participation in his son's presidency in any meaningful way ended in December 1961 before Jack had completed his first year in office. While golfing at the Palm Beach Country Club, Joe suddenly lost his balance and staggered off the course without finishing his round. At home, he briefly fell asleep, then awoke "coughing and unable to speak or move on the right side," his niece Ann Gargan recalled. Joe's incapacitation from his stroke wrought a sudden change in the family dynamic. In an instant, as biographer David Nasaw brilliantly described the grim scene in *The Patriarch*, Joe was "transformed from the most vital, the smartest, the dominant one in the room to a . . . speechless, wheelchair-bound, utterly dependent shell of a man. His right arm and leg were paralyzed, his right hand had frozen into a clawlike appendage curled up at the wrist; the right side of his face drooped; he could not dress himself, feed himself, shave or shower, or communicate his thoughts, desires, fears, or hopes in spoken or written language. Yet he appeared to understand everything that was said to him, everything he read or heard or saw."

He fought against his debility with ferocity but progressed only so far. He was able to feed himself with assistance and communicate in a limited way, using the sole word still at his command: no. "He would bellow, 'No!' until the question came to which he could answer yes, and then he would change his tone of voice and signal with a smile, his blue eyes blazing, and say, 'No,' again but in such a way that everyone who heard him knew it mean yes," Nasaw wrote.

⸎

On that Sunday, the old man and his son the president spent all day together. Joe was rolled in his wheelchair down a ramp onto the *Marlin*, his fifty-two-foot motor yacht, and Jack took him out for a spin under an overcast sky on Nantucket Sound. They were joined by Gargan, who served as nurse and companion to Joe. Later, father and son spent part of the afternoon watching football on television. In the evening, Jack decided to stay overnight and leave early the next morning for Washington.

Around 8 a.m. on Monday, Joe was positioned on the porch to watch Jack take off. The onetime lord of the Kennedy clan was now a feeble spectator. "He had been a handsome young man, and he'd aged gracefully into the most handsome of older men," Nasaw recounted. "The stroke reversed all that. He was now—and he had to have known it—a twisted, gaunt old skeleton."

Whenever Jack bid his father farewell, he typically stuck to a familiar ritual. But today something inspired him to behave differently. As Ken O'Donnell wrote in his joint memoir with Dave Powers, "the President went to his father, put his arm around the old man's shoulders, and kissed his forehead. Then he started to walk away, turned and looked at his father for a moment, and went back and kissed him a second time, something Dave had never seen him do before."

Aboard the helicopter, Jack gazed through the window at his father up on the porch, and his eyes welled with tears. Whatever Joe's excesses as a father, his brazen philandering, his travesty of a marriage, Jack couldn't help feeling sentimental. The old man in the wheelchair—once so formidable—was now wizened into what a rehabilitative physician described as "a tragic figure." Gazing at his father before his chopper lifted off, Jack told Powers: "He's the one who made all this possible, and look at him now."

It was Jack's last trip to Hyannis Port.

TWENTY

—•••—

"I'll Campaign with You Anywhere You Want"

The week of John F. Kennedy's inauguration in 1961, First Lady-to-be Jacqueline graced the cover of *Time* magazine. The issue traced Jackie's life story, from her birth through her parents' divorce, her mother's remarriage, her debutante life, schooling at Vassar, her year at the Sorbonne in Paris, her courtship by Jack, engagement, and marriage, and her husband's obsession with politics and campaigning. The magazine was surprisingly candid on some points about their early life together, revealing: "In the gossipy circle they moved in, it was an open secret that the Kennedys' married life was far from serene."

The article then leaped ahead four years—gliding silently past any mention of the couple's miscarriages and stillbirth—to the arrival of Caroline. Jackie's "motherly instincts," her dedication to her daughter, and her commitment to her husband became the main features of her life, according *Time*, which superficially presumed that by this time "the Kennedys were well clear of the marital reefs."

Then, as Jack's ambition for the White House moved into the Kennedy narrative, so, too, did Jackie's aversion to politics. The *Time* piece veered back to an uncomfortable truth: "Jackie's biggest hurdle was her husband's profession," the article said. "Completely apolitical and shrinking instinctively from the hail-fellow habits of politicians, she has had a hard time adapting."

Jackie's distaste for politics was on full display even before Jack announced his candidacy for president in 1960. In September 1959, Ben Bradlee, then a political reporter for *Newsweek*, covered a Kennedy political event at a motel in Prince George's County, Maryland. "I remember most watching Jackie," he recounted, "and the almost physical discomfort she showed, as she walked slowly into this crowded hall to get stared at—not talked to, just simply stared at. Her reaction, later to become so familiar, was simply to pull some invisible shade down across the face, and cut out spiritually. She was physically present, but intellectually long gone. We were to see that expression a hundred times in the years to come."

When Jack's presidential campaign got underway, she kept her distance, using her pregnancy as the excuse. Readers of the *Time* inauguration article were reminded that gossip columnists had contended "Jackie was not pregnant—that it was all an elaborate hoax to remove her from the campaign scene." Underscoring her distaste for the political limelight, *Time* repeated a quip she had made to a friend about how she would organize her life once she was resident in the White House: "I'll get pregnant and stay pregnant. It's the only way out."

⸻

Now with the 1964 reelection campaign on the horizon, Jackie confronted a critical decision: Could she swallow her loathing of politics and get out on the hustings to support her husband's bid to retain his job? A lot had changed in the short time since Patrick's death. In the eyes of close friends and staff, Jack and Jackie were different with each other: more in step, more casual and nonchalant. Their moments of public affection were no longer shocking. The president "seemed much more attentive to her," recalled Secret Service agent Larry Newman (who had the same name as Jack's longtime Cape Cod friend journalist Larry Newman). The First Couple would seek each other out far more often now than at any previous time. At the end of the day Jackie was seen strolling into the West Wing to meet Jack and, Newman observed, the couple would leave the Oval Office walking "arm in arm to the mansion."

Jackie knew she had let Jack down by deserting him for the Aegean, and she admitted later to Father McSorley that since her return she wasn't as good to him as she might have been. She still fell into periods of darkness over Patrick's death and behaved poorly. "When I came back, he was trying to get me out of my grief and maybe I was a bit snappish," she said. "But I could have made his life so much happier, especially for the last few weeks. I could have tried harder to get over my melancholy."

On October 22, the First Couple invited the Bradlees for a private dinner at the White House, where discussion inevitably turned to Jackie's Aegean adventure. Jackie and Tony gossiped across the table about Onassis, while Jack and Ben spoke on their own about the ramifications of the trip. The unflattering press coverage still smarted: the vivid reports about the "brilliantly lighted luxury yacht," and "lavish shipboard dinners," and "dancing music." Jackie singled out a story in *Newsweek*, "which she felt went a little heavy on hi-jinks," according to Bradlee, who served as the magazine's Washington bureau chief. But, Bradlee added, Jackie seemed "a little remorseful about all the publicity" and said Jack was "really nice and understanding."

The president acknowledged that the trip was "potentially damaging to him politically." But he saw Jackie's mischief as a personal opportunity, telling Bradlee her "guilt feelings" could "work to his advantage." He wanted Jackie by his side a few weeks later when he was to set off on an early three-day campaign swing down South. Hoping to win her over, he turned to her and said: "Maybe now, you'll come with us to Texas next month."

Without hesitation, Jackie replied: "Sure I will, Jack."

Her response floored Ken O'Donnell: "I almost fell over when he told me Jackie was coming with us." It was to be Jackie's "first appearance on a Presidential campaign tour, much to [Jack's] delight and to the astonishment of all of us." Later, she confirmed her commitment, assuring Jack: "I'll campaign with you anywhere you want." And, as William Manchester reported, "She flipped open her red leather appointments book and scrawled 'Texas' across November 21, November 22, and November 23."

⸻

As planning got underway for their joint appearances in Texas, Jackie had one principal wish: she wanted to remain in the background. She did not want the kind of attention she attracted on their trip to Paris in 1961 when, with her excellent French, she charmed President Charles de Gaulle and took Paris by storm. Her presence so upstaged the president that he memorably delivered a witty opening at a Paris press conference: "I do not think it altogether inappropriate to introduce myself to this audience. I am the man who accompanied Jacqueline Kennedy to Paris, and I have enjoyed it." But he was apparently irritated by her inadvertent scene-stealing; it was early in his administration and he was still proving himself as president, especially in light of the debacle of the Bay of Pigs less than two months earlier. Journalist and author Marianne Means, who wrote a book on first ladies, told historian Robert Dallek that when she interviewed President Kennedy "it was clear to her that he had actually resented Jackie's spectacular emergence from his shadow."

Pamela Turnure said that on the upcoming campaign swing, Jackie "wanted to be the woman to accompany John Kennedy to Texas." She made clear "she wanted . . . to be with him—his helpmate—rather than be a predominant person in her own right."

Jackie planned to take, by her standards, a pared-down wardrobe; she would depart Washington without her personal maid, who normally helped her dress and pack on her travels. "She would do her own hair," Turnure said, and would be accompanied by only Mary Gallagher.

In response to press inquiries, Jackie instructed Turnure to say: "I am going out with my husband on this trip and that it will be the first of many that I hope to make with him." If anyone questioned her willingness to campaign, Turnure was to quote Jackie as saying: "I plan to campaign with him . . . I will do anything to help my husband be elected President again."

TWENTY-ONE

Bagpipes on the South Lawn

In the late afternoon of November 13, Jackie appeared before seventeen hundred guests on the South Lawn of the White House at her first official public event since Patrick's death. She had planned to resume her first lady duties at the beginning of the year, but her recovery progressed so well she pushed her return ahead by several weeks. It was to be a special day for children, many underprivileged, some disabled, others belonging to the president's brothers and sisters, close friends, and White House staff. Kids had started pouring through the White House gate at 3:30 p.m., scrambling across the South Lawn and clambering onto temporary bleachers.

Standing in formation on the lawn awaiting orders to march and play were musicians in kilts and feather hats, their instruments at the ready: bagpipes, trumpets, French horns, trombones, tubas, saxophones, clarinets, and drums. These performers were members of the Scottish Black Watch Band of the Black Watch Royal Highland Regiment. The young spectators were invited not only to watch a military band performance unlike anything they had ever seen but afterward to dig into mountains of cookies and gallons of hot chocolate.

The president and first lady had taken their seats with Caroline and John Jr. on the Blue Room Balcony overlooking the South Lawn. The occasion gave the nation a rare chance to see the First Family together. The joint appearance of the foursome marked the changing times. As Helen Thomas of United Press International wrote: "The image of the First Family these days is 'togetherness.'" She commended the Kennedys for their recent willingness to share family photos with the nation. "The President and Mrs. Kennedy have permitted more newspaper photographs of themselves with their children in the past month than they have in all their previous time in the White House," Thomas wrote.

Before the entertainment kicked off, the president and first lady came down from their perch on the balcony and crossed the lawn for a welcoming ceremony. Nancy Tuckerman advised the president to walk in front of the bleachers "so the children can see you." But it was Jackie who caught the attention of the crowd. She looked rested, even happy, *The Boston Globe* said, and suggested that her early public appearance came at the expense of the Black Watch. "It would be hard to convince those present that the main attraction was not a buoyant young woman in an off-white autumn coat, her tidy black hair dancing in the late afternoon breeze," the *Globe* wrote. "Mrs. Kennedy's eyes seem to glitter with that special delight of a woman fully convalescent and anxious to pick up the tempo of an active life."

At a microphone on the lawn, the president told the crowd that the history of Scotland had fascinated him from his youngest days. He spoke of the many contributions of the regiment to Britain's defense over the years and praised the Black Watch for siding with the United States in World War I, World War II, and the Korean War. "We regard it as a great honor to have the representatives of a great country here as our guests," he said. "That green and misty country has sent hundreds and thousands of Scottish men and women to the United States. And they have been among our finest citizens."

Major W. M. Wingate Gray, the Black Watch commander, stepped to the mic and presented the president with a small sword—an officer's dirk. Kennedy lowered his head to examine it, nearly bumping his forehead against the major's fluffy feather hat. The president and the major huddled, studying the dagger, as Wingate Gray explained in a quiet private exchange faintly picked up by the microphone: "It has an engraving on the blade, sir."

The president, captivated, held the dirk by its handle and slowly ran his thumb along the blade, and wondered out loud to the major: "What is the motto of the regiment?"

"'Nobody wounds us with impunity, sir,'" the major murmured as he reinserted the dirk into its scabbard.

Caroline and John Jr. kept an eye on their parents from the balcony. While the president and Major Gray exchanged remarks, Caroline, in a blue coat and white headband, stood up on an upholstered chair to reach a cup of hot chocolate served on a tray by the tuxedoed White House doorman Preston Bruce.

Stepping back to the mic, the president thanked the major for the dirk. He told the crowd that he just learned that the motto of the Black Watch was "Nobody wounds us with impunity." Jackie took a step closer to the president and was smiling as he added: "I think that's a very good motto for some of the rest of us."

The First Couple then strode back across the lawn in the autumn chill to rejoin their children on the balcony. The president had left his overcoat inside the White House, preferring the crisp look he achieved in just a suit jacket. When he returned to the porch, Preston Bruce had the winter coat in hand ready to help him into it: "Mr. President, would you like your overcoat now?"

"No, you put it on," Jack proposed to the doorman.

Bruce, in his light tuxedo jacket, was grateful. "I immediately put it around my shoulders because I was cold."

Major Gray came onto the balcony to view the performance in a seat next to the president. John Jr. marched over to him and bowed. Caroline leaped off her father's upholstered chair and curtsied. The family then settled in to watch the show. White House photographer Cecil Stoughton captured the Kennedys from behind, Caroline snuggled against her father with her arm around his shoulder and John Jr. propped on his mother's lap. Some fifty years later, Caroline had that photo on display in her home, she told the newsmagazine *60 Minutes* in 2015. The image, framed and inscribed "The Black Watch November 13, 1963," was dear to her mother. "It was the last picture of the four of us," Caroline said.

During the extended demonstration of music, marching, and sword-dancing, John Jr. became fidgety. Caroline eventually couldn't sit still either. And the president was called upon to give a stoic display of parental patience. "He sat there for about an hour with John-John and Caroline crawling all over him," doorman Bruce recalled. "At one point little John had his legs laced around his daddy's neck." It was, in Bruce's estimation, proof of the president as a "marvelous" father who took "extreme pleasure" in his children no matter the circumstances. In her appraisal of the afternoon, UPI's Helen Thomas concluded the Kennedys huddled on the balcony presented "a close family picture."

It was their last public appearance together.

That same evening, Caroline and John Jr. got a few minutes privately with their dad before going to bed. He was standing near Evelyn Lincoln's desk in the West Wing when nanny Shaw brought his daughter and son in for a final romp of the day. The president got down on the carpet and lay there as they pounced on him. Lincoln looked on, thinking this was not really the way one would expect a president to behave. "What would people think," she asked him, "if they saw the President down on the floor?"

"Mrs. Lincoln, I am also a father," he replied.

"There's no doubt about that," she agreed.

The kids then scrambled out onto the steps of the Rose Garden.

John Jr. took off chasing the cocker spaniel Shannon.

Caroline gazed up into the darkened sky.

"Star light, star bright," she said.

The president suddenly appeared beside her and looked skyward.

Caroline spoke again: "Star light, star bright."

Mrs. Lincoln prompted her: "First star I've seen tonight."

Caroline echoed: "First star I've seen tonight."

The president chimed in: "Up above the world so high."

Caroline responded: "Up above the world so high."

Lincoln was overcome "by the strangest feeling . . . eerie, like a warning" when the president instructed Caroline to go find "mommy" and recite those lines to her. "Then he slowly walked away."

The week before they left for Texas, Jack and Jackie didn't see much of each other. On Thursday, November 14, the day after the Black Watch performance, Jack set off on a five-day swing through New York and Florida while Jackie and the children spent time at Wexford, the family's 166-acre estate in the horse country of Atoka, Virginia.

In Manhattan, Jack dined at the Fifth Avenue apartment of his sister Jean and her husband, Steve Smith, in the company of his brother Bobby and wife Ethel, Oleg Cassini, Adlai Stevenson, and novelist William Styron. Jack spoke at two national conventions: the AFL-CIO and the Catholic Youth Organization. By Friday evening, the president was in Florida for a weekend of rest at his father's Palm Beach estate. On Saturday, he went to Cape Canaveral to witness a test submarine launch of a Polaris missile, a fairly recent addition to the nation's nuclear arsenal. He also surveyed the construction site of a Saturn rocket, which was intended to lift a man toward the moon.

While apart, Jack and Jackie contemplated their upcoming trip, each with their own shiver of trepidation. George Smathers, a longtime friend and Florida senator, recalled the president's growing obsession with death. Jack often asked Smathers how he would like to die and offered options: drowning, strangling, hanging. "He talked about that a *lot*," Smathers told journalist and author Ralph Martin. That weekend in Florida, Smathers remembered, the president had a note of doom in his voice. "God, I hate to go out to Texas," Jack confided to his friend. "I have a terrible feeling about going. I wish this was a week from today. Wish we had this thing over with."

At Atoka, Jackie had reservations about Texas but for less dire reasons. She passed the weekend horseback riding and visiting with British journalist and novelist Robin Douglas-Home, the nephew of the recently installed British prime minister, Alec Douglas-Home. Robin recounted his conversation and several others in a revealing portrait of the first lady which was published in 1967 first in the British magazine *Queen* then reprinted in newspapers around the world. (The profile caused a storm within the Kennedy family for its disclosures of Jackie's private ruminations.) Jackie confided to Robin that she preferred to stay away from Texas and all the glad-handing it required of her. "Jack knows I hate that sort of thing," she told him. "But all he said to me was 'I'd love you to come with me, but only if you really want to come.'" She was determined to be by his side now as part of her new commitment, as proof of their rejuvenated relationship. "If he wants me there, then that's all that matters," she told Robin. "It's a tiny sacrifice on my part for something that he feels is very important to him."

Jackie lingered in the comfort and seclusion at Wexford until Wednesday, the day before the departure to Texas. In the morning, she took a five-mile ride on her beloved horse Sardar, a gift from President Mohammad Ayub Khan during her 1962 visit to Pakistan. She left Wexford in the afternoon for a reunion with Jack and her first official White House event since Patrick's death: a traditional reception for Supreme Court justices and federal judges. She looked splendid mingling with some six hundred guests in a red velvet suit with a pale pink satin blouse and a diamond-and-ruby necklace. Though the evening was meant to honor Chief Justice Earl Warren and the associate justices, it was Jackie who "drew a crowd everywhere she went," a society reporter wrote. Even a federal judge acknowledged that for him Jackie was the center of attention. "I didn't come to see the president," he told the Associated Press. "I came to see her."

With the Texas trip looming, Jackie had come to believe that better times lay ahead for her and Jack. "She was convinced that the atmosphere in their marriage had changed," observed historian Thurston Clarke at a John F. Kennedy Library forum in 2013. Her husband's personal growth had altered the tenor of their relationship to such a degree that Jackie felt confident enough to insist to her friend Bill Walton: "I think we're going to make it. I think we're going to be a couple. I've won."

Jackie had finally arrived at the comfort she had chased throughout their years together. As she told Father Richard McSorley: "I had worked so hard at the marriage. I had made an effort and succeeded and he had really come to love me and to congratulate me on what I did for him." Jackie had stretched herself to accommodate Jack's wishes, and now she was prepared to drop her previous qualms about campaigning and hit the trail with him in Texas.

On Thursday morning, November 21, President Kennedy dressed in front of his bedroom mirror in clothes his valet had laid out for him: he secured his back brace, pulled on his shirt, and snapped his PT boat clip onto his tie. The frame of the mirror held a miscellany of memories: family photographs, a handwritten list of Masses at churches in Washington, a snapshot of Jackie, a postcard from Caroline written while vacationing with her mother in Italy in 1962: "I miss you daddy very much X Caroline," and an image of Caroline in her mother's high heels.

The president clapped his hands and called out: "Caroline! John!"

Waiting outside his door, the kids raced in on command and were at his side while he ate his breakfast from a tray.

Nanny Maud Shaw had prepped them about their parents' trip to Texas. It meant little to John Jr. other than his excited expectation of a helicopter landing on the White House lawn. For Caroline, separations from her father took on special meaning. "She liked to make the partings . . . memorable," author William Manchester observed. She liked to choose a special outfit to wear to say goodbye. On this morning, she had a last-minute change of mind and change of clothing; finally satisfied, she showed up in a dark blue velvet dress and a blue leotard and cheerily accepted her father's compliment.

It was a typical busy morning. As he ate, the president flipped through a stack of newspapers, studied briefing books, and got on the phone with Under Secretary of Defense Roswell Gilpatric, briefly tuning out John and Caroline's chatter.

At 9:15, Caroline hugged her father and whispered: "Bye, Daddy." Then she headed upstairs to her kindergarten classroom in the third-floor White House Solarium.

John Jr. stayed in the second-floor residence. A treat lay ahead for him.

At about 9:30, the president went downstairs to the Oval Office to meet with two U.S. ambassadors on their way to postings in Africa. In the hurried hour before his own departure, Kennedy wrote condolence notes to two Texas children of a U.S. serviceman who had died in a plane crash in Germany. "As you grow older," he told them, "you will realize the full importance of the service your father rendered his country and will take pride and comfort in the knowledge that his countrymen are deeply grateful for his contribution to the security of the Nation."

The president then went back upstairs to the residence. When three Marine helicopters touched down on the White House lawn, John Jr. watched from a window with unbridled joy. He knew what was coming.

Playing to Little John's love of flying machines, Jack had begun taking him aboard his Marine helicopter for the brief flight to Andrews Air Force Base whenever he set off on a trip.

Father and son rode downstairs holding hands in the wood-paneled elevator. Seeing Bob Foster of the Secret Service Kiddie Detail awaiting them, the boy cried out: "We're going in the helicopter, Mr. Foster!"

The day was gray and rainy, and John Jr. was outfitted in a London Fog raincoat and sou'wester of Army fatigue style. The president, first lady, and John Jr. climbed aboard Marine One along with Agent Foster and others in their entourage. As the choppers lifted off at 10:50,

Caroline briefly escaped from her classroom and waved goodbye from the White House roof.

During the roughly ten-minute flight to Andrews, John Jr.'s bubbliness was infectious. "President Kennedy got such a kick out of seeing John's enthusiasm," Agent Hill recounted, "I don't know who enjoyed it more—the president or his son."

But when the boy realized both his mother and his father were going away, his mood sank. Worst of all, he was not going to be clambering aboard Air Force One. From the chopper window, John Jr. locked the aircraft in his sights and his eyes gleamed.

As his father hugged him and said goodbye, the boy whimpered: "I want to come."

Jack gently explained: "You can't."

The tears came. His mother kissed him.

"It's just a few days, darling. And when we come back, it will be your birthday," she said. "Maybe we'll have a surprise or two."

His father patted his leg. "John, like Mummy said, we'll be back in a few days."

The president, worrying about photos of a crying son in the next day's newspapers, left John Jr. aboard the chopper. "The President kissed his sobbing son for the last time and patted the trembling shoulders in the small London Fog coat," Manchester wrote in *The Death of a President.*

He then said to the agent who was staying behind: "You take care of John, Mr. Foster."

"Yes, sir," Foster said. The agent thought the president's request was "odd." Though John Jr. had cried at other farewells, the president had never asked Foster to look after him.

When the First Couple left the helicopter, Agent Foster climbed into the president's seat and brought the boy onto his lap. To distract him, he told him tales of Bertram the Beaver, Jaggy the Jaguar, and Jasper the Jet.

As Air Force One lifted off, the three-year-old watched it slant skyward, pierce the clouds, and disappear.

Then John Jr. sighed.

As Manchester wrote, “he always loved to watch that plane.”

TWENTY-TWO

Texas: Animosity and Adulation

As Air Force One approached San Antonio International Airport, a moment of panic erupted on the ground. The skies had been closed. All aircraft were ordered to stay clear of the field until the president's jet was safely on the ground. But air traffic controllers suddenly flew into a flurry when a private jet on the eastern horizon radioed that it was heading for the runway. Communicating in air-traffic speak, the pilot insisted: "DV arriving." DV meant Distinguished Visitor, and the plane's pilot was immediately warned that those call letters at that moment referred only to the president. In seconds, another voice radioed from the white Jetstar on approach: John Connally, the governor of Texas, informed the control tower that he, too, was a distinguished visitor.

Connally, who was expected to greet the arriving president got a terribly late start after a speaking engagement in Houston. The tower took pity on him, broke the rules, and let his jet slip in ahead of the president's. On the ground, Connally hurried along the tarmac, shook some hands, and took up his place in the reception line joining Vice President Lyndon Johnson and others.

When the president's plane was spotted at the far end of the airfield taxiing toward the terminal, a man hollered: "There it is!" and the crowd of about five thousand let loose with wild cheers. The air was filled with cries of "Jackieee! Jackieee!"

Thus began the First Couple's nonstop sweep through the Lone Star State. Over two days, the president intended to hit five cities. On November 21, he and Jackie were to speed through San Antonio and Houston and arrive in the evening at Fort Worth. On November 22, the day was to begin with a breakfast appearance in Fort Worth, then it was on to Dallas for a nine-and-a-half-mile motorcade journey from Love Field to a luncheon at the Trade Mart; in midafternoon, the president was to fly to Austin for a fundraiser in the evening.

During the hectic swing, Kennedy hoped to heal rifts in the Texas Democratic Party. Among other issues, conservative Democrats abhorred his enlightened views on civil rights. Through much of his political career, Kennedy had little interest in the plight of Black Americans. But as president, he became appalled by the racist way of life in the South. Educated and prodded by Martin Luther King Jr., Kennedy was slowly emboldened to confront the scourge of white supremacist brutality. He evolved in stops and starts over his first two years as president until finally he had enough of racists like Alabama governor George Wallace. On June 11, 1963, the day Wallace stood in the schoolhouse door at the University of Alabama to block the admission of two Black students, the president rushed onto live national television to announce he was introducing civil rights legislation. The language of his speech reflected King's rhetoric, and the president's urgency revealed his newfound passion for civil rights. Asserting the need for change, Jack Kennedy declared: "We are confronted primarily with a moral issue."

Martin Luther King, watching the speech in Atlanta, leaped out of his seat and cried to a friend: "Can you believe that white man not only stepped up to the plate, he hit it over the fence!" King sent a telegram to the White House, praising the address as "one of the most eloquent, profound and unequivocal pleas for justice and freedom for all men ever made by any president."

Kennedy was emerging as the country's first civil rights president, a laudable mark of political transformation but one that enraged a wide swath of Southern voters. It was no secret that many Texans despised the president and bluntly expressed it. Before Kennedy arrived, Abraham Zapruder, a Dallas dressmaker, had a disturbing conversation with a young man in a department store. The encounter began as a brief debate on civil rights. The man seemed to resent Kennedy's power to alter the longstanding culture of Southern racial relations. "God made big people," he said, referring to Kennedy. Indicating himself, he said: "And God made little people." The young man's final comment chilled Zapruder: "But Colt made the 45 to even things out."

With the 1964 election looming, Kennedy needed to soften Southern rancor. And he had to win Texas for a second time. But in early polls he was lagging. The state was leaning toward right-wing Arizona senator Barry Goldwater.

At the San Antonio airport, however, the president and first lady couldn't have received a warmer welcome. As they stepped onto the tarmac and walked along the line of waiting dignitaries, chatting and shaking hands, boisterous spectators called out to them. Signs reading "Kennedy in '64" bobbed in the crowd.

Suddenly Jack threw the Secret Service into a scramble. Instead of heading directly to the limousine, as planned, he moved toward the throng barricaded behind a low fence. That he went to chat and shake hands was no surprise—he "couldn't resist," Agent Hill explained. Jackie, by contrast, was never comfortable in a crush of well-wishers. "This was the kind of thing she tried to avoid," the agent recalled. But something had changed. "Mrs. Kennedy took me completely by surprise," Hill said, "and followed the president toward the crowd. She had never done this before." Demonstrating a surprising boldness, Jackie plunged into the exultant mob right behind her husband. "She followed the President's lead, tentatively reaching her gloved hand into the crowd," Hill recounted. "Ladies were shrieking at the sight of the president and calling out 'Jackie! Jackie!' "

The trip to Texas marked the start of something new for Jack and Jackie. Very late in their complicated marriage, they had attained "a mutual understanding, a greater love for each other," concluded author Thomas Maier. Patrick's tragedy was, with sad irony, a gift to his parents. As historian Thurston Clarke observed, his loss "haunted them and brought them together."

Jackie's confidant Robin Douglas-Home asserted that the loss of Patrick "acted as a kind of catalyst in the relationship between Jacqueline Kennedy and her husband. His reaction to the child's death, as recounted by her [and] her own reactions to his. This tragedy brought them closer together than ever before, to a new plateau of understanding, respect, and affection."

That Jackie accompanied him to Texas reinforced their mutual resolve to be together. Her presence had a collateral impact: it kept other women at bay. As Mimi Beardsley recounted, "I had been scheduled to take one last trip with the president." But in late October, around the time Jackie agreed to campaign with Jack, Beardsley got a call from Dave Powers. He told her the plans had changed: "I was no longer on that trip."

In San Antonio, the president and first lady climbed into their Secret Service limousine, a 1961 midnight-blue Lincoln Continental convertible, the same open vehicle that would carry them through Dealey Plaza in Dallas the following day. As the motorcade moved along its fifteen-mile route in bright sunshine, an estimated 125,000 people packed the sidewalks and spilled into the streets. Handwritten signs bobbed here and there: "Welcome, JFK," "Bienvenido, Mr. President," "Jackie, Come Waterski in Texas!" Schoolchildren waved American flags.

In the downtown district, confetti fluttered over the motorcade. The car carrying the press stalled, blocking the vehicles behind it. Chaos briefly ensued. With a busy schedule and no time to lose, the Secret Service agent at the wheel of the limo hit the gas to hurry the president to his first destination: Brooks Air Force Base.

Shortly before 3 p.m., President Kennedy and the first lady mounted a speaker's platform erected on a vast lawn outside the headquarters of the United States Air Force Aerospace Medical Division. Here the School of Aerospace Medicine was conducting crucial research to advance President Kennedy's dream of landing a man on the moon.

Seated on folding chairs, some ten thousand Air Force personnel and guests strained for a look at the "youthful Commander in Chief," wrote Green Peyton, chief historian of the Aerospace Medical Division, in a rather idolatrous re-creation of the scene. The president appeared onstage, Peyton observed, as "if he had been evoked by some feat of magic out of the brisk November air." Peyton highlighted the president's "rather mischievous smile" and enthused that his "infectious gaiety [and] personal magnetism had never been more evident than it was at this moment. He gave the impression of being at the height of all his powers, supremely confident, enjoying himself and the effect that he produced on his audience."

In a rousing New Frontier speech underscoring the essential challenge of space exploration, the president undertook his purpose of the visit: to dedicate a collection of buildings making up a new Aerospace Medical Health Center. He promised that not only did advances in space medicine safely lift astronauts into orbit, they also pointed the way to understanding a variety of health issues affecting the community at large. Experiments aimed at protecting astronauts from radiation in space were applicable to similar dangers on Earth. New devices developed to measure astronauts' heart and breathing rates, brain waves, and eye movements would prove useful for everyday patients. Leaps in science, technology, and medicine in one field, the president's message was, would eventually benefit all of humanity. "Just as the wartime development of radar gave us the transistor, and all that made possible, so research in space medicine holds the promise of substantial benefit for those of us who are earthbound," he told the crowd.

The research was already delivering U.S. astronauts into space and returning them home. In the latest success just six months earlier, Gordon Cooper had circled the Earth twenty-two times over thirty-four hours in a Project Mercury spacecraft, and the next phase, Project Gemini, was moving forward apace, with hopes pinned on the future prize of a moon landing.

But daunting obstacles lay ahead. To illustrate his determination, the president drew on the words of the Irish writer Frank O'Connor. In his youth, O'Connor was hiking through the countryside with friends when they found their path blocked by an orchard wall that looked too high to climb. Refusing to be deterred, the boys told themselves it was impossible not to carry on. "They took off their hats," Kennedy told the audience, "and tossed them over the wall—and then they had no choice but to follow them." The space program, the president promised, was just as committed to its task. "This Nation," Kennedy concluded, "has tossed its cap over the wall of space and we have no choice but to follow it. Whatever the difficulties, they will be overcome. . . . We will climb this wall with safety and with speed—and we shall then explore the wonders on the other side."

The crowd erupted in raucous applause.

The president and first lady were behind schedule, and the Secret Service team wanted to rush him along. But there was one location on the vast base that the president had to visit. With Major General T. C. Bedwell Jr., commander of the Aerospace Medical Division, leading the way, the president's small procession filed back inside the Medical Division headquarters, strolled along the corridors, then exited outdoors again and crossed a driveway and a lawn, and passed a new Aeromedical Library. The parade stepped into another building and followed the major general to the Altitude Laboratory.

Awaiting the president was Billy E. Welch, a thirty-four-year-old scientist who led the Medical Division's research into the complex atmospheric conditions inside a spacecraft. Welch was warned at the last minute that the president might stop by. "We did tidy up," he said, "and told our people to be on their best behavior."

What sparked Kennedy's interest was an intriguing human experiment underway in the Altitude Lab. Welch briefly explained the project to the president: four airmen, seventeen to nineteen years old, from nearby Lackland Air Force Base had taken up residence for a month inside a hyperbaric oxygen chamber and were breathing pure oxygen in a simulated altitude of 27,500 feet. The aim was to study the body's reactions to space travel in an environment that replicated cabin conditions expected to exist aboard the Gemini and Apollo spacecraft.

Alerted their high-profile visitor was on the way, the airmen quickly donned new gowns. When the president stepped up to a window for a look inside, the movement "caught the attention of one of the airmen, and he glanced up. His jaw dropped," wrote Peyton, the Medical Division historian. Kennedy then placed a headset with a mic "over the celebrated shock of auburn hair."

Seventeen-year-old Airman Third Class Phillip Jameson, known as "Flip," was thrilled when he heard the president's famous Boston accent. "I can't tell you how big the grins were on all four of our faces—they were just huge," he recalled.

The president "gave us a wide smile and waved," remembered eighteen-year-old Airman Third Class Thomas Rusiecki.

With his usual curiosity, the president peppered the men with questions about their experiences inside the chamber. What were their days like? How did they sleep? What had they learned? Airman Jameson quickly realized the man in the headset wasn't that different from him: "He wasn't the president when he talked to us, he was just a person that was into space."

The president gave the men his highest praise, Jameson recalled: "He says you are the perfect model of 'ask not what your country can do for you but what you can do for your country.'" Jameson knew the expression from the president's inaugural address, "but for him to say we were the model . . . was very exciting. Very very exciting."

The experience became even more thrilling when Jackie stepped into full view in the window.

"Here, Jackie," the president said, peeling off his headset and inviting her to try it on, "have a talk with the men."

The first lady, wearing a beret on her well-coifed hair, politely declined her husband's offer with a laugh and shake of her head.

The young captives nonetheless were bowled over by the sight of her. All four of the guys were "taken by Jackie's beauty," Rusiecki recalled. Writing to his mother later, he said: "She didn't say anything, but smiled and gave us a good luck sign."

Speaking into the headset, President Kennedy signed off, telling the men: "Good luck."

"Thank you, Sir. Good luck to *you*."

As passionate as he was about the space program, the president had an ulterior motive for looking in on the high-altitude project. The Air Force's experimental use of a hyperbaric oxygen chamber held special resonance for him. "The death of his infant son, Patrick Bouvier Kennedy, was still weighing on his mind," observed Ken O'Donnell. And the president had some questions for lead researcher Billy Welch.

Taking the scientist aside, the president said, "Apart from the space research, there must be other medical implications here. Do you think your work might improve oxygen chambers for, say, premature babies?"

Without mentioning his son, Kennedy spoke of the fragile lungs of premature infants and hoped that possible treatment in an oxygen chamber might one day prove beneficial.

Welch thought it was an intriguing idea, but he was puzzled why the president had such deep interest in the subject. Welch had been obsessed with his own research in recent months and had paid scant attention to the news. He had missed not only the headlines about Mrs. Kennedy's pregnancy but also the national trauma over Patrick, including deployment of the hyperbaric chamber. "He wondered why the President should be concerned with infant mortality," Manchester wrote, "and why, as Kennedy turned for a final glance into the steel tank, his tanned face should seem so pensive."

Welch told the president that the work he was overseeing would benefit a range of medical endeavors—he outlined a few—and, yes, it might have implications for oxygen-chamber treatment of premature infants. "President Kennedy looks at his wife, and their eyes lock," Hill recalled. "Nothing is said, but I know they are both thinking about their baby Patrick."

After the visit, when Welch learned the reason for the president's interest in prematurity and oxygen chambers, he was moved by the profound sorrow that inspired the questions. "As a father myself," he said, "I think . . . it was something that was deep in his heart. We forget that Presidents are human. We forget that they have emotions just like the rest of us do. . . . They hurt just like we do."

After a stop in Houston, the president and first lady attended a Chamber of Commerce breakfast in Fort Worth. Jackie was twenty minutes late coming downstairs to the grand ballroom of the Texas Hotel. Jack wanted her looking her best for Dallas, their next stop just a thirteen-minute flight away, and Jackie lost track of time while dressing. The crowd of two thousand, the president knew, was more interested in seeing her than in anything he had to say. When she walked in, giving breakfast-goers the first peek at her Chanel-inspired pink suit and pillbox hat, pandemonium broke out. People stood on their chairs cheering, straining for a look at her. Jackie smiled slightly into the bright lights but the uproar frightened her. Her eye fell on Jack at the podium, and she calmed a little.

As William Manchester described it: "She saw her husband smiling at her. He seemed far away, but he was beckoning reassuringly, standing steadfast as she moved toward him through the strange valley of clamor, her hand outstretched, her eyes on his. Their hands touched. The tumult subsided." Jack was reminded of the adoration Jackie inspired on a previous trip, telling the audience: "Two years ago I introduced myself in Paris by saying that I was the man who had accompanied Mrs. Kennedy to Paris." But this time he had no reservations; in fact, he was delighted by the public response to his wife. "I am getting somewhat the same sensation as I travel around Texas. Nobody wonders what Lyndon and I wear."

After the breakfast, Jack and Jackie rested a short while upstairs in their hotel suite. When Ken O'Donnell popped in, he found them in a cheerful mood, pleased by their reception in the grand ballroom. In his memoir, he re-created the camaraderie that now existed between them: "Jackie was saying, 'I'll go anywhere with you this year.' The President, laughing, said to her, 'How about California in the next two weeks?' She said, 'I'll be there.' He turned to me and said, 'Did you hear *that*?' " O'Donnell, knowing what a boon Jackie was to her husband's campaign, couldn't contain his excitement: "I was grinning like an ape."

Then it was on to Dallas.

TWENTY-THREE

Red Roses for Jackie

As Air Force One rolled to a stop at Love Field, President Kennedy saw the large, enthusiastic crowd waiting behind a fence. He was aware of ugly false accusations against him circulating to the large readership of the respected *Dallas Morning News*, claiming Kennedy was soft on communism and had even signed a secret agreement with the U.S. Communist Party. That, and other dark provocations, some charging the president with treason, were fluttering from lip to lip. But gazing out at the warm welcome awaiting him in Dallas, Jack preferred to lean toward the positive. "This trip is turning out to be terrific," he told O'Donnell. "It looks like everything in Texas is going to be fine for us."

Among the dignitaries at Love Field to greet the First Couple were Vice President Lyndon Johnson and Dallas mayor Earle Cabell. The mayor's wife, Dearie, presented Jackie with a robust bouquet of red roses. The flowers were a surprise: at their other stops in Texas, Jackie had received yellow roses that had brought to mind the unofficial state song: "The Yellow Rose of Texas." "But in Dallas they gave me red roses," she told writer Theodore White. "I thought how funny, red roses." When she climbed into the limousine, she placed the bouquet on the backseat between her and her husband.

As the motorcade made its way toward Dealey Plaza, Abraham Zapruder climbed onto a four-foot-high concrete block overlooking Elm Street opposite the Texas School Book Depository. It wasn't long before the president and first lady came into view in the open limousine crawling through the plaza at about eleven miles per hour. Zapruder flicked the run button on his top-of-the-line, Bell & Howell eight-millimeter movie camera.

"OK, here we go," he murmured.

What happened in Dealey Plaza that afternoon not only shocked America, it also forever defined a young mother and her two small children. In the nation's collective imagination, those few seconds in Dallas locked Jacqueline Kennedy, Caroline, and John Jr. in a historical moment. The horror that streamed across Zapruder's lens turned Jackie into a courageous survivor; it also snuffed out her dream that she and Jack might grow old together in a love they had rediscovered too late. For millions of Americans, Dealey Plaza left Caroline and John Jr. frozen forever as adorable youngsters whose lives were shattered before they began to take shape.

Zapruder's film gave rise to an afterlife of unanswered questions. Thirty-five years later, *The New York Times* opined that of all of America's cultural artifacts, Zapruder's brief thread of color Kodachrome film was perhaps the most closely examined. "It has been sped up, slowed down, reversed, enhanced," the newspaper wrote. "People will always remember where they were when President Kennedy was shot. But in a sense the one place we all were is behind the lens of Mr. Zapruder's camera."

Zapruder's film also occasions us to wonder: Had no bullets flown that day, how would Jack and Jackie have fared together in their next chapter?

At Parkland Memorial Hospital, Jackie sat on a folding chair outside Trauma Room 1, certain her husband was already dead. There was no way he could have survived the bullets that slammed into his neck and head. *She saw.* She saw a "flesh-colored . . . piece of his skull," at first strangely there was no blood, then blood everywhere, splashing onto her pink suit and the bouquet of flowers. As she recalled later: "all the seat was full of blood and red roses."

During the six-minute dash to the hospital at speeds of up to eighty miles per hour, she cradled her husband's limp body in her arms, his head resting in her lap, muttering again and again: "He's dead—they've killed him—oh Jack, oh Jack, I love you."

At the emergency dock, she tried to hide him from eyes prying into the open limo, a last chance to protect his privacy. She was in shock, reality reaching her only in small bursts. When they wanted to get the president onto a gurney, she resisted.

"Mrs. Kennedy, please let us help the president," Agent Hill said. "Please let us get him into the hospital."

Only after Hill understood her hesitation and draped his coat over her husband's head and upper body, concealing his gruesome appearance, did Jackie let them take him. She ran alongside the gurney, keeping her hand on it all the way to Trauma Room 1. When they rolled him inside, she settled onto that folding chair outside the door.

"Mrs. Kennedy was sitting there, the epitome, the total epitome of forlornness, she was totally traumatized," remembered Elizabeth Harris, who had helped with advance planning for the Dallas stopover. "People would try to speak to her, she didn't want to talk to anybody—she just simply did not respond."

When Jackie heard someone inside the trauma room say "resuscitation," she couldn't believe it. "He's still alive," she thought. "Could there be a chance that he could live?" Standing nearby were a few of Jack's closest aides, Ken O'Donnell, Larry O'Brien, and Dave Powers. She whispered to them, "Do you think . . . ?"

"I did not have the heart to tell her what I was thinking," O'Donnell recalled. He couldn't stay there next to her. "I walked down the hall with Dave and said to him, 'If he's got a chance, it's a thousand to one.'"

When the men said nothing and just walked away, Jackie understood and was determined to be by Jack's side when he died. "I'm going in there," she announced to the collection of people huddled outside the trauma room.

"You can't come in here," a nurse said, blocking the door. Relatives weren't allowed inside for their own good—and the patient's.

But it was her husband who was in there. "I'm coming in," Jackie repeated, "and I'm staying."

She had to get past the nurse in her white uniform and rubber-soled shoes. Their contest became gently physical: a show of pushing, and a show of obstructing, and Jackie whispering, "I'm going to get in that room."

The White House physician, George Burkley, who was struggling to hold himself together, was drawn toward the commotion. "Mrs. Kennedy," he said with a quavering voice, "you need a sedative."

Jackie was adamant: "I want to be in there when he dies."

Burkley heard her plea: if that was what she needed, he was going to get her into that room. He angled her through the nurse's blockade, repeating: "It's her right, it's her right, it's her prerogative." The nurse, thinking Burkley was a Secret Service agent, grudgingly stepped aside.

Inside, Burkley and Mrs. Kennedy were crammed against a back wall of the cold, sterile tomb that was Trauma Room 1. No windows, no natural light, just a medical-industrial glare from overhead hitting the black rubber floor, gray metal cabinets, stacks of gauze, a green oxygen cannister. In the center was her husband, the president of the United States, lying on his back on a thick leather pad, naked except for his undershorts. The assassin's bullets had caught only Jack's head and neck. His torso was just as it was when he was dressing that morning, if you ignored a couple of chest tubes and a doctor massaging the skin over his rib cage in hopes of keeping his heart beating. Though well-meaning doctors were working hard to save his life, it was impossible to believe that Trauma Room 1 could ever be anything more than an unlovely, impersonal place where no wife would want her husband to spend his final moments.

Burkley hovered protectively around Jackie in case she fainted or someone tried to drag her out of there. "She leaned forward," William Manchester recounted, "and rested her spattered cheek on Burkley's shoulder. Then she dropped briefly to the floor, knelt in the President's blood, and closed her eyes in prayer. She rose again and stood erect."

At 1 p.m. (Dallas time), after heroic medical interventions proved futile, Dr. Marion Jenkins performed the definitive act: he pulled a sheet over the face of President John F. Kennedy. Dr. Burkley confirmed the absence of a pulse, then cleared the room. Everything had happened so fast: only thirty minutes earlier, at 12:30 p.m., the fatal shots were heard in Dealey Plaza.

Jackie stayed with Jack. Two doctors also remained briefly. Dr. Robert McClelland, a surgeon who had assisted in the emergency measures to save her husband, recalled that throughout the crisis, the first lady, in her bloodied pink suit, behaved "in a truly wonderful, regal, self-contained manner." In the stillness afterward, she approached Jack, kissed his foot, which was protruding from the sheet, kissed his hand, kissed his forehead, and laid her head on his chest. McClelland had witnessed the gore in the cramped room that day, and his own clothing was stained with the president's blood. But watching Jackie bid farewell to her husband, he wrote to a friend, was "the most poignant and worst moment for all of us."

⁂

At the White House, Caroline and John Jr. had finished their lunch, all the while chattering with nanny Maud Shaw about their birthdays: little John would be three in three days; Caroline would turn six two days later. The kids retired to the sitting room in the private residence. Caroline was in an easy chair reading a book. John Jr. lay on the floor on his stomach, doing his best to stay within the lines of his coloring book.

Shaw was in her room about to go scoop them up for their afternoon naps when the phone rang. Information was filtering out slowly in bits and pieces. Downstairs in the East Wing, news that the president had been shot—nothing more—had reached the first lady's social secretary Nancy Tuckerman, a friend of Jackie's for twenty years. Tuckerman began making phone calls to break the news gently to the family's inner circle: Jackie's mother Janet, sister Lee. When the Kennedys' nanny picked up the phone, she heard Tuckerman's voice: "Miss Shaw."

The line fell silent for a moment. Tuckerman's genteel style was to build up to the point, beginning with a casual inquiry: Was her listener busy? Then moving on tactfully, until she came to the reason for the call. "I have some bad news for you," Tuckerman told Shaw. "I'm afraid the President has been shot."

She had no further details.

Shaw went to get the kids.

"Come along, children," she said, putting on a bright face. "It's time for your rest now."

She escorted them to their rooms.

John fell asleep immediately.

Caroline sat up reading.

Shaw was unable to sit still. Wandering through the White House, she bumped into Bob Foster of the Kiddie Detail. Usually he was a cheerful companion, "big and suntanned," easygoing with the kids.

But at that moment "he looked ghastly—pale-faced and ill," Shaw recalled.

Foster, a Republican known for his sense of humor and fine clothing, which earned him the code name Dresser, was staring straight ahead with tears in his eyes.

"The President's dead," he said.

⁂

Jackie sat on the folding chair outside the trauma room at Parkland Memorial while nurses and orderlies cleaned the president's body. She wanted to leave something with Jack, something of hers he would carry with him to eternity. She remembered the St. Christopher medal that Jack had placed in Patrick's casket. She wanted to do something like that. But what?

Gradually Jackie was reconnecting to reality. In Manchester's telling, she was still weak, still faint, but "she retained her heightened sense of awareness. She was thinking clearly, and she was thinking ahead."

She realized there was one thing that meant more than anything to her, one thing that tied her and Jack together both symbolically and emotionally. She asked O'Donnell to make sure she could get back inside the trauma room while Jack was still there. She needed a moment with him. When the last nurse came out, she and O'Donnell got their chance. Inside, Jackie slid off her wedding ring. It was an ordinary band Jack had hurriedly bought in Newport prior to their wedding. "The ring," she thought, "would be exactly right." As she told Theodore White later, "it's the closest thing I have to the memory of him." She lifted Jack's hand and tried to work the ring on but it stopped at his knuckle. An orderly stepped forward helpfully with some cream. "I put the ring on," she recalled, "then I kissed his hand."

Outside the room, she was stricken with doubt.

"Do you think I did the right thing?" she asked O'Donnell.

His sympathy for Jackie was absolute: "I was not going to disagree with anything she wanted to do right now," he recalled. He told her: "You leave it right where it is."

But her regret nagged at him. Had she acted too impulsively in a haze of grief?

White House aides were anxious to get Jackie and her late husband back to Washington. When a casket arrived from a local mortuary, the president's body was wheeled out to a white hearse parked at the emergency entrance. From the trauma room to the hearse, Jackie didn't leave his side. "As soon as they came out of that little room," advance planner Elizabeth Harris said, "she walked with them and never took her hand off the casket. She wasn't going to be parted from him at that point. There was this feeling that you got from her that she was almost fixed, tied to him, tied to the casket."

At the emergency loading dock, Agent Hill proposed that he and Jackie ride in a car behind the hearse back to Love Field, where Air Force One waited. But as Hill recounted in his book *Five Days in November*, written with Lisa McCubbin, Jackie refused to be separated from her husband.

"No," she insisted. "I'm going to ride in the hearse with the president."

Jackie, Hill, and Dr. Burkley crowded into the hearse with the casket. Andy Berger, the Secret Service agent whose son had survived hyaline membrane disease, climbed behind the wheel and sped to the airport. On the drive, Dr. Burkley rummaged for something in his pockets. Before departing, he had slipped into the trauma room to make sure none of the president's belongings were left behind. When he flipped open the stainless-steel trash can, his eye fell on a red rose lying amid the mess of used sponges and gauze and empty drug boxes. On the floor next to the trash can lay another remnant of the first lady's welcome bouquet. In the hearse, Burkley pulled from his pocket an envelope containing the two roses. He shook them onto his palm and presented them to Jackie.

She silently slipped them into her suit pocket.

At the airport, Secret Service agents struggled to lift the casket onto Air Force One, its engines already whirring. It was placed in the rear compartment in a space widened by the removal of several seats. Jackie settled in near her husband's body. She was joined by Dr. Burkley and the president's buddies Ken O'Donnell and Dave Powers. The presidential jet rolled down the runway at 2:47 p.m. (Dallas time) and lifted off for Andrews Air Force Base.

⊰◇⊱

At the White House, the afternoon had dissolved into disbelief and confusion. The staff learned that Mrs. Kennedy was flying back from Dallas and was expected to return by six o'clock. Then word came she couldn't bear to see the children just yet: they had to go somewhere. Suitcases were quickly packed. Shaw, explaining only in the vaguest terms, whisked the kids to Jackie's mother on O Street. But no sooner had they settled in than the plans changed. At around 7:30, as Shaw was about to take Caroline and John Jr. upstairs to bed, Agent Foster came in looking "more harassed than ever." Everyone had to gather their belongings, it was time to go. "Mrs. Kennedy is coming back tonight," Foster announced, "and wants the children in the house with her."

Shaw tried to turn all the to-and-froing into a form of play.

"Dear me, what a night!" she chirped, explaining: "Mummy wants us." She asked Caroline to be her "bestest friend" and make sure John Jr. got into his coat.

"Caroline slapped her hand across her mouth to smother a giggle," Shaw remembered. "It was all a big game."

While Air Force One was streaking through the night sky toward Washington, Jackie, O'Donnell, and Powers traded stories of the man they had lost. "Our talk with Jackie beside the casket," O'Donnell recalled, "was like the talk at an Irish wake, filled with sentimental reminiscences." Jackie had begun sketching out the funeral, calling up memories that she turned into essential elements of the Mass. Jack loved Luigi Vena, a Boston tenor who performed at their wedding, so Vena would sing "Ave Maria" and "Agnus Dei." Jackie recalled how much Jack loved the Black Watch performance at the White House: "They must be at the funeral too."

Jackie, who had a special fondness for Joe Kennedy, listened raptly as Powers recounted Jack's final visit with his father. He told her about Jack putting his arm around the patriarch's shoulders and kissing him on the forehead—and then, after walking away, looking back and going to the old man again to plant a second kiss on him. "It almost seemed," Powers told Jackie, "as if the President had a feeling that he was seeing his father for the last time."

O'Donnell and Powers both recounted Jack's visit to Patrick's grave on his last trip to Boston—and his remark about their infant looking "so alone" there. Jackie told them she would fix that. Her intention was to bury Jack at Arlington National Cemetery and bring Patrick from Holyhood in Brookline to lie beside his father. She promised, "I'll bring them together now."

At the White House, butlers, maids, and ushers had fallen into dazed, tearful paralysis. Chief usher J. B. West, though numb himself, set the staff in motion, knowing the White House would soon fill with aides, friends, family, and overnight visitors.

"I summoned everybody, had the butlers prepare to serve coffee, had the maids prepare all the guest rooms, little meaningless things," he said, "but a signal that our work must go on."

Nanny Shaw had hurried the kids back to the residence. No one was sure of Mrs. Kennedy's exact whereabouts or when she would arrive. Then word came she was going to the Naval Hospital in Bethesda. She would stay with the president's body during his autopsy. Her delay gave Shaw time to hustle Caroline and John Jr. into their beds. The little ones still had no idea what was going on or what had happened to their father.

Janet Auchincloss was at Bethesda Naval Hospital to meet Jackie. Mother and daughter had a difficult conversation about the children: Who was going to break the news to them? Mrs. Auchincloss was not the right person for it. And Jackie was too distraught. Bobby Kennedy, who had an ease with children, was shattered and fixated on looking after Jackie and planning the funeral. The task fell to the woman who, after their parents, was closest to the young Kennedys.

Outside the Otis hospital suite, press secretary Pierre Salinger briefed reporters on plans for Patrick's funeral. Cardinal Richard Cushing would preside over a private Mass in a small chapel on the grounds of his residence. Jackie, still recovering from her caesarean operation, was too weak to attend.

Cecil Stoughton, White House/John F. Kennedy Presidential Library and Museum

After the Mass on August 10, the funeral cortege set off to Holyhood Cemetery in Brookline for the burial. Jack was so distraught he at first refused to leave the chapel. "He literally put his arms around that casket [and shed] copious tears," Cardinal Cushing recalled.

Calvin Campbell/Boston Herald/John F. Kennedy Presidential Library and Museum

On her first visit to see her mother at the Otis hospital, Caroline brought a bouquet of larkspur, black-eyed susans, and pink trumpet lilies she had picked herself. As she approached the VIP suite, Caroline lifted her father's hand to her lips and kissed it. As one observer noted: "It will be a long time before any photographer snaps a better picture."
Bettmann/GettyImages

Five days after Patrick's death, Jackie left the hospital. Surprising onlookers, she and Jack came out of the suite holding hands in a rare public display of affection from the famously reserved couple.
Bettmann/GettyImages

At their summer home with their lively brood of dogs later the same day, the family faced their sorrow. Patrick's loss changed Jack Kennedy—as biographer Donald Spoto observed: "This man was never more attentive to his wife and children than during . . . the last three months of his life."
Cecil Stoughton, White House/John F. Kennedy Presidential Library and Museum

Several staff members at Otis Air Force Base Hospital, including Dr. Charles Sanislow, the chief of surgery, received a signed, framed lithograph of the White House inscribed: "With deep appreciation, Jacqueline Kennedy, August 1963."
Courtesy of Dr. Charles A. Sanislow

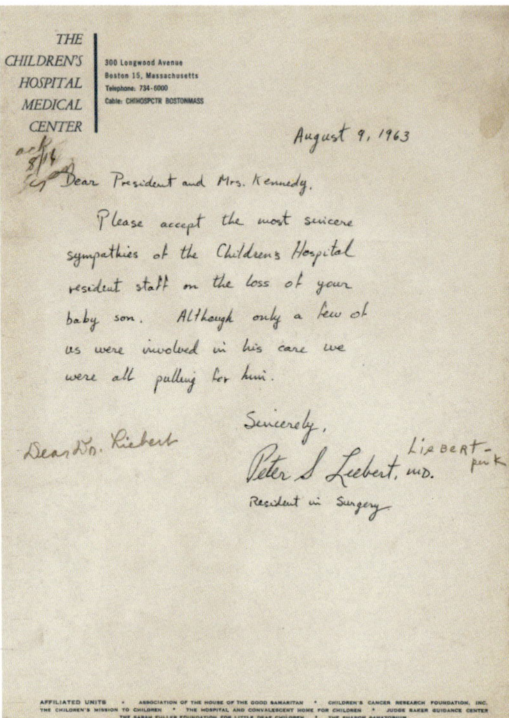

THE CHILDREN'S HOSPITAL MEDICAL CENTER

300 Longwood Avenue
Boston 15, Massachusetts
Telephone: 734-6000
Cable: CHIHOSPCTR BOSTONMASS

August 9, 1963

ack 8/14

Dear President and Mrs. Kennedy,

Please accept the most sincere sympathies of the Childrens Hospital resident staff on the loss of your baby son. Although only a few of us were involved in his care we were all pulling for him.

Sincerely,

Peter S Liebert, MD.
Resident in Surgery

Dear Dr. Liebert

LIEBERT - pink

AFFILIATED UNITS • ASSOCIATION OF THE HOUSE OF THE GOOD SAMARITAN • CHILDREN'S CANCER RESEARCH FOUNDATION, INC.
THE CHILDREN'S MISSION TO CHILDREN • THE HOSPITAL AND CONVALESCENT HOME FOR CHILDREN • JUDGE BAKER GUIDANCE CENTER
THE SARAH FULLER FOUNDATION FOR LITTLE DEAF CHILDREN • THE SHARON SANATORIUM

Dr. Peter Liebert, a twenty-seven-year-old pediatric resident at Children's Hospital, was one of the many medical staff members who developed a deep attachment to the distraught First Family and their son. Liebert was moved to write a note expressing the staff's "most sincere sympathies" for Patrick's loss. Days later, he got a signed response from the president with a personal inscription: "Many thanks for all that you did."
John F. Kennedy Presidential Library and Museum

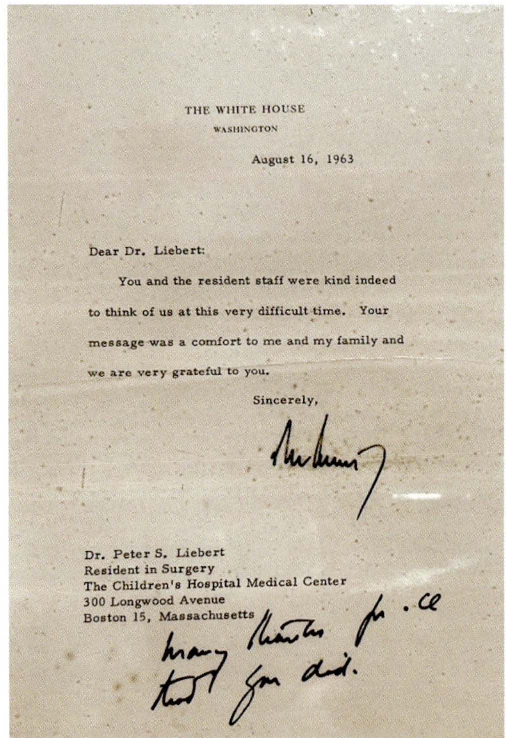

THE WHITE HOUSE
WASHINGTON

August 16, 1963

Dear Dr. Liebert:

You and the resident staff were kind indeed to think of us at this very difficult time. Your message was a comfort to me and my family and we are very grateful to you.

Sincerely,

[signature]

Dr. Peter S. Liebert
Resident in Surgery
The Children's Hospital Medical Center
300 Longwood Avenue
Boston 15, Massachusetts

Many thanks for all that you did.

Courtesy of Dr. Peter S. Liebert

To ease her grief, Jackie escaped to Greece in October to be with her sister Lee and Aristotle Onassis aboard his luxury yacht. In her absence, Jack invited Stanley Tretick of *Look* magazine to do a photo feature titled "The President and His Son." In a classic image, Tretick captured the pair in soft-focus, holding hands as they walked toward the living quarters.
Estate of Stanley Tretick/Corbis/GettyImages

On October 17, the excited family was reunited at National Airport. Caroline and John Jr. bounded up the airline stairs each at their own pace. When Jack reached the cabin door, Jackie wrapped a white-gloved hand around his neck and drew him inside for a private moment.
National Archives/GettyImages

After sitting through the first half of the Harvard-Columbia football game at Harvard Stadium, Jack sneaked out to visit the grave of his son, the sole Kennedy buried in the family plot at Holyhood Cemetery. He stared at the headstone—PATRICK BOUVIER KENNEDY AUGUST 7, 1963–AUGUST 9, 1963—then turned to his aides and said, "He seems so alone here."
Cecil Stoughton, White House/John F. Kennedy Presidential Library and Museum

On November 13, 1963, the Scottish Black Watch Band performed on the White House lawn for an audience of fifteen hundred children. Caroline sat with her arm around her father, while John Jr. was perched on his mother's lap. It was the last photo of the Kennedy family together at an official function.
Cecil Stoughton, White House/John F. Kennedy Presidential Library and Museum

During his trip to Texas, the president viewed a space-program experiment that involved a hyperbaric oxygen chamber. With Patrick in mind, Jack asked the chief scientist if the research could help development of new treatments for premature infants.
Cecil Stoughton, White House/John F. Kennedy Presidential Library and Museum

Their newfound closeness inspired Jackie to set aside her aversion to campaigning and she agreed to go out early on the trail for Jack's 1964 re-election bid. On November 22, Jackie plunged into the crowd at Love Field in Dallas.
Art Rickerby/The LIFE Picture Collection/Shutterstock

After her husband's death, Jackie moved the remains of their two lost children to rest on either side of him at Arlington National Cemetery. On the right is a cross marking the grave of their daughter who was stillborn in 1956 while Jack was on a Mediterranean cruise gallivanting with beautiful women. To the left is the headstone of their last child, Patrick, whose brief life completed Jack's complicated journey as a father, and a husband.
AP Images/Bob Schutz

The phone rang in the residence. Neither child had fallen asleep yet. Mrs. Auchincloss was on the line, asking: "How are the children doing?"

Shaw said they were fine but a little dizzy from their day.

Mrs. Auchincloss came to the point: "Mrs. Kennedy wants you to tell Caroline."

Shaw stifled a gasp and begged to be spared the duty.

"You must," Mrs. Auchincloss persisted. "There's no one else."

Shaw had been at Caroline's side almost every day since the girl was eleven days old. She spent more time with Caroline and John Jr. than either of their parents. She had become a nurturing, trusted friend. Just three months ago, she helped Caroline through the loss of her baby brother Patrick, consoling her with prayers at bedtime.

Shaw had no choice: she accepted the task and embraced it with confidence. "Caroline . . . had been so dear to her father and so close to him," she recalled, "and she was old enough to understand."

John Jr., it was agreed, could wait until morning; he was too young to immediately take in the full meaning. Shaw tucked him into his bed, and together she and the boy recited their standard evening prayers.

Then she went in to see Caroline.

Shaw sat on the edge of her bed, as usual, and began reading a book to her—Caroline "loved this moment of the day," her nanny remembered. But soon Shaw's eyes clouded with tears. Caroline, a bright, alert little girl, looked at her nanny with concern. Shaw took her into her arms and told her the truth.

Her father had been shot: "God had taken him to heaven because they just couldn't make him better in a hospital."

Caroline understood: her father was now in heaven.

"He was there with Patrick," Shaw told her. "He was very glad to go to see Patrick." She explained: "Patrick was so lonely in heaven. He didn't know anybody there. Now he has the best friend anyone could have." She continued: "God gives each of us a thing to do. God is making your father a guardian angel over you and your mother, and his light will shine down on you always. His light is shining now, and he's watching you, and he's loving you, and he always will."

The reality of it—perhaps the finality—hit Caroline. She crumbled. She put her face in her pillow and sobbed.

"It was a dreadful time for us both," Shaw recalled. "Eventually she fell asleep while I sat on the bed, still patting her."

Jackie arrived at Bethesda Naval Hospital, along with Jack's body, not long after 6 p.m. and settled into a private suite on the seventeenth floor to wait out the autopsy. Her rooms were soon filled with family, friends, and staff. Many advised her to change out of her stained dress, put on something fresh. But her answer was invariably a headshake. She was fine, she just wanted to talk. Her obstetrician Dr. John Walsh defended her refusal to shed the bloodied suit. "If she doesn't want it, O.K. Leave her alone," he said. "Let her talk herself out."

And talk she did—her wake-like unburdening that began on Air Force One continued at the hospital in what Walsh dubbed "a talkathon." She described the horrible scene inside the president's convertible Lincoln and her last moments in the trauma room when she placed her ring on Jack's finger. Memories of her husband reminded her of another loss: her infant son so recently buried. Husband and son, lost just months apart, in a year that had dawned so full of hope. "Always the two deaths were intertwined," Manchester observed. "For the country the assassination of the President stood alone; for her the two acts of the double tragedy were inseparable."

The hours dragged on. Midnight came and went, and the autopsy was still incomplete. Making use of the time, Jackie and Bobby concentrated on organizing the funeral for the thirty-fifth president, drawing inspiration from the farewell to Abraham Lincoln.

At 3:30 a.m., the autopsy came to a close. But one last-minute matter still needed to be addressed. Ken O'Donnell hadn't stopped thinking about Jackie's question about her wedding ring—"Do you think I did the right thing?" Nothing linked a couple quite like a wedding band. If children were the fruits of love, the ring was its symbol. Wishing to send Jack off with hers was a tender gesture. But her doubts weighed on O'Donnell: Would she miss being able to hold in her hand that solid testament to their love in the years ahead?

"Jackie, I'm going to get that ring back for you," O'Donnell told her.

Down in the morgue Dr. Burkley was still with the president's body. At O'Donnell's request, Burkley carefully pried off the ring, then hurried out, wishing to deliver it to Jackie himself. On the seventeenth floor, he ran into Bobby Kennedy outside Jackie's bedroom and told him what he had in his palm. "I want to give it to her myself," he said, "so I can be sure she has it."

On seeing the ring, Jackie lighted up. She told Burkely she was grateful for everything he had done over the years. She then dug her hand into her jacket pocket and drew out one of the two red roses. She offered it to the doctor, and as he accepted it, he lowered his head and in a quiet voice said, "This is the greatest treasure of my life."

The president's body, in a new mahogany casket draped in the Stars and Stripes, left Bethesda Naval Hospital in a discreet motorcade, arriving at the North Portico of the White House at 4:24 a.m. A team of seven military men carried the coffin inside, crossed a marble hall, and placed it on the waiting Lincoln catafalque in the East Room. Two butlers lit tall candles with trembling fingers. A priest delivered a few words to a small assembly of Jackie, Bobby, several family members and close friends and aides.

Shortly before dawn on November 23, Jacqueline Bouvier Kennedy, who was widowed sixteen hours earlier, went upstairs alone to her bed in the second-floor residence.

⁂

Caroline came into nanny Shaw's room very early in the morning. Her face was pale, her eyes were large, now she wished to understand. Her inquisitive mind—a trait she inherited from her father—was swirling with questions.

"It has always struck me, since then, how terribly logical children can be," Shaw recalled. "Some of the questions Caroline asked could only have come from a child, and they had to be answered plainly and without emotion, for to her they were real problems."

Shaw took each one seriously. "Only by replying to every question logically did I think the child could be eased in her mind," she explained. "It seemed essential never to try to sidestep any of her questions."

When their father's coffin was moved to the Capitol Rotunda the next day, Caroline and John Jr. accompanied their mother, hand in hand, for the solemn ceremony of the president lying in state.

John Jr. didn't last long amid the stillness, the flood of words, the sad faces all around. He began behaving like any three-year-old trapped in the slow-moving, monotonous world of adults. His arms came up like airplane wings and he hummed like an engine. Mrs. Kennedy nodded at Agent Foster, who moved in, took the child's hand, and guided him toward a room just beyond the Rotunda.

John Jr. had been told that his father was gone and could not come back. Like his sister, he had his own questions. When Foster saw one was ready to pop from the boy's lips, he stooped down to John's eye level. "Mr. Foster," the boy asked, "what happened to my daddy?"

Inside the Rotunda, Jackie and Caroline were standing some distance away from the coffin when Jackie whispered: "We're going to go say good-bye to Daddy, and we're going to kiss him good-bye, and tell Daddy how much we love him and how much we'll always miss him."

Caroline and her mother clasped hands and approached the flag-draped casket. Her eye on her mother, Caroline followed her lead. Together they knelt beside the coffin.

Jackie quietly instructed: "You know. You just kiss."

Eyes closed, they touched their lips to the flag.

Jackie placed her black-gloved hand on the Stars and Stripes.

Caroline, as if wanting to get closer to her father, slid her white-gloved hand under the flag and patted the casket in a final farewell.

TWENTY-FOUR

The Salute

The following day, November 25, was John Jr.'s third birthday. It was also the day of his father's funeral. Caroline would turn six in two days. Jackie and nanny Shaw wanted to make sure John Jr.'s third life milestone was not overlooked. At a quiet breakfast together, Shaw and Caroline sang "Happy Birthday to You" and presented the boy with their gifts: a toy helicopter from Caroline, and Beatrix Potter's *Peter Rabbit* from his nanny. Additional muted celebrations for both children attended by extended family would follow in coming days.

Shaw dressed both kids in matching powder blue coats and red shoes with white socks. She helped Caroline put on her black mourning headband.

At 10:43 a.m., an honor guard muscled the president's casket down the steps of the Capitol and strapped it onto a horse-drawn caisson for the 1.2-mile march to the White House.

Jackie had wanted to lead a walking procession of more than one hundred dignitaries and world leaders all the way from the Capitol to the funeral Mass at St. Matthew's Cathedral. But she was dissuaded by the Secret Service and agreed to a shorter route of eight blocks from the White House to the church.

When the caisson rolled up to the mansion, the dignitaries were waiting in a mass assemblage on the North Portico, among them: Prince Philip, Duke of Edinburgh, President Charles de Gaulle of France, Emperor Haile Selassie of Ethiopia, Crown Prince Harald of Norway, Prime Minister Golda Meir of Israel. The leaders fell in behind the caisson. Following them were Caroline, John Jr., and nanny Shaw in a Chrysler limousine. Around the car were several Secret Service agents, including Bob Foster, who was positioned next to Caroline's closed backseat window.

Before the procession set off, Jackie raised a small alarm: she wanted her children "as close to her as possible" during the walk to the Mass. The dignitaries were already in their assigned places, their global prominence denoted by their closeness to the front. Jackie's need to have her children nearby ignited a last-minute rearrangement, sending Secret Service agents through the mob of royalty, prime ministers, and ambassadors, waving their arms, calling out, "Pardon me, excuse me." Finally, the agents had cleared a path for the Chrysler to inch past the world leaders to a spot right behind the black-veiled first lady flanked by Jack's brothers Bobby and Ted.

Only the French Sûreté guarding President de Gaulle, and protecting his pride of place at the front, resisted, crying *"Non, non, non! C'est impossible!"* But once a startled de Gaulle realized it was the president's children moving ahead of him, he stepped aside.

The procession behind the caisson slow-rolled toward the cathedral to the wailing of the Black Watch bagpipers. From inside the Chrysler, Caroline rolled down the back window and poked her tiny hand out toward Agent Foster walking beside her. In his suit, overcoat, and crew cut, he glanced over and saw the little hand and clasped it, and immediately looked away. He was staggered by the small action of this hurting child. He held her hand all the way to the cathedral. His eyes wet with tears, he told himself: "Stay on task. Scan the crowd. Good God, you can't let anything happen to this little girl."

Taking his seat in St. Matthew's Cathedral next to his mother, John Jr. caught sight of Haile Selassie, the emperor of Ethiopia. On his visit to the White House in the summer Selassie had given John Jr. a small warrior figurine carved from ivory, a keepsake the boy loved so much he often took it to bed with him. Little John pointed at the emperor as though wanting to race over to him. But the commencement of his father's Mass had begun.

Cardinal Cushing, who barely three months earlier had presided over baby Patrick's funeral, was now called upon to send Jack to his eternal rest. John Jr. paid little attention: he was unmoved by the solemnity of the moment and Cardinal Cushing's reverent chanting of long passages in Latin. The "Ave Maria" sung by Boston tenor Luigi Vena didn't crush the three-year-old the way it did his mother. Stuck in this crowded, dull place, the boy fidgeted: if only he had a toy helicopter to play with. If only his father were here to amuse him. "Where's my daddy?" he called out. He shot his arms into the air pleading: "Somebody pick me up."

At the nod of Mrs. Kennedy, Agent Foster swooped in and whisked him off to a room at the back of the church. Foster entertained the boy with tales of Jasper the Jet, then switched to an activity certain to engage him. Two weeks earlier, John had performed a perfect military salute in his father's presence at a Veterans Day commemoration at Arlington

National Cemetery. It was the climax of considerable practice. But lately the boy had lost his cadet polish and was guilty of a breach of protocol. Every time he saluted he now performed the hallowed action with his left hand.

In the back room of the church, Foster was working to correct the error, putting the boy through the proper motions, when a Marine colonel walked in. Majestic in his uniform bursting with ribbons and medals, the colonel commanded respect and enthralled John Jr. After watching the boy's left-hand faux pas, the colonel explained: "John, no, son, you've got it all wrong. That is not how you salute." Snapping to attention, the colonel demonstrated the proper motion with his right hand in crisp Marine style. "*This* is how you salute," he barked. In earnest mimicry John Jr. straightened up, imagining himself tall as a Marine, and whipped his right hand up to his brow.

⸻

Inside the church Jackie was absorbed in the sights and sounds of the mournful ceremony: the prayers she and Jack had shared, the presence of the cardinal who had married them, and christened Caroline. And, impossibly, within view was her husband's coffin. She broke down and sobbed unreservedly. A handkerchief appeared over her shoulder from Agent Hill. Her body quaking, Jackie felt a hand squeeze hers. "Caroline couldn't see her mother's face," Manchester recounted, "but she felt her spasms; she was comforting her."

A short time later, Cardinal Cushing, breaking into tears himself, used an unexpected, affectionate phrasing in reference to the president: "May the angels, dear Jack, lead you into Paradise." Jackie again shook with sobs. Caroline, all of a sudden the grown-up child, saw tears streaming down her mother's face. Her small fingers took hold of her mother's hand. "You'll be all right, Mummy," Caroline whispered. "Don't cry. I'll take care of you."

After the service, Jackie, holding hands with Caroline and John Jr., followed her husband's casket covered in the Stars and Stripes down the cathedral steps and watched as it was fastened onto the caisson. Deferential strains of "Hail to the Chief" swept over the crowd in a final performance for this president. Every person in uniform—soldiers, policemen, and the lead horseman at the front of the caisson—saluted.

The caisson was now set to carry President Kennedy's body to his final resting place at Arlington National Cemetery. In the brilliant midday sun, Jackie, veiled in black, bent down and whispered to her son:

"John, you can salute Daddy now and say good-bye to him."

Of all the images captured on the day of the funeral, William Manchester observed, "nothing approached the force of John's salute." While it looms large as a heart-stirring public moment, John Jr.'s farewell to his father was personal, an expression of the confused sadness of a young child who would never again see the most important man in his life. The respect and love that Jack roused in his children was plainly evident in his boy's raised arm. It seemed to some observers that little John in the split second of his salute acknowledged the fate that had befallen him.

"Somehow the mood and meaning of the day had reached the President's son," Manchester wrote. "His elbow was cocked at precisely the right angle, his hand was touching his shock of hair, his left arm was rigidly at his side, his shoulders were squared, and his chin in." He had aced the salute, and in doing so he had crossed into pint-sized manhood. "His bearing was militant," Manchester observed, "and to see it in a three-year-old, with his bare legs stiff below his short coat, his knees dimpled and his blunt red shoes side by side—to hear the slow swell of the music, and recall how the President idolized him—was almost insupportable. Cardinal Cushing looked down on the small face. He saw the shadow of sadness crossing it and felt a burning sensation in his chest."

The caisson drawn by six gray horses rolled away from St. Matthew's for the procession to Arlington National Cemetery. The cortege of one hundred and seven vehicles crept along cordoned streets lined with spectators. Along Seventeenth Street, one limousine peeled off: Caroline and John Jr. were returning to the White House, their day was over.

An hour and twenty-five minutes later, the funeral motorcade pulled up to the Memorial Gate entrance to the cemetery.

⁂

A few days later, Caroline was taken to see her father's resting place. Jackie organized a secret evening visit to Arlington Cemetery after the crowds had vanished and the gates were locked.

"We're going to visit Daddy's grave," Jackie told her daughter, "and we won't take John."

It occurred to Caroline that her father would probably like to see the family dogs and, after some begging—"Daddy loved them so much"—Jackie gave in. It was impossible to take all of them. The companions were whittled down to three: the German shepherd Clipper, the Irish wolfhound Wolf, and the cocker spaniel Shannon. Clint Hill packed the hounds into the back of the family station wagon.

At the cemetery, Jackie leashed the bigger dogs Clipper and Wolf, but Shannon bounded out of the car and raced off. Moments later he was heard barking furiously. The small cocker had come upon a soldier standing guard at the president's grave whose sidekick was a massive police dog.

Shannon, who landed in the United States from Ireland a few days after Patrick died, had immediately forged a special bond with Jack. Not only did his timing offer a happy diversion, but his feisty nature evoked the fighting spirit of Patrick. Having arrived as a tiny newcomer, the puppy came to be known for his fearlessness: he staked out his place on the sands and fields of Hyannis Port, yipping at the much larger animals that were already settled into the pecking order of the Kennedy pets. "Daddy always loved Shannon the best because he was so brave," Caroline said.

In the heat of the canine confrontation, Jackie scooped up Shannon and deposited him back in the car. The soldier retreated with his large brute. He was in tears, visibly mortified to have played a part in a snarling fracas on Caroline's first visit to her father's grave.

Approaching the burial site, Jackie carried lilies of the valley, and Caroline a nosegay she had collected at home. It was a cold, wet night, and both mourners knelt in the mud, prayed, and stared at the now-lighted eternal flame.

Leaving the cemetery, Caroline came upon the sad-eyed soldier. She stopped and stroked his big dog and asked its name.

"I call him Baron, Caroline," the solider said.

"Baron," she said, running her fingers across his fur.

On the ride back to the White House, she and her mother sat close together in silence, holding hands. Caroline was thinking about her cardboard dollhouse with punchout figures. She mentioned to her mother that one of the cutouts was a police dog. Wanting to memorialize her first visit to her father's grave, she said excitedly: "Oh Mummy, I'm going to name him Baron, after the dog who's watching Daddy."

TWENTY-FIVE

"We Were About to Have a Real Life Together"

Death had visited the family too much in too short a time.

When Ted Kennedy's wife Joan first heard the president had been shot and his condition was unknown, she refused to believe that another tragedy could strike Jack and his family. "Thinking of Patrick—it was inconceivable to her that her brother-in-law would not recover," William Manchester wrote. "She said, 'Oh, they've had so much trouble this year!' "

Inevitably, the president's death overshadowed Patrick's. Many accounts of the president's assassination mentioned the baby's loss only in passing. But that third child always had a larger place in the Kennedys' lives than the public accounts conveyed. By the time of Jack's death, Patrick had seeped into his marrow. Jackie was already deeply traumatized by her loss of Patrick before she was stunned by her husband's assassination. The twin blows of Patrick then Jack, coming in rapid succession, caused Jackie to question not only her faith in God but life itself.

In one of her many searching conversations with the Jesuit priest Father Richard McSorley, Jackie couldn't stop wondering: "Does God know everything?" God's ways, of course, were inscrutable, but Jackie needed to discern some hint of a divine plan in all of her suffering. But there was no answer to the mystery she begged McSorley to explain: "Why did He take my son Patrick if He knew my husband was going to die?"

⁂

On December 4, two days before Jackie and the kids were to move out of the White House, the former first lady launched an elaborate stealth mission. It began in the morning almost simultaneously in Brookline, Massachusetts, and Newport, Rhode Island, and ended under cover of darkness around 9 p.m. at Arlington National Cemetery.

In Brookline, the body of baby Patrick was removed from its resting place at Holyhood Cemetery. It was placed in a funeral director's car and driven seventy miles to Quonset, Rhode Island, in the company of two close Kennedy friends, Cardinal Richard Cushing and Judge Francis X. Morrissey.

In Newport, the Kennedys' stillborn daughter, Arabella, was disinterred from her grave. Her casket was escorted by a Catholic priest to a rendezvous with Patrick roughly fifteen miles away at Quonset. There Jack's brother Ted was waiting to transport both caskets to Washington aboard the Kennedy plane the *Caroline*. Cardinal Cushing blessed the coffins as they were placed aboard the aircraft. Jackie deemed this clandestine, one-day operation the least likely to attract public attention.

At 7:15 p.m., the *Caroline* landed at National Airport in Washington and taxied to a field far away from the terminals. The remains were loaded into two waiting Army vehicles, which then drove off into the night.

At 8:45 p.m., Jackie arrived at Arlington National Cemetery along with eight others: close friends and five family members, including Jack's brothers Bobby and Ted and Jackie's sister, Lee. Jackie, in a black dress and veil, approached the white picket fence surrounding the president's gravesite. The auxiliary bishop of Washington, the Most Reverend Philip Hannan, who spoke at Jack's funeral, led the small group in prayer. The brief ceremony lasted less than twenty minutes.

The mourners watched as the tiny caskets containing the remains of Patrick and Arabella were placed into the earth, on either side of their father on a slope overlooking the Potomac and the Lincoln Memorial.

Within a week, the original granite headstones that marked the children's graves in Brookline and Newport were installed at Arlington. On one side of the president was the arched headstone, designed by Jack himself, that read "Patrick Bouvier Kennedy August 7, 1963–August 9, 1963." On the other side was the simple cross that adorned Arabella's gravesite. Across it were the words "Baby Girl Kennedy Aug. 23, 1956." Engraved at the base were the words: "Suffer Little Children to Come Unto Me." The cross did not bear the name Arabella that Jack and Jackie had planned to give their daughter because, having been born dead, the child had never been christened.

⁂

For a man who at first hadn't envisioned himself as a father, it was a fitting emblem of his profound evolution: to be flanked by two of his children who represented the two poles of his long journey. On the right side lay his baby girl, whose stillbirth he greeted seven years earlier with confusion and hesitancy from four thousand miles away. On the left side lay his final child, whose illness at birth drove him immediately to his side to seek every possible measure to save his life, and whose death tore his heart out.

John Kennedy, though far from perfect, had grown into his role not just as a father but as a husband. His love of Jackie in his final year was in many respects a reigniting of the first spark that had sizzled between them back in the early 1950s. Dave Powers recounted that a month before Jack proposed to Jackie in 1953, he came to Powers with a series of photos taken in a cramped camera booth. "I have never met anyone like her—she's different from any girl I know," he told Powers. "Do you want to see what she looks like?" Jack pulled four photos out of his pocket, "the kind you get in a penny arcade," Powers recalled in *Life* magazine in 1995. They were, he noted, "the first pictures ever of Jack and Jackie together." Three of the photos showed the couple looking straight into the camera: Jack in suit and tie, Jackie in three strands of pearls and glossy lipstick. Jack wore an easy smile, while Jackie cuddled against him, her head resting on his shoulder. In another shot, they were in profile nose-to-nose, staring into each other's eyes, Jackie's pinkie appeared to be hooked in the lapel of his jacket tugging him toward her: it was a sultry image suggesting the moment before their lips met. "The pictures," Powers concluded, "clearly show two people in love."

But that early flame flickered and struggled to stay lit over ten years of a twisted journey together. The marriage floundered early on, dragged down by Jack's affairs, Jackie's anger and absences. Yet Jack's career blossomed as their private life withered. The nation, however, saw only their charm and glamour. As Jackie told a friend, she and her husband were like two icebergs: "the public life is above the water—& the private life—is submerged." And icy it was down below: they each struggled to overcome scars from their troubled home life as youngsters. "Jack just had a fear of intimacy and I guess Jackie did too," recalled their mutual friend Betty Spalding. Breakthroughs were nearly impossible. "They were both . . . silent as if afraid that conversation would deepen the wound," said Jack's friend Lem Billings.

Then along came the children—and everything changed: Caroline and John Jr., with unintentional ease, gave their parents lessons in affection and intimacy. And Patrick—first the expectation, then the sorrow—drove Jack and Jackie into each other's arms as never before. "They folded into each other on the couch. You couldn't tell where one ended and the other began," said their friend Charles Spalding, Betty's husband, who witnessed their transformation at Brambletyde following Patrick's death. When Jackie broke down, Jack was up "at her side with a tissue, wiping her tears and holding her," Spalding said. They were now a loving couple unafraid of intimacy even in the presence of friends. "They didn't seem interested in hiding their feelings anymore."

It was a testament to how far they had come. "There had always been this wall between them," writer Theodore White observed, "but their shared grief tore that wall down. At long last, they were truly coming closer together. But it would prove to be too late."

Jackie knew all too well that she and Jack had survived bittersweet years to reach this hopeful new plateau—and then all of a sudden he was snatched away. "It took a very long time for us to work everything out, but we did," she told interior designer Billy Baldwin in January 1964. "We were about to have a real life together."

EPILOGUE

Patrick's Legacy

"We Can Fix This"

In December 2020, Holly Jordan gave birth to an extremely premature son in an emergency caesarean delivery at Lenox Hill Hospital in New York. Her boy arrived three and a half months early, weighing just one and a half pounds. In Patrick Bouvier Kennedy's day, very small newborns were not even considered for treatment. Parents of a baby weighing less than 2.2 pounds (1,000 grams) were told there was no hope of survival. Doctors advised these mothers and fathers to hold their child in their arms, spend a little time together, before nature took its course.

But this was not 1963. Holly's son had the good fortune to be born into the modern era of neonatal intensive care units, baby ventilators, sophisticated drugs, and life-saving treatments. This is Patrick's legacy. His brief life and tragic death inspired a revolution in premature care which, sixty years later, gave Holly's very early little boy a fighting chance.

As her son's days in the neonatal intensive care unit turned into weeks and then months, Holly wished she could talk to Patrick's big sister, Caroline, the sole surviving member of the president's immediate family. She had something she wanted to tell her. Then, on the day before Easter in 2021, her wish came true, as she recounted in a first-person piece for *People* magazine.

Holly and her husband, Pete, were walking their dog in New York's Central Park near the Jacqueline Kennedy Onassis Reservoir, of all places, when she spotted the president's daughter.

"Pete, there's Caroline," Holly recounted in an interview for this book.

What happened next was what Holly described as "one of those wonderful, magical moments."

Holly and Caroline fell into conversation. Caroline was no longer the six-year-old big sister but a sixty-four-year-old former U.S. ambassador to Japan and imminent ambassador to Australia. As she was about to move on with her day, Holly composed herself to say what she longed for Caroline to know.

"Caroline," Holly told her, "my son is alive because of your brother Patrick."

For a moment, Caroline looked confused, even shocked.

"She wanted to know more," Holly recalled. "And that's when I began to explain."

Holly's harrowing odyssey through premature birth began on a routine visit to her doctor at six months, or twenty-four weeks, when she was shocked to learn she had developed hypertension. Her doctor admitted her to the hospital in hopes of controlling her condition until she got to the targeted goal of a delivery at eight-and-a-half months, or thirty-four weeks. If her child were born at that time, doctors had full confidence they could nurse the infant to health and a normal life. In a sign of how far neonatal medicine had come, Patrick Kennedy had been born in line with the modern target point of thirty-four weeks, or six weeks early. But in his day, his early birth was a probable death sentence.

Holly was unable to reach thirty-four weeks. Just two weeks after her distressing doctor's visit, her health deteriorated. She was diagnosed with two life-threatening conditions: preeclampsia, a serious form of high blood pressure that sometimes strikes pregnant women, and HELLP syndrome, which threatened the health of her blood and liver.

Her baby had to be born, without delay, fourteen weeks early. "When I told Caroline that, her face fell," Holly said. "She knew how serious it was, and she had a look of concern."

Holly and her husband began alternating shifts in the NICU beside their baby day and night. It was a grueling one hundred and forty-four days. "We didn't know if he was going to make it," Holly said. "There were some really scary days. I didn't know if he'd be able to walk. I didn't know if he would be verbal."

Holly's newborn had an excellent chance of a happy outcome because legions of doctors and researchers in the wake of Patrick's death dedicated their lives to advancing premature care. Robert deLemos was a twenty-six-year-old pediatric resident on the team treating the president's baby at Children's Hospital, and he was devastated by Patrick's loss. "There was nothing we could do," he later lamented to a friend. "The experts were all trying to think of things but none of it was working." Losing Patrick was "incredibly depressing"—and unacceptable for the quiet, driven cum laude graduate of Harvard Medical School. On the day Patrick died, deLemos discovered his life's work. "What, are you kidding me? We can't fix this?" the young, bespectacled doctor said. "Yes, we can fix this. I know we can fix this." The indefatigable deLemos would go on to introduce innovative care for premature newborns and collaborate on crucial advances in baby ventilators.

President Kennedy motivated researchers like deLemos by ensuring they had abundant government funding to pursue their ambitions. Kennedy had already turned a spotlight on the health of children and infants by creating the National Institute of Child Health and Human Development in 1962. At that time, the diseases of children and newborns attracted far less funding and scientific inquiry than adult afflictions. "What you have to remember is back then most everything was the push on adults," recalled Dr. Donald Null, professor emeritus of neonatology at the University of Utah. The lion's share of funding went to adult medicine, with a small portion going to pediatrics. "The newborn," Null added, "really wasn't getting much of anything."

After Patrick's death, the president accelerated funding for prenatal and prematurity research. In October 1963, a month before his assassination, he signed a two-bill package totaling $594 million ($6.1 billion in today's dollars) that targeted mental retardation and mental health: the bills included $40 million ($410 million today) for research into maternal and child health, $110 million ($1.1 billion today) for improved prenatal care in impoverished areas, and another $26 million ($266 million today) for building research centers. By November 1963, the National Institutes of Health had allocated $800,000 ($8.21 million today) for forty-four grants to study hyaline membrane disease, the lung ailment that killed Patrick. The National Institute of Child Health and Human Development designated prematurity for intensive research.

In 1963, hyaline membrane disease was killing an average of 25,000 babies a year in the United States. The chance of survival at that time was about 50 percent for a baby, like Patrick, born six weeks early with a lung ailment. By the 1990s, after three decades of intensive innovation, doctors had largely eliminated respiratory disease as a primary cause of death for premature babies.

Following Patrick's death, researchers chased answers to the crucial question facing lung-impaired preterm newborns: How could doctors keep these fragile infants breathing long enough to boost their chances of survival? Two clear goals emerged: to uncover the secret of how healthy lungs work and to perfect a baby ventilator.

In the 1950s, two trailblazing researchers working separately delivered transformative insights into the mystery of the breathing process. A young doctor named John Clements, assigned to the U.S. Army Chemical Center in Edgewood, Maryland, was tasked with learning everything he could about the physiology of the lungs. At the time, the U.S. government feared that the Soviet Union might one day deploy chemical weapons. "My assignment was to find out how nerve gases worked on the lungs," recalled Clements, a graduate of the Cornell University Medical College. He landed on a brilliant discovery: the lungs contained a foamy liquid substance that was essential for breathing. This substance, which he dubbed surfactant, coated the lungs' thin, balloon-like air sacs known as alveoli, thereby facilitating respiration.

A few years later, Dr. Mary Ellen Avery was engaged in pediatric research at Harvard Medical School when she heard about Clements's work. Avery had become fascinated by diseases of the lungs after she came down with tuberculosis following her graduation in 1952 from Johns Hopkins University School of Medicine. She had since turned her attention to studying the lungs of infants who died of hyaline membrane disease. Clements had not set out to cure any diseases; his work was pure scientific research. But Avery realized he had something important to teach her.

So, off she went to visit him. She and Clements became lifelong friends. "He had never heard of hyaline membrane disease," Avery recalled. But with his background, he taught her how to do essential scientific measurements to assess the loss of function in the lungs of babies who died of HMD. "He knew what I didn't know, and vice versa," she said. "So this was a wonderful relationship."

Avery soon delivered a foundational breakthrough. By studying the autopsied lungs of premature babies and comparing them with healthy animals, she discovered what was behind the infants' breathing problems: an absence, or insufficient amount, of surfactant. In the lungs of babies lacking surfactant, a glassy film or membrane forms and covers the alveoli, impairing respiration and often causing the tiny sacs to collapse. Surfactant prevents this process. Babies born at full term typically have developed enough of the substance to breathe on their own at birth, while surfactant-deprived premature infants must fight for each breath. In a seminal 1959 paper, Avery and her lab director, Jere Mead, noted what doctors saw all too often—that preterm newborns lacking surfactant "could not live more than a day or two."

In the 1960s, following Patrick's death, scientists sought practical applications of Clements's and Avery's discoveries. The goal was to create a synthetic version of this crucial lung lubricant. "Within a year [of Patrick's death], trials with synthetic surfactants had begun," Dr. Henry L. Halliday, a neonatologist who specialized in surfactant research, wrote in the *Journal of Paediatrics and Child Health*. By 1968, research into surfactant had accelerated: references to the substance in medical journals had more than doubled since Patrick died.

But significant hurdles slowed progress. In 1967, a major clinical trial of an inhaled synthetic surfactant was so disappointing that afterward the field was considered "dead," according to one expert.

With synthetic surfactants elusive, researchers turned their attention to finding natural sources of the substance. Studies discovered similarities between human and mammal lung surfactants across various species.

In 1980, Japanese scientist Tetsuro Fujiwara became the first researcher to successfully use surfactant culled from cows. He reported that ten premature infants administered the substance through an endotracheal tube benefited from it. In subsequent clinical trials, the lungs of pigs as well as cows and calves proved good sources of natural surfactant. Researchers would spend years studying how to harvest animal-sourced surfactant, sterilize it, test it, and make sure it was safe to manufacture.

The application of natural surfactant was a major advance for premature babies whose bodies were unable to create the substance fast enough on their own. But its widespread use was slow in coming. "It took forty years—from the initial discovery in the early '50s to the first approval of the FDA in the 1990s," said Dr. Sam Hawgood, a neonatologist and former colleague of Clements's. But if that development timeline seems slow, Hawgood believes that four decades was "pretty remarkable," given no one even knew that surfactant existed in the 1950s.

The creation of surfactant was "one of the greatest breakthroughs in neonatology," wrote Roland Hentschel and colleagues in *Pediatric Research*. It "led to a spectacular increase in survival, pushing back the boundaries of premature viability" and improving the short- and long-term health of premature babies.

Meanwhile, medical scientists were also racing to create effective breathing devices for babies. This work was forging ahead on the path laid in the late 1950s and early 1960s by researchers such as Mildred Stahlman of Vanderbilt University and Maria Delivoria-Papadopoulos at the Hospital for Sick Children in Toronto. Known for pushing boundaries, the two doctor-scientists cobbled together makeshift breathing devices for use on premature infants so critically ill they had little chance of survival anyway. Some doctors, however, refused to allow Delivoria-Papadopoulos to treat their infant patients, believing her untested approach strayed into unethical territory. "They said, 'You are experimenting on our babies,'" Delivoria-Papadopoulos remembered nearly sixty years later.

Pioneers in neonatal research like Stahlman and Delivoria-Papadopoulos operated in what was essentially an unregulated Wild West of medical discovery. Researchers relied on trial and error, not unlike early practitioners trying to determine how much chemotherapy to give cancer patients to bring benefits rather than additional harm. Early efforts at ventilation likewise required the acceptance of considerable risk. President Kennedy himself consented to a risky, last-ditch experiment to save his son in a hyperbaric oxygen chamber. While doctors worked in the best interest of their patients, Federal Drug Administration oversight that is standard in medical research today did not exist. "It was a different era in terms of research regulation and consent," James deLemos, a professor and division chief of cardiology at the UT Southwestern Medical Center and one of Robert deLemos's sons, explained in an interview for this book.

Today, Stahlman and Delivoria-Papadopoulos are revered for their contributions to life-saving treatments for struggling newborns. Dr. John Lantos, a pediatrician and expert on medical ethics, has called some of Delivoria-Papadopoulos's early activities "morally complex." But the result, he said, "changed the world. There's probably half a million people in the world today who wouldn't be here but for her work."

Building on Stahlman's and Delivoria-Papadopoulos's work, later innovators acquired insights that turned the early rudimentary ventilators into the miracle lifesavers of the modern era.

In 1968, Dr. George Gregory was a thirty-four-year-old anesthesiologist who was versed in the use of adult ventilators; he also had clinical interest in hyaline membrane disease and the treatment of newborns. A graduate of the University of California, San Francisco

School of Medicine, he was invited to join the staff of the UCSF neonatal intensive care unit. "Newborn intensive care units were practically nonexistent," Gregory recalled in an interview for this book. The first rudimentary NICU had opened in 1960 at Yale University Hospital, but it wasn't until Patrick's death that these crisis locations began to take root. Tracing the history of NICUs, neonatal nurse practitioner Anne Jorgensen noted in *NICU Currents*, a publication for health care professionals, that Patrick was lost because crisis care for babies like him was inadequate. "More than any other single event," she wrote, "the death of this infant served to ignite public and medical awareness to the need for neonatal intensive care and soon led to the establishment of NICUs around the country."

Six months after taking up his position—he was one of the few anesthesiologists at work in a NICU—Gregory happened upon an article in the journal *Pediatrics* that investigated the grunting noise made by babies afflicted with hyaline membrane disease. South African researchers reported that the grunting was a sign of a lung-impaired baby working hard to keep its collapsing airway open each time it exhaled.

That insight prompted Gregory to ponder a possible adjustment to the adult ventilators then used to assist the breathing of these struggling premature babies. The ventilating approach at the time pumped oxygen into the lungs, then shut off the flow. The impaired lungs would then collapse without any air pressure from the ventilator to keep them open. Gregory wondered, what if a ventilating system not only delivered oxygen but also maintained air pressure in the lungs to assist the infant in the act of exhaling?

Gregory, now a UCSF Professor Emeritus of Anesthesia and Pediatrics, soon got the chance to test his theory. One night in the NICU, he came upon a premature boy in the throes of respiratory distress. The infant was the son of a Navy officer, a doctor himself serving at a nearby naval hospital. Gregory went to work: he inserted an endotracheal tube attached to a supplement device that applied what he called continuous positive airway pressure on the weakened lungs. The continuous positive airway pressure kept the passageway open for the baby to exhale. The process, in effect, did "the same thing the baby was doing, only the baby didn't have to work as hard," Gregory explained. Aided by Gregory's ventilatory innovation, the newborn was able to exhale without struggling: his breathing smoothed and his blood oxygen level improved markedly in a very short time. The Navy officer's son survived.

Thus was born a groundbreaking ventilation approach known as continuous positive airway pressure, or CPAP. In June 1971, Gregory published his landmark study of his first thirty-six CPAP cases in *The New England Journal of Medicine*. The turnaround in survival rates was startling. Eighty percent of the first wave of premature CPAP patients survived. By comparison, less than half that percentage pulled through on the earlier ventilators. Within a year, doctors in Japan, South Africa, and Europe adopted the CPAP system.

Forty years later, the journal *Pediatric Anesthesia* observed: "Gregory's innovation saved not just one baby that night but subsequently improved the odds for countless other infants." Over his career, Gregory, now in his nineties, was also hailed for his achievements in pediatric anesthesia; he is the author of a leading textbook on the subject. But he believes that his chief contribution lies in four letters: CPAP. His ventilating innovation, as his peers have written, "revolutionized the treatment of premature infants with respiratory failure."

CPAP led to other ventilator innovations. Robert deLemos, the pediatric resident who helped treat Patrick, was so intrigued by CPAP that he traveled to a conference in San Francisco to meet Gregory. By then, nearly a decade after his frustrating experience with the president's son at Children's in 1963, deLemos was well along on his journey to find solutions to save ill premature infants. He joined the military, conducted research under Mary Ellen Avery at Johns Hopkins, and led the newborn nursery at Wilford Hall USAF Medical Center at Lackland Air Force Base in San Antonio. At the time of his visit with Gregory, deLemos was serving as the first neonatologist in the Air Force.

Like Gregory and others, deLemos and his team had been focusing on the use of ventilators for struggling babies. The device they used, an early ventilator called the Mark II, had achieved a 30 to 40 percent success rate. The problem with the Mark II was that it, like other early ventilators, blasted oxygen into a baby's lungs but did not have CPAP to keep the passageway open to smooth the infant's exhalation; often the bursts of oxygen generated by these early ventilators tore the newborn's fragile lungs, causing serious injury, even death.

DeLemos, along with his Wilford Hall colleagues anesthesiologist Robert Kirby and head respiratory therapist Jimmy Schultz, adapted Gregory's CPAP device to create a ventilator for babies that produced constant pressure to keep the lungs open during exhalation. Their efforts resulted in much less damage to infants' lungs and considerably more success in keeping newborns alive long enough to produce their own surfactant and breathe on their own.

DeLemos also collaborated with a leading ventilator designer, Forrest Bird, to incorporate CPAP into a new device. The Baby Bird respirator, as it was known, would be designed and manufactured specifically for the needs of infants. In the 1970s and 1980s, it was regarded as "the workhorse mechanical ventilator" for newborns with respiratory illness. Dr. Null, who was a colleague of deLemos's at Wilford Hall, noted that if baby Patrick had had access to the Baby Bird ventilator, he probably would have had "a 99 percent chance of survival. That's how much things had changed."

Though Patrick Kennedy was given only a day and a half on earth, his legacy has lived on for more than half a century through the spirit and work of neonatal professionals. Medical journals still refer to Patrick's case as the starting point for major advances in the field. Professors lecturing on neonatal history remind their students of the transformation in premature care Patrick and his father inspired. DeLemos mentored a generation of neonatology students, first in the Air Force, then as chairman of the Southwest Foundation for Biomedical Research (an independent research nonprofit now known as the Texas Biomedical Research Institute), and finally as a professor of pediatrics and head of neonatology at the University of Southern California.

Over the years, Patrick's story informed deLemos's teaching. The loss of the president's baby had a powerful impact on him, one he never forgot. "It was evident in his personal reflections, moments typically clouded with emotion that you could see in his face and in his speech," said deLemos's former student Bradley Yoder, who is a professor of pediatrics in the division of neonatology at the University of Utah and a retired Air Force colonel. In professional presentations, deLemos acknowledged Patrick's case by displaying a slide of the front page of the *Detroit Free Press* from August 8, 1963, bearing the headline: "New Kennedy Son Is Hit by Breathing Ailment; Baby Rushed to Specialists; Born 5½ weeks early/Named Patrick Bouvier."

DeLemos often pointed out to students that Patrick's case motivated neonatology researchers to push the boundaries of innovation. "If we had not been fired up because of Patrick, if we had not done our research since then, we never would have learned how to take care of babies who are surviving in our neonatal ICUs now," Parviz Minoo, a longtime research colleague of deLemos's, said in an interview for this book. Minoo, a professor of pediatrics at USC's Keck School of Medicine, uses deLemos's Kennedy slide in his own scientific presentations to audiences around the world.

DeLemos died suddenly in 1997, at the age of sixty. Twenty of his former students were moved to submit a tribute letter to the *Journal of Pediatrics* in his memory. They noted that deLemos's career began at the bedside of a president's dying son and afterward, his "own feeling of helplessness drove him to the research that is now his legacy." In their careers, deLemos's students not only handed down the story of Patrick but also contributed their own advances to pediatrics and neonatology. Dr. Null, a former student of deLemos's and a retired Air Force colonel, has published more than one hundred articles and chapters in pediatric medicine. After leaving the Air Force, Dr. Null went to Pittsburgh Allegheny General Hospital. In his presentations, he would remind residents and practitioners of Patrick's legacy. "I'm sure some of you know of Patrick Kennedy who was a baby who died of RDS," he would tell them, using the modern name, respiratory distress syndrome, instead of the earlier hyaline membrane disease. Then he would ask: "Did you know he was an almost 35-week-old baby who weighed 4 pounds 10 ounces and he died."

Null's students, raised in the new world of neonatology, would gasp in disbelief: "Are you kidding me?"

Advances in neonatology since Patrick have reenvisioned the parameters of prematurity. Preterm is typically defined as babies born before 37 weeks, but there are now three subcategories: moderate to late preterm (32 to 37 weeks); very preterm (28 to less than 32 weeks); and extremely preterm (less than 28 weeks), according to the World Health Organization.

Thanks to years of advances in treatment, technology, and care, the odds of survival are very different from 1963. Babies born six weeks early like Patrick, at 34 weeks, will likely need only a short stay in the

NICU before heading home. Compared to Patrick's day, survival rates are quite hopeful for other early arrivals: a 32-week-old preemie often has as high as a 95 percent chance of pulling through; for a 28-week newborn, that figure slips to 80–90 percent, with a 10 percent risk of long-term health problems; for a 24-week-old infant, the survival rate is 60–70 percent. Viability before 24 weeks becomes tougher, declining to 50 percent, with 40 percent experiencing long-term health problems. Despite tremendous advances, prematurity remains a risk. Yet sixty years since Patrick, doctors have not only new tools but also greater precision in applying them. "We're light-years away" from what medical science had to offer in 1963, Dr. Yoder explained in an interview.

◈

As Holly Jordan described her premature son's journey, Caroline Kennedy listened intently, drawing a deep, sympathetic breath now and then. "She was really struck by it all," Holly recalled. Her son received state-of-the-art NICU care, first at Lenox Hill, then at NewYork-Presbyterian/Weill Cornell Hospital. He was on a ventilator for two weeks; he was introduced to CPAP; he was given surfactant; he had nine blood transfusions; he was administered steroids; monitors tracked every second of his blood oxygen level, and when it fell, alarms went off and the oxygen flow was increased, always with care to prevent any risk to the eyes. "It really is an art," Holly said.

Holly mentioned that she had learned a lot about the arc of care from *Early: An Intimate History of Premature Birth and What It Teaches Us About Being Human* by Sarah DiGregorio, who is herself a mother of a preterm daughter. The book introduced Holly to Patrick's plight and President Kennedy's campaign to help all children, especially infants born early.

Caroline was unaware of her father's advocacy for premature children and his funding of neonatal research. "To me," Holly said, "that's totally understandable." Caroline was just a child when Patrick died, and just three months later her father's assassination overwhelmed her and the nation.

It was at this time during the nation's mourning that Jackie became obsessed with ensuring that her husband's achievements were not forgotten. In an interview with journalist Theodore White, she referred to the Broadway musical *Camelot*, a brew of romance, sentiment, and heroics centered on the legend of King Arthur. In the popular stage show, she found the Jack Kennedy she wished to bequeath to history. "Jack's life had more to do with myth, magic, legend, saga, and story," Jackie insisted to White. Jack's favorite lyrics were: "Don't let it be forgot, that once there was a spot, for one brief shining moment that was known as Camelot." As White explained to biographer C. David Heymann, "So the epitaph of the Kennedy administration became Camelot—a magic moment in American history when gallant men danced with beautiful women, when great deeds were done and when the White House became the center of the universe." Thus, Camelot became synonymous with the Kennedy era.

Baby Patrick, the beloved son born in the twilight of Camelot, was eclipsed by the prolonged sorrow over his father's assassination and the rise of the Kennedy myth. Americans largely forgot his short life and his father's leadership in advancing neonatal care. "The reason I wanted to meet Caroline," Holly explained, "was because I didn't feel there was enough awareness about what her father did. There's something about the fact that he was a father who went through this and had the power to do something about it. And he did."

When the women were parting, Caroline asked for the title of the book Holly had mentioned. "I could tell she made a mental note,"

Holly said. She was interested and wanted to learn more." And indeed, sometime later, Caroline emailed Holly to let her know she had read it.

Holly sends Caroline a Christmas card annually; last year's featured her active son walking the family dog, Wally. Holly is fully aware that had her family's ordeal occurred in Patrick's era, her son would not be with her today. But he has emerged from his daunting trial in excellent physical and intellectual health. When Holly moved her boy to a new pediatrician at around age three and a half, she was cheered immeasurably to hear the doctor say her son was as healthy and vibrant as any child. "If I had not seen this kid's medical file," the doctor told her, "I would never have known what he's been through and that he was born so premature." It brought his mother to tears.

Back when her son was in the NICU, Holly lay awake some nights thinking about Patrick and his family. She often talked to her husband Pete about the heartache Jackie must have experienced. Her sympathy for the Kennedys helped her work through some of her own dark moments. Now, as she and her husband raise their thriving son, Holly can't help feeling a special connection to the Kennedys. In her living room hangs a portrait of JFK. "I thank God for Patrick and what his father did," Holly said. "I just feel so grateful to them."

ACKNOWLEDGMENTS

Every book reflects its era, some intentionally, others by pure chance.

While writing *Twilight of Camelot*, I took special pleasure in re-creating the story of the trailblazing doctors, scientists, and researchers who revolutionized neonatal medicine in the wake of Patrick Kennedy's death. It was President John F. Kennedy's commitment to the nation's public health that made their advances possible. In the depths of his grief, Kennedy guaranteed federal money to propel America beyond its primitive state of premature baby care in the 1960s to the miracles performed daily in today's neonatal intensive care units.

I never anticipated that this work of history would have such current-day resonance and relevance. Some sixty years ago, Kennedy championed a long tradition of presidential support of science and medicine to protect the well-being of all Americans. Today, however, that norm of compassion and public service has been defiled, making *Twilight of Camelot* an unexpected commentary on the politics of cruelty and greed that exist today. History has a way of shining a light on the sins of the present.

Researching this book, I was honored to speak with a few of the medical pioneers who led the charge to modernize neonatal care. Their recollections were supplemented by stories of doctors and medical specialists who have followed in their footsteps, inspired by Patrick's plight and the dream of saving ill premature infants. I was fortunate to hear stories of Jackie's and Patrick's medical experiences from doctors on staff in 1963 at Otis Air Force Base hospital on Cape Cod and at Children's Hospital Medical Center in Boston. I am grateful to all, some now in their eighties and nineties, for filling in illuminating historical details and offering clarity on complicated medical and scientific questions. My appreciation goes out to David deLemos, James deLemos, George Gregory, James Hughes, Peter S. Liebert, Parviz Minoo, Donald Null, Charles Sanislow, and Bradley Yoder.

My wife, Suzanne, a longtime science and medical journalist, has been at my side for all of my books. Her medical knowledge, insights, and indefatigable research were instrumental in the writing of this one. She compiled a mountain of material from medical journals, contemporary and historical media, and other sources to gain a picture of the evolution of neonatal care from the 1960s to today. She tracked down the medical specialists whose recollections and insights helped shaped the story of Patrick's legacy. Suzanne also helped research and develop the book's two other parallel narrative threads: the thirty-nine frantic hours of Patrick's life, and Jack and Jackie's evolving relationship in the twilight months of Camelot. She found untapped documents in library archives and excavated little-seen historical newspaper clippings. Working with staffers at the John F. Kennedy Presidential Library, she unearthed two thousand unpublished condolence notes sent to the Kennedys after Patrick's death from the famous and the unheralded. She examined hundreds of photographs to best tell this story visually, selected scores for possible inclusion, and oversaw myriad details on their publishing rights. With inexplicable good cheer, she took on the blinding task of preparing more than five hundred chapter-by-chapter endnotes that identify sources for every quoted reference in the book.

In addition to all her legwork and organization, Suzanne was always ready with encouragement and astute guidance as I struggled through one draft after another. The braided narratives made this my most difficult book to write. Forgive me for going on so long about my partner in this task. But any writer who plunges alone into the travail of book writing knows how much it means to have a compassionate companion along for the ride. I am blessed not only for all Suzanne has contributed to all of my books but, more important, for her presence in my life every day over the past thirty-seven years.

I am grateful to many others for their participation and support during the writing of this book. In addition to the doctors who were on the scene in 1963, I was fortunate to speak to people who played roles in the Kennedy era, including Secret Service agents Clint Hill and Paul Landis, journalists Alvin Spivak and Marvin Kalb, and Kennedy friend Martha Bartlett. Their recollections supplemented the rich material in the JFK Library's magnificent collection of oral histories that speak for those of the era who are no longer with us. Careful combing of the oral histories turned up unexpected gems pertinent to the telling of Patrick's story and the waning days of Camelot.

This book has benefited immensely from the superlative editing team at Gallery Books, led by Aimée Bell, herself a specialist in Kennedy history. These pages were enhanced from beginning to end thanks to Aimée's incisive, sharp-eyed suggestions, and the contributions of editors Sierra Fang-Horvath, Paul Choix, and Hanna Preston. Suzanne and I both greatly appreciated Aimée's kind consideration of our thoughts on the book's title, photo selections, and cover design. We felt a warm part of the team. Gallery Books publisher Jennifer Bergstrom and director of publicity Sally Marvin and executive publicist Jennifer Robinson were instrumental to the book's launch. Nicholas Poser provided comfort by carefully poring over the text with his lawyer's eye. Fred Chase and Stephen Breslin applied impeccable editing rigor line by line.

My agent Keith Urbahn was a generous partner in this project, always a willing ear, and a savvy adviser at every stage from the book's proposal to publication. His instincts and wisdom are unparalleled.

Several writer friends and sources were kind enough to read early drafts of the book. I'm indebted to Katie Hafner, Tim Smith, Bradley Yoder, Donald Null, and Holly Jordan for their nudges big and small on the writing and their clarifications on medical language.

Others who were kind enough to offer their insights and stories were Lisa McCubbin, Suzanne Salisbury, Anne Krupman, Sam Jellinek, and Gloria Seiler.

I tend to keep pretty tight-lipped about a book in progress—perhaps it's superstition, fear of draining inspiration into the ether, I don't know—yet I did jawbone with a few folks (outside the many participants in the project). It's always a joy to talk books with Brenna Maloney, Del Wilber, David Rowell, Judd Levingston, Ron Charles, Nora Krug, Sara Kehaulani Goo, Steve Roberts, Alexis Coe, Lucinda Robb, and Steve Namm. Fred Logevall was a wise sounding board as I puzzled through the themes and history of this work. I'm indebted to registered respiratory therapist and neonatal pediatric specialist Michael Ryan and his book *Patrick Bouvier Kennedy: A Brief Life That Changed the History of Newborn Care*, in particular its oral histories of two of Patrick's attending physicians at Children's James Drorbaugh and William Bernhard. Sarah DiGregorio offered perceptive historical context on prematurity and the efforts to improve treatments in her book *Early: An Intimate History of Premature Birth and What It Teaches Us About Being Human.*

It is here I have to raise the obligatory caution: While this book has gained in myriad ways from the guidance, suggestions, and work of many people, I am solely responsible for any gaffes, misinterpretations, or errors.

Suzanne and I thank Roberta Schnoor for kindly accommodating us during a period of research at the JFK Library.

Karen Abramson, Stacey Chandler, Abigail Malangone, and James B. Hill at the JFK Library kindly chased down answers to our many questions and assisted in digging out a wealth of material for us; Hill was an invaluable partner in our search for rarely published photos. Our thanks go to Heidi Smith, Julia Johnas, and Cynthia Medrano at the Highland Park Public Library; Teri Hedgpeth at the Boston Children's Hospital archives; and Erin Wright at *The New England Journal of Medicine*. I'm also indebted to wizard Sean Tyree for helping ease me through a technological nightmare during the book's editing process.

When people ask me what I am writing about, I often begin by saying: "Not that we need another Kennedy book, but . . ." I hope this work fills a gap long neglected in Kennedy history. Its birth has relied on a stack of excellent previous Kennedy works. Their titles are listed in the bibliography, but I want to mention a few authors whose work has enlightened my own with their deep research and rich detail across the spectrum of the Kennedy years: Michael Beschloss, Benjamin Bradlee, Thurston Clarke, Peter Collier and David Horowitz, Robert Dallek, Paul Fay, Doris Kearns Goodwin, Clint Hill and Lisa McCubbin, Evelyn Lincoln, Fredrik Logevall, Thomas Maier, William Manchester, Ralph Martin, David Nasaw, Kenneth O'Donnell, David Powers and Joe McCarthy, Michael S. Ryan, Arthur Schlesinger, Maud Shaw, Sally Bedell Smith, Daniel Spoto, J. B. West and Mary Lynn Kotz, and Garry Wills.

Finally, my abiding gratitude goes to my family: as always, Suzanne, and our two sparkling children, Katie and Ben, whose enthusiasm for a writer's life keeps me going. Katie brought a new member into the family during the writing of this book, her husband, Trevor Gill, who jumped right in with his own curiosity and questions about Patrick, the Kennedys, and the nature of book publishing. Katie was an early reader of the manuscript, casting her fearless millennial eye on every word and posing perceptive questions. I always enjoy talking with Ben, the musician in the family, about the similarities between writing a book and composing music. Our processes are alike, except that I think in words and he thinks in notes and melodies. That he can think in music astonishes me.

NOTES

Abbreviations used in the notes:

AP: Associated Press

BG: Boston Globe

JFKL: John F. Kennedy Presidential Library and Museum, Boston, Massachusetts

JFKLOHP: John F. Kennedy Presidential Library Oral History Project

JFKWHCSF: JFK Library White House Central Subject Files

JFKWHSFPS: JFK Library White House Staff Files, Pierre Salinger

JFKWHSFTR: JFK Library White House Staff Files, Ted Reardon

NYT: New York Times

UPI: United Press International

WES: Washington Evening Star

WHSF: White House Social Files (not digitized)

WP: Washington Post

ONE: "White House—Color It Pink or Blue?"

1 *"The president wrapped":* AP, "Jackie Extends Warm Greeting to J.F.K.," *Kansas City* (MO) *Times*, April 12, 1963, 4.

2 *"There was obviously":* Christopher Andersen, *These Few Precious Days: The Final Year of Jack with Jackie* (New York: Gallery, 2013), 231.

2 *"Mr. Hill," she said*: Clint Hill and Lisa McCubbin, *Mrs. Kennedy and Me* (New York: Gallery, 2012), 209.

3 *"It was challenging":* Ibid., 214.

3 *"in a happy holiday mood":* UPI, "No Easter Bonnet for Mrs. Kennedy," *The Morning Call* (Allentown, PA), April 15, 1963, 8.

5 *"Silly Daddy":* Paul B. Fay, Jr., *The Pleasure of His Company* (New York: Harper & Row, 1966), 221–22.

6 *"was blue and rolling":* Tom Wicker, "Kennedys Attend Easter Mass in Father's Palm Beach Home," *New York Times*, April 15, 1963, 18.

6 *"Stoughton. Stoughton":* UPI, "No Easter Bonnet for Mrs. Kennedy."

6 *"in a jovial mood":* Wicker, "Kennedys Attend Easter Mass in Father's Palm Beach Home."

7 *"Will you give us":* Pierre Salinger, News Conferences, #1033, April 15, 1963, 11:10 a.m., 1, JFKL.

7 *"No," Ted replied:* "The Presidency: Big Year for the Clan," *Time*, April 26, 1963, 23.

7 *"a matter so":* UPI, "Jackie Begins Four Months Seclusion to Await Third Child," *Tucson Daily Citizen*, April 16, 1963, 12.

7 *"One of the treasures":* Pierre Salinger, *With Kennedy* (New York: Avon, 1967), 383.

8 *"Let me say":* Pierre Salinger, News Conferences, #1034, April 15, 1963, 5:30 p.m., 1, JFKL; "April 16, 1963—Pierre Salinger Announces That Jacqueline Kennedy Is Expecting Her Third Child," posted March 5, 2014, by HelmerReenberg, https://www.youtube.com/watch?v=7acT3y0BP1k.

9 *"Actually," United Press International:* UPI, "First Family Awaits Visit from Stork," *News-Review* (Roseburg, OR), April 16, 1963, 1.

9 *"During the past few":* UPI and AP, "Only Four Others 'In All the World' Were Told News," *The Times* (San Mateo, CA), April 16, 1963, 1.

9 *"history of difficult":* Maxine Cheshire, "For First Lady: Date in August Clears Calendar," *WP*, April 17, 1963, D1.

9 *"was attended by secrecy":* UPI, "First Family Awaits Visit from Stork."

10 *"one of the":* UPI, "News of Jackie's Baby Takes Capital by Storm," *El Paso Herald-Post*, April 16, 1963, 22.

10 *"First Family Awaits":* UPI, "First Family Awaits Visit from Stork," 1.

10 *"News of Jackie's":* UPI, "News of Jackie's Baby Takes Capital by Storm," 22.

10 *"A prospective little":* Betty Beale, "Mrs. Kennedy Owned Capital's Best-Kept Secret," *BG*, April 21, 1963, A39.

10 *"I would say":* Clint Hill, interview with author.

10 *"in a very chic"*: "White House—Color It Pink or Blue?," *Billings* (MT) *Gazette*, April 16, 1963, 1.

10 *"radiant"*: UPI, "Radiant Jackie Waves to 'Fans,'" *Bend* (OR) *Bulletin*, April 17, 1963, 12.

10 *"aglow"*: Helen Thomas, UPI, "Friends Say First Lady 'Aglow,'" *Medford* (OR) *Mail Tribune*, May 17, 1963, 7.

10 *"a beaming Pierre"*: "White House—Color It Pink or Blue?," *Billings* (MT) *Gazette*.

11 *"Kennedys Play Waiting Game"*: *The Record* (Hackensack, NJ), April 16, 1963, 5.

11 *"vacations with the Kennedys"*: Alvin Spivak, UPI, "Washington Notes," *The Times-News* (Twin Falls, ID), April 19, 1963, 4.

11 *"will be a very healthy"* and other letter comments: UPI, "300 Letters a Day: Fan Club Grows for Kennedys' Third Child," *Pasadena Independent*, August 6, 1963, 24.

12 *"Caroline had her"*: Maud Shaw, *White House Nannie: My Years with Caroline and John Kennedy, Jr.* (New York: New American Library, 1966), 157.

13 *"goldfish bowl"*: Arthur M. Schlesinger, Jr., *Jacqueline Kennedy: Historic Conversations on Life with John F. Kennedy* (New York: Hyperion, 2011), 202.

13 *"an indefinite 'vacation'"*: Marie Smith, "D.C. Obstetrician Vacations Nearby, Air Force Hospital at Hyannis Port Alerted for Mrs. Kennedy's Arrival," *WP*, July 24, 1963, A1.

13 *"provided the best"*: Janet Travell, M.D., *Office Hours: Day and Night* (New York: New American Library, 1969), 418.

13 *"rather charming"*: Janet G. Travell, recorded interview by Theodore C. Sorensen, January 20, 1966, 28, JFKLOHP.

13 *Walter Reed Army Medical Center:* Winzola McLendon, "Army Leading Navy in Stork Classic," *WP*, June 6, 1963, E1.

14 *redecorating and upgrading:* UPI, "Ready AF Base for Jackie's Baby," *New York Daily News*, July 24, 1963, 5.

15 *"From here"*: Mary Barelli Gallagher, *My Life with Jacqueline Kennedy* (New York: Paperback Library, 1970), 278.

15 *"July was the month"*: Ibid., 277.

TWO: Heartbreak Worth the Pain

17 *"The old man"*: Joan Blair and Clay Blair, Jr., *The Search for JFK* (New York: Berkley, 1976), 318.

17 *"But I was always"*: Ibid., 521.

17 "extraordinarily *personal questions*": Ibid.

17 *"I think all this"*: Ibid., 522.

17 *"a convent-bred girl"*: David Nasaw, *The Patriarch: The Remarkable Life and Turbulent Times of Joseph P. Kennedy* (New York: Penguin, 2012), 76.

17 *"She had found in God"*: Doris Kearns Goodwin, *The Fitzgeralds and the Kennedys: An American Saga* (New York: Simon & Schuster, 1987), 188.

18 *"Mrs. Kennedy had"*: Michael O'Brien, *John F. Kennedy: A Biography* (New York: Thomas Dunne, 2005), 35.

18 *"One of the characteristics"*: Thomas Maier, *The Kennedys: America's Emerald Kings* (New York: Basic Books, 2003), 260.

18 *"No more sex"*: Goodwin, *The Fitzgeralds and the Kennedys*, 392.

18 *"Gee, you're a great"*: Nasaw, *The Patriarch*, 86; noted in Rose Kennedy's diary.

19 *"He was always"*: Blair and Blair, *The Search for JFK*, 353.

19 *"In a flash"*: Mary Van Rensselaer Thayer, *Jacqueline Bouvier Kennedy* (New York: Doubleday, 1961), 95.

19 *"He really brightened"*: Robert Dallek, *An Unfinished Life: John F. Kennedy, 1917–1963* (New York: Back Bay, 2013), 193.

19 *"with a great clinking"*: William Manchester, *Portrait of a President* (New York: Macfadden, 1967), 115.

20 Wish you were here: Ibid.

20 *"cool cat exterior"*: Laura Bergquist Knebel, Oral History #1, recorded interview by Nelson Aldrich, December 8, 1965, 13, JFKLOHP.

20 *"He disliked emotion"*: Theodore C. Sorensen, *Kennedy* (New York: Harper & Row, 1965), 14.

20 *"We both have curious"*: Mary Cremmen, "Wives of Candidates: Jackie Can't Campaign, Pat Helps Husband," *Tampa Tribune*, September 29, 1960, D1.

21 *diagnosed as leukemia:* Fredrik Logevall, *JFK: Coming of Age in the American Century, 1917–1956* (New York: Random House, 2020), 107.

21 *"My mother never really"*: Ralph G. Martin, *A Hero for Our Time* (New York: Macmillan, 1983), 31.

21 *"Emotions resonated"*: Goodwin, *The Fitzgeralds and the Kennedys*, 352.

21 *"he was inclined"*: Rose Fitzgerald Kennedy, *Times to Remember* (New York: Doubleday, 1974), 97.

22 *"a tough, constant"*: Goodwin, *The Fitzgeralds and the Kennedys*, 353.

22 *"Toward his mother":* Ibid.

22 *"a monster" and "utterly charming":* Sarah Bradford, *America's Queen: The Life of Jacqueline Kennedy Onassis* (New York: Penguin, 2000), 22.

22 *"highly strung":* Ibid., 23.

22 *"excelling and perfection":* Ibid., 12.

23 *"In public":* Ibid., 13.

24 *"noble blood lines":* Ibid., 21.

24 *Catherine the Great's:* Ibid.

24 *"large, cumbersome":* Ibid. See also Gore Vidal, *Palimpsest* (New York: Penguin, 1995), 14.

24 *stash of pornography:* Bradford, *America's Queen*, 21; Vidal, *Palimpsest*, 17.

24 *An excellent equestrian:* Bradford, *America's Queen*, 9.

24 *"She was so shy":* Laurence Leamer, *The Kennedy Women: The Saga of an American Family* (New York: Fawcett, 1994), 428.

25 *"cartoon example":* Bradford, *America's Queen*, 27.

25 *"I don't know if":* Carl Sferrazza Anthony, *As We Remember Her: Jacqueline Kennedy Onassis in the Words of Her Family and Friends* (New York: Perennial, 2003), 75.

26 *"it will be":* Tom Leonard, "How JFK's Wife Became Enchanted by a 73-Year-Old Irish Priest Who Took Her for Dinner," *Daily Mail*, May 15, 2014.

26 *"She wasn't sexually":* Peter Collier and David Horowitz, *The Kennedys: An American Drama* (New York: Summit, 1984), 194.

26 *"He's like my father":* Leonard, "How JFK's Wife Became Enchanted by a 73-Year-Old Irish Priest Who Took Her for Dinner."

27 *"this little boy":* Theodore H. White, "For President Kennedy: An Epilogue," *Life*, December 6, 1963, 159.

27 *"His vulnerability aroused":* Goodwin, *The Fitzgeralds and the Kennedys*, 770.

27 *"They had both taken":* Ibid.

27 *"manly skill":* "Life Goes Courting with a U.S. Senator," *Life*, July 20, 1953, 96.

28 *"just like the coronation":* "The Senator Weds," *Life*, September 28, 1953, 45.

28 *"I was alone":* Goodwin, *The Fitzgeralds and the Kennedys*, 772.

28 *"Jackie . . . learned":* Kenneth P. O'Donnell, David F. Powers, and Joe McCarthy, *"Johnny, We Hardly Knew Ye"* (New York: Pocket Books, 1973), 109.

29 *"How can you live":* From an interview with Marie Ridder in Leamer, *The Kennedy Women*, 433.

29 *"After the first year":* Collier and Horowitz, *The Kennedys*, 197.

29 *"We didn't fully":* Daniel Spoto, *Jacqueline Bouvier Kennedy Onassis: A Life* (New York: St. Martin's, 2000), 136.

29 *"The point is":* Collier and Horowitz, *The Kennedys*, 172.

30 *"There is no doubt":* Christopher Andersen, *Jack and Jackie: Portrait of an American Marriage* (New York: Avon, 1996), 149.

30 *"For the moment":* Spoto, *Jaqueline Bouvier Kennedy Onassis*, 111.

31 *"I have to tell you":* Gunilla von Post and Carl Johnes, *Love, Jack* (New York: Crown, 1997), 32.

31 *"long, deeply passionate kiss":* Ibid., 33.

31 *"With a truly":* Garry Wills, *The Kennedy Imprisonment: A Meditation on Power* (Boston: Mariner, 2002), 32.

31 *"the tickle of lust":* Ibid.

31 *"It is only fair":* Ibid., 33.

31 *"His back trouble":* Von Post and Johnes, *Love, Jack*, 64.

31 *"Jack came in":* Ibid., 66.

32 *"rumor that":* Bradford, *America's Queen,* 104.

32 *"I'm never going back":* Ibid.

32 *"She did love":* Ibid., 105.

32 *"exchanged eyes":* William Manchester, *The Death of a President* (New York: Harper & Row, 1967), 84; Sally Bedell Smith, *Grace and Power: The Private World of the Kennedy White House* (New York: Random House, 2004), 7.

32 *"an intensity, an electrical":* Andersen, *These Few Precious Days*, 60.

THREE: Marriage in a Shambles

33 *"bacchanale":* Collier and Horowitz, *The Kennedys*, 209.

34 *"Sen. Kennedy on":* Winzola McLendon, "Sen. Kennedy on Mediterranean Trip Unaware His Wife Has Lost Baby," *WP*, August 25, 1956, 1.

34 *"Why the hell":* Kitty Kelley, *Jackie Oh!* (Secaucus, NJ: Lyle Stuart, 1978), 58.

34 *"terrible obtuseness":* Leamer, *The Kennedy Women*, 462.

34 *"If you want":* Kelley, *Jackie Oh!*, 57–58.

35 *"slow maturer":* Wills, *The Kennedy Imprisonment*, 73.

35 *"Surely no one":* Spoto, *Jacqueline Bouvier Kennedy Onassis*, 135.

35 *"deep emotions":* Lord Harlech (William David Ormsby-Gore), recorded interview by Richard E. Neustadt, March 12, 1965, 88, JFKLOHP.

35 *"For Jack too":* Goodwin, *The Fitzgeralds and the Kennedys*, 785.

35 *"Children evoked":* Ibid., 785–86.

35 *"They were all":* Ibid., 786.

36 *"Though the Kennedys":* C. David Heymann, *A Woman Named Jackie* (New York: Lyle Stuart, 1989), 191.

36 *"It was terribly":* Luella R. Hennessey and Margot Murphy, "Bringing Up the Kennedys," *Good Housekeeping*, August 1961, 116.

37 *"called him a":* Andersen, *Jack and Jackie*, 175; Heymann, *A Woman Named Jackie*, 193.

37 *"By all accounts":* Spoto, *Jacqueline Bouvier Kennedy Onassis*, 137.

37 *"As for Joe paying":* David Nasaw, interview with author. Note that Kitty Kelley (68) in *Jackie Oh!* says discussion of divorce was "untrue": it was out of the question, arguing that Jackie realized her life as a divorcee would be severely limited.

38 *"Don't think that":* Michael Kelly, "Letters to Irish Priest Reveal Jackie Kennedy's Struggles with Faith," catholicregister.org, May 14, 2014.

38 *"She . . . had a":* Drew Pearson, "Washington Merry-Go-Round: Mrs. Kennedy Felt Some Remorse," *WP*, December 23, 1966, B11.

38 *"He blamed himself":* Ibid.

FOUR: "At Last a Baby We Both Love"

39 *"As the Senator":* Evelyn Lincoln, *My Twelve Years with John F. Kennedy* (New York: David McKay, 1965), 108.

40 *"He paced the":* Hennessey and Murphy, "Bringing Up the Kennedys," 52–57, 117.

40 *"very pretty":* Janet Lee Bouvier Auchincloss, recorded interview #1 by Joan Braden, September 5, 1963, 9, JFKLOHP.

40 *"Jack seemed completely":* Fay, *The Pleasure of His Company*, 54.

40 *"And not just":* Lincoln, *My Twelve Years with John F. Kennedy*, 109.

41 *"Jack was more":* Goodwin, *The Fitzgeralds and the Kennedys*, 793.

41 *"Now Lem":* Andersen, *These Few Precious Days*, 188.

41 *"I don't think":* Barbara Leaming, *Jacqueline Bouvier Kennedy Onassis: The Untold Story* (New York: Thomas Dunne, 2014), 90.

41 *"It was the first":* Blair and Blair, *The Search for JFK*, 318.

41 *"Being Caroline's father":* Travell, *Office Hours*, 422.

41 *"at last a baby":* Dialynn Dwyer, "Handwritten Letter Penned by Jacqueline Kennedy to JFK Donated to Kennedy Library Foundation," boston.com, January 7, 2020, https://www.boston.com/news/local-news/2020/01/07/handwritten-letter-jacqueline-kennedy-donated-jfk-library-foundation/; "Jacqueline Kennedy Handwritten Letter to Jack," RR Auction, Remarkable Rarities: Elite 100, Lot #2043.

42 *"No matter how tired":* Shaw, *White House Nannie*, 63.

42 *"This life is very":* Bruce Biossat, Newspaper Enterprise Association, "An Afternoon with Jacqueline Kennedy," *Shawnee* (OK) *News-Star*, July 31, 1960.

42 *"Every time a plane":* Ruth Montgomery, "At Home with Jacqueline Kennedy: She Yearns to Be in Vortex of Current Political Cyclone," *The Morning Call* (Allentown, PA), September 25, 1960.

FIVE: "I'm Never There When She Needs Me"

43 *by the smallest margin:* "1960 Presidential Returns," JFKL, www.jfklibrary.org.

44 *"She's all right":* "Acceptance Speech, Hyannis Armory, Hyannis, Massachusetts, November 9, 1960," JFKL, https://www.jfklibrary.org/archives/other-resources/john-f-kennedy-speeches/hyannis-ma-acceptance-speech-19601109; "November 9, 1963, President-Elect Kennedy's Acceptance Speech," posted November 4, 2022, by HelmerReenberg, https://www.youtube.com/watch?v=odkc15Y90YA.

44 *"Jackie never looked":* Martin, *A Hero for Our Time*, 246.

44 *"Can you come":* Shaw, *White House Nannie*, 75.

44 *white sweater:* "The President-Elect: John Jr.," *Time*, December 5, 1960; Warren Duffee and Helen Thomas, UPI, "President-Elect Flies Back from Fla. Trip," *Courier-Post* (Camden, NJ), November 25, 1960, 1.

45 *"She looked so tiny":* "Bet Winner Pilots Trip to Hospital," *WES*, November 25, 1960, B1.

45 *"Will I lose":* "The President-Elect: John Jr.," *Time*.

45 *"Everything's going to be":* Willard Baucom and Walt Myers as told to UPI, "Future First Lady Calm on Stork Run," *Indianapolis Star*, November 25, 1960, 1.

45 *"I was the low man":* Phil Gianficaro, "If JFK Was Killed Today," *The Times* (Beaver County, PA), timesonline, November 14, 2013. Sam Jellinek, seventeen, grandson of Dr. Ira Seiler, interviewed his grandfather about his memories of his experiences with Kennedy as one of several reader submissions for the article.

46 *"[Jack] became tense":* O'Donnell, Powers, and McCarthy, *"Johnny, We Hardly Knew Ye,"* 268.

46 *"He handed the baby":* Dean R. Owen, *November 22, 1963: Reflections on the Life, Assassination, and Legacy of John F. Kennedy* (New York: Skyhorse, 2013), 339.

46 *"was nervous and":* Gianficaro, "If JFK Was Killed Today."

46 *"I took the baby":* Ibid.

47 *"It was a very tense":* Dorothy McCardle, "This Was a 'First' That Thrilled Nurse Carol," *WP*, November 29, 1960, B5.

47 *"Why was he going":* Martin, *A Hero for Our Time*, 247.

48 *"We have just been advised":* Marvin L. Arrowsmith, AP, "Father Mostly in the Air," *WES*, November 25, 1960, B1.

48 *"out of your regular":* Martin, *A Hero for Our Time*, 247.

48 *"she just smiled":* UPI, "It's a JFK Jr. for the Kennedys," *New York Newsday*, 93.

48 *"The mother is":* Lee Walsh, "Kennedy Son Born, Mother Doing Well," *WES*, November 25, 1960, B-1.

48 *"pronounced him healthy":* Duffee and Thomas, UPI, "Jacqueline Has a Boy; President-Elect Flies Back from Fla. Trip," 3.

48 *"It was premature":* Walsh, "Kennedy Son Born, Mother Doing Well," 1.

48 *"lusty cry":* Stanley Meisler, AP, "JFK Jr. and Mother Reported Doing Well," *Indianapolis News*, November 25, 1960, 1.

49 *"Three beautiful shots":* "Cameraman Loses Exclusive Films of Mrs. Kennedy," *WES*, November 25, 1960, B-1.

49 *"I feel as though":* "Women: Jackie," *Time*, January 20, 1961.

49 *"jubilant":* Duffee and Thomas, "Jacqueline Has a Boy," 1.

49 *"It was really":* Merriman Smith, UPI, "His Name Will Be John F. Jr, The Proud Father Declares," *Courier-Post* (Camden, NJ), November 25, 1963, 1.

50 *"I was so terribly":* Hennessey and Murphy, "Bringing Up the Kennedys," 118.

50 *"Jack always seemed":* Ibid.

51 *"I just walked along":* "Mrs. Kennedy Sees Son for First Time; Reveal Baby Was Ill," *Philadelphia Inquirer*, November 27, 1960, 1.

51 *slight respiratory ailment:* Ibid.

51 *"It was obvious":* Hill and McCubbin, *Mrs. Kennedy and Me*, 22.

52 *"Everything's beautifully normal":* AP, "Everything Is Fine with the Kennedy Folks," *Bradenton* (FL) *Herald*, December 1, 1960, 6.

52 *"But what she":* Hennessey and Murphy, "Bringing Up the Kennedys," 119.

52 *"Do you think":* Ibid.

53 *"I am very very":* Robert Healy, "Jack Jr. Fine," *BG*, November 25, 1960, 1.

53 *"I haven't thought":* UPI, "Kennedy Startled About Presidency Wish for Son," *Anderson* (IN) *Herald*, November 30, 1960, 3.

53 *"It was one of the":* Mary Van Rensselaer Thayer, "Jacqueline Kennedy," *Ladies' Home Journal*, April 1961, 78, 4, 132.

54 *"for the many kindnesses":* Owen, *November 22, 1963*, 340.

54 *"had not been":* Ibid., 341.

SIX: A Bewildering Portrait of a President

55 *"that the torch":* "President John F. Kennedy's Inaugural Address (1961)," Milestone Documents, National Archives, https://www.archives.gov/milestone-documents/president-john-f-kennedys-inaugural-address#transcript.

55 *"I was so proud":* Mary Van Rensselaer Thayer, *Jacqueline Kennedy: The White House Years* (New York: Popular Library, 1971), 75.

55 *"I so badly wanted":* Schlesinger, *Jacqueline Kennedy*, 152.

56 *"I could scarcely":* Thayer, *Jacqueline Kennedy*, 75.

56 *"There's a picture":* Schlesinger, *Jacqueline Kennedy*, 152–53.

56 *"I used to worry":* Ibid., 126.

57 *"I didn't realize":* Ibid.

57 *"My life here":* Ibid., 127n27.

57 *"awful exercise man":* Ibid., 334.

57 *"He loved those children":* Ibid.

57 *"to amuse John":* Ibid., 158.

58 *"He often stepped":* J. B. West and Mary Lynn Kotz, *Upstairs at the White House: My Life with the First Ladies* (New York: Open Road, 1973), 201.

58 *"for about a half":* Schlesinger, *Jacqueline Kennedy*, 156.

58 *"He really would":* Ibid., 334.

58 *"He'd get on":* Ibid., 337.

58 *"Nothing alters a man":* Alastair Granville Forbes, Oral History #2, recorded interview by Joseph E. O'Connor, October 31, 1966, 36, JFKLOHP.

58 *"There is a rapport":* Laura Bergquist, *A Very Special President* (New York: McGraw-Hill, 1965), 121.

59 *"This is the girl":* Barbara Gamarekian, recorded interview by Diane T. Michaelis, June 10, 1963, 31, JFKLOHP.

59 *"I've always wondered":* Ibid.

59 *"He'd have absolutely":* Hugo Vickers, ed., *Beaton in the Sixties: More Unexpurgated Diaries* (London: Phoenix, 2003), 278–79.

60 *"She could accept":* Bradford, *America's Queen*, 111.

60 *"She had brought":* Carly Simon, *Touched by the Sun: My Friendship with Jackie* (New York: Farrar, Straus & Giroux, 2019), 182.

61 *"One of the many":* Alan Brinkley, *John F. Kennedy*, The American Presidents (New York: Times Books/Henry Holt, 2012), 55. Brinkley draws on William Chafe, *Private Lives/Public Consequences: Personality and Politics in Modern America* (Cambridge: Harvard University Press, 2005), 122–23. See also Rose McDermott, *Presidential Leadership, Illness, and Decision-Making* (Cambridge: Cambridge University Press, 2007), 141–44.

61 *"Kennedy's womanizing had":* Dallek, *An Unfinished Life*, 475.

61 *"His right hand":* Manchester, *Portrait of a President*, 18.

61 *"displaying symptoms of":* Ibid., 22.

61 *"always on the edge":* Ibid., 18.

62 *"We cannot discount":* Dallek, *An Unfinished Life*, 408.

62 *"He treated me":* Ibid.

62 *"he just beat":* Michael R. Beschloss, *The Crisis Years: Kennedy and Khrushchev, 1960–1963* (New York: Edward Burlingame, 1991), 225.

62 *"probable long-term worsening":* Nassir Ghaemi, "What Jackie Kennedy Didn't Say—and Didn't Know," *Psychology Today*, September 14, 2011, http://www.psychologytoday.com/us/blog.

63 *"Within months"*: T. Glenn Pait and Justin T. Dowdy, "John F. Kennedy's Back: Chronic Pain, Failed Surgeries, and the Story of Its Effects on His Life and Death," *Journal of Neurosurgery: Spine* 27 (September 2017): 252.

63 *"No president with his"*: Dallek, *An Unfinished Life*, 581. Note: Dallek writes that Jacobson managed to treat Kennedy through 1962.

63 *"One day when"*: Lincoln, *My Twelve Years with John F. Kennedy*, 338.

64 *"it seemed that 1963"*: Hill and McCubbin, *Mrs. Kennedy and Me*, 209.

64 *"He seemed to us"*: O'Donnell, Powers, and McCarthy, *"Johnny, We Hardly Knew Ye,"* 434–35.

65 *"the tides of human"*: John F. Kennedy, "January 14, 1963: State of Union Address," University of Virginia Miller Center, millercenter.org.

65 *"buoyantly hopeful"*: James Reston, "Kennedy Reflects Progress of the U.S.," *NYT*, January 15, 1963, 6.

65 *"the serenity of"*: James Cannon Personal Papers, Draft 4/11/63, Talk with President Kennedy, April 5, 1963, 2, Box 1, JFKL.

65 *"Well, I think it's"*: Ibid., 3.

66 *"One crisis ebbs"*: E. B. White, "Burdens of High Office," *The New Yorker*, October 12, 1963, 56. Inspired by short UPI item, "Son Accompanies Kennedy in Limousine to a Parley," *NYT*, October 1, 1963, 9.

66 *"flamboyant eyebrows, piercing"*: Sally Bedell Smith, *Grace and Power*, 226.

66 *"there was no"*: Dallek, *An Unfinished Life*, 476.

66 *"He could talk in"*: Ibid.

67 *"I didn't sleep"*: Mimi Alford, *Once Upon a Secret: My Affair with President John F. Kennedy and Its Aftermath* (New York: Random House, 2013), 118–19. Note: Alford didn't respond to interview requests.

67 *"and it was"*: Ibid., 124.

67 *"The president was"*: Ibid., 125.

SEVEN: Signs of a Healthy, Full-Term Delivery

68 *"Thursday had to be"*: Robert V. Leary, "Old Style 4th Captivates N.E.," *BG*, July 5, 1963, 7.

69 *"He made one"*: Frank Falacci, "President Has Day Off," *BG*, July 6, 1963, 3.

69 *"greatest Hyannis Port"*: O'Donnell, Powers, and McCarthy, *"Johnny, We Hardly Knew Ye,"* 434.

70 *"Every mother in"*: Fay, *The Pleasure of His Company*, 217.

70 *"the breath of death"*: Dallek, *An Unfinished Life*, 626.

71 *"Can you imagine"*: Beschloss, *The Crisis Years*, 487, from "Crisis Hits Younger Set," *Boston Herald*, October 26, 1962, 5.

71 *"logical and unemotional"*: Martin, *A Hero for Our Time*, 504.

71 *"That's when he"*: Ibid.

71 *"Where's my daddy?"*: Lincoln, *My Twelve Years with John F. Kennedy*, 325.

72 *"all mankind has"*: John F. Kennedy, "Radio and Television Address to the American People on the Nuclear Test Ban Treaty," July 26, 1963, The American Presidency Project, https://www.presidency.ucsb.edu/node/237272.

72 *refurbishments:* "Hospital Readied for First Lady," *WES*, July 25, 1963, B6; Frank Falacci, "Otis Hospital Shines Suite," *BG*, July 25, 1963.

73 *"I'd just like to send"*: Ted Widmer, comp., *Listening In: The Secret White House Recordings of John F. Kennedy* (New York: Hyperion, 2012), 273–75.

73 *"See that fellow's"*: Ibid., 275–76.

74 *"If the stork"*: Falacci, "Otis Hospital Shines Suite."

74 *"Children almost too numerous"*: "Kennedys Galore Frolic on Birthday of the First Lady," *NYT*, July 29, 1963, 1.

74 *"It's my daddy's turn!"*: Thurston Clarke, *JFK's Last Hundred Days* (New York: Penguin, 2013), 68, quoting Joan Meyers, *John Fitzgerald Kennedy: As We Remember Him* (New York: Antheneum, 1965), 207.

74 *"The kids all yelling"*: Stanley Tretick, recorded interview by Diana Michaelis, September 15, 1964, 21, JFKLOHP.

74 *"He spent a lot"*: Laura Bergquist Knebel, Oral History #2, recorded interview by Sheldon Stern, August 1, 1977, 13, JFKLOHP.

74 *"The one thing"*: Alastair Granville Forbes, Oral History #1, recorded interview by Joseph E. O'Connor, October 19, 1966, 13, JFKLOHP.

75 *"What's the limit?"*: Clarke, *JFK's Last Hundred Days*, 68.

75 *"Friends at Cape Cod"*: UPI, "Jacqueline Plans Quiet 34th Birthday Fete Today," *BG*, July 28, 1963, 2.

75 *"had excellent"*: Ibid.

75 *"One of the best"*: Frank Falacci, "JFK Gift to Wife? CIA Not Told," *BG*, July 29, 1963, 4.

76 *"a lovely ceramic":* Gallagher, *My Life with Jacqueline Kennedy*, 283.

76 *"All I want":* West and Kotz, *Upstairs at the White House*, 247.

77 *"a vibrator with a":* Gallagher, *My Life with Jacqueline Kennedy*, 285.

77 *"post-natal wardrobe":* Ibid.

77 *"Enough work went into":* West and Kotz, *Upstairs at the White House*, 246.

77 *"Jacqueline Kennedy enjoyed":* Ibid., 201.

78 *"Will one of you":* Gallagher, *My Life with Jacqueline Kennedy*, 282.

79 *"President Kennedy was":* James A. Reed, recorded interview by Robert J. Donovan, June 16, 1964, 69, JFKLOHP.

79 *"I just hope":* Ibid., 70.

79 *"thoughtlessly carousing":* Barbara Leaming, *Mrs. Kennedy: The Missing History of the Kennedy Years* (New York: Touchstone, 2001), 295.

79 *"He was a man":* Ibid., 296.

80 *"he was feeling":* Ibid.

80 *"a friendly familiar":* Sally Bedell Smith, *Grace and Power*, 393.

80 "*Certain women from*": Bradford, *America's Queen*, 99.

EIGHT: "This Baby Mustn't Be Born Dead"

81 *"I noticed that":* Shaw, *White House Nannie*, 157.

81 *"Oh no you":* Ibid., 158.

82 *"OFF THE RECORD":* Evelyn Lincoln Personal Papers, Schedules and Diaries, 1953–1963, President's appointments, August 1963, ELPP-006-009, JFKL.

82 *"troubled genius":* William J. Broad and Walter Sullivan, "Edward Teller, a Fierce Architect of the Atom Bomb, Is Dead at 95," *NYT*, September 11, 2003, A22.

82 *"cherished ambition":* O'Donnell, Powers, and McCarthy, *"Johnny, We Hardly Knew Ye,"* 417.

84 *"Mr. Landis":* Paul Landis, interview with author.

84 *"Mr. Landis, I":* Hill and McCubbin, *Mrs. Kennedy and Me*, 239.

85 *"If we could":* Landis, author interview.

85 *"I think she's":* Paul Landis, *The Final Witness* (Chicago: Chicago Press, 2024), 105.

85 *"Call and have":* Ibid.

86 *"Clint, Mrs. Kennedy":* Hill and McCubbin, *Mrs. Kennedy and Me*, 240.

86 *"No member of":* Frances Lewine, AP, "Kennedy Saga: Planning, Luck Pay Off at Hospital," *Austin* (TX) *American*, August 19, 1963, 16.

86 *"several weeks ahead":* Gallagher, *My Life with Jacqueline Kennedy*, 285.

87 *"I was going":* Landis, author interview.

87 *"'Mr. Landis, can'":* Landis, author interview; Landis, *The Final Witness*, 105.

87 *"So, there I":* Landis, *The Final Witness*, 105.

87 *"She keeps saying":* Landis, author interview.

88 *"Please God":* Hill and McCubbin, *Mrs. Kennedy and Me*, 239.

88 *"Jackie's gone into":* Kate Storey, *White House by the Sea: A Century of Kennedys at Hyannis Port* (New York: Scribner, 2023), 137.

89 *"Wow," he sighed:* Landis, author interview.

89 *"I think I'm going":* "The Presidency: The Struggle of the Baby Boy," *Time*, August 16, 1963, 8–9.

89 *"I felt there":* Gallagher, *My Life with Jacqueline Kennedy*, 285.

90 *"feminine intuition":* Ibid.

90 *"Hi, Jackie":* Ibid., 286.

90 *"I'm bringing Mrs.":* Lewine, "Kennedy Saga: Planning, Luck Pay Off at Hospital," 16.

91 *"I went right":* Dr. Charles Sanislow, interview with author.

91 *"We need to":* Hill and McCubbin, *Mrs. Kennedy and Me*, 240.

91 *"I couldn't stand":* Gallagher, *My Life with Jacqueline Kennedy*, 286.

91 *"Mrs. Kennedy!":* Ibid.

92 *"No Clint!":* Landis, author interview.

92 *"By the time":* Landis, *The Final Witness*, 107.

92 *"Clint, they're taking":* Hill and McCubbin, *Mrs. Kennedy and Me*, 240.

92 *"Dr. Walsh," she:* Gallagher, *My Life with Jacqueline Kennedy*, 286.

92 *"far more at":* "It's Dr. Walsh on Job When Crisis Calls," *BG*, August 8, 1963, 6.

92 *"This baby":* Gallagher, *My Life with Jacqueline Kennedy*, 286.

93 *Jerry Behn:* "Secret Service Man Promoted to Head of White House Detail," *NYT*, August 3, 1961, 24.

93 *"They called me":* Lincoln, *My Twelve Years with John F. Kennedy*, 349.

93 *"Why did she":* Ibid., 350.

94 *"he could navigate":* Hugh Sidey, "The Boy We Called John-John," *Time*, July 26, 1999, 58.

94 *"Mrs. Lincoln, soon":* Lincoln, *My Twelve Years with John F. Kennedy*, 338.

94 *"Jerry tells me":* Ibid., 350.

94 *"Mr. President":* Travell, *Office Hours*, 421.

95 *"I was in":* Salinger, *With Kennedy*, 139.

95 *"cigar in hand":* William M. Blair, "2d Son Born to Kennedys; Has Lung Illness," *NYT*, August 8, 1963, 1.

95 *"Salinger burst into":* Helen Thomas, *Front Row at the White House: My Life and Times* (New York: Touchstone, 2000), 248.

95 *"had been rushed":* Shaw, *White House Nannie*, 158.

96 *Three twelve-passenger helicopters:* Alvin Spivak, UPI, "When JFK Calls, Helicopters Rise to the Occasion," *BG*, August 14, 1963, 28.

96 *"Thirty minutes":* Martin, *A Hero for Our Time*, 525.

96 *"We had trouble":* O'Donnell, Powers, and McCarthy, *"Johnny, We Hardly Knew Ye,"* 435.

97 *"We'll need three":* Martin, *A Hero for Our Time*, 435.

97 *"Here he was":* Storey, *White House by the Sea*, 105.

97 *"I want you":* Martin, *A Hero for Our Time*, 525.

97 *"just to be":* Andersen, *These Few Precious Days*, 258.

97 *"I'll go right":* Martin, *A Hero for Our Time*, 525.

98 *"I've never seen":* Bradford, *America's Queen*, 252.

98 *"We all sat":* Lincoln, *My Twelve Years with John F. Kennedy*, 351.

98 *"It was a very":* Pamela Turnure and Nancy Tuckerman, recorded interview by Mrs. Wayne Fredericks, 1964, 20, JFKLOHP.

NINE: "Please Let the Baby Be All Right"

99 *"She did not":* Gallagher, *My Life with Jacqueline Kennedy*, 287.

99 *"deeply worried":* Hill and McCubbin, *Mrs. Kennedy and Me*, 240.

100 *"You clean the patient":* Sanislow, author interview.

100 *"She wanted a cigarette":* Ibid.

100 *"Why don't you":* E. B. McKee, "A Brush with History," *Providence Journal*, November 10, 2013.

100 *"Devoid of makeup":* Ibid.

101 *"beautiful, normal":* Lewine, "Kennedy Saga: Planning, Luck Pay Off at Hospital," 16.

101 *"Who needs to":* Hill and McCubbin *Mrs. Kennedy and Me*, 240.

101 *"The next hour":* Gallagher, *My Life with Jacqueline Kennedy*, 287.

101 *"I kept watching":* Ibid.

102 *"We have some concerns":* Ibid., 241.

102 *"Immediately, it was":* McKee, "A Brush with History."

102 *"Then, most":* Ibid.

103 *"difficulty in breathing":* Michael S. Ryan, *Patrick Bouvier Kennedy: A Brief Life That Changed the History of Newborn Care* (Minneapolis: MCP Books, 2015), 45.

103 *"Mrs. Kennedy has":* Gallagher, *My Life with Jacqueline Kennedy*, 287.

103 *"We were all":* Ibid.

103 *"nice, old fashioned":* Gloria Negri, "Whole World Taken by Littlest Kennedy," *BG*, August 8, 1963 (a.m.), 4.

104 *"We'd known each":* Andersen, *These Few Precious Days*, 258.

104 *"His eyes were wide":* Gallagher, *My Life with Jacqueline Kennedy*, 288.

104 *"I didn't know":* Hill and McCubbin, *Mrs. Kennedy and Me*, 242.

105 *"they were trying":* Gallagher, *My Life with Jacqueline Kennedy*, 288.

105 *Jackie's heavy smoking:* Bradford, *America's Queen*, 108; Heymann, *A Woman Named Jackie*, 191.

106 *"was almost certainly":* Bradford, *America's Queen*, 95.

106 *"Although in fairness":* Ibid.

106 *"The next thing":* Bill Nemetz, "Airman's Admiration Grew as JFK, Jackie Grieved Son," *Portland Press Herald*, November 21, 2003, 7.

107 *"grunting":* Details of Patrick's condition found in Ryan, *Patrick Bouvier Kennedy*, 55.

108 *"cautiously optimistic":* McKee, "A Brush with History."

108 *"tanned, shorter":* Ibid.

108 *"Mrs. Kennedy has":* "August 7, 1963—Press Secretary Pierre Salinger Announces the Birth of Patrick Bouvier Kennedy," posted February 6, 2013, by HelmerReenberg, https://www.youtube.com/watch?v=dU7z7KOeizM.

109 *"Clint":* Hill and McCubbin, *Mrs. Kennedy and Me*, 242.

109 *"They're on Pat's":* "They're on Pat's Medical Team," *BG*, September 9, 1963, 3.

110 *"He was beautiful":* Hill and McCubbin, *Mrs. Kennedy and Me*, 242.

110 *"What do you":* Nemetz, "Airman's Admiration Grew as JFK, Jackie Grieved Son."

110 *"I yield":* 88th Congress, 1st Session, *Congressional Record*, Vol. 109, Part 11, 14479, Congress.gov.

111 *Children's Hospital Medical Center:* In 1963, the institution was the Children's Hospital Medical Center. Today it is called Boston Children's Hospital.

111 *"I would like to transfer":* Dr. James Hughes, interview with author. Dr. Roy Heffernan, a Kennedy family physician, also called Hughes to discuss Patrick's condition. Kennedy had phoned Heffernan seeking his advice and tracked him down on his golf course, according to Heffernan's JFK Library oral history, 4.

111 *"Could this be":* Hughes, author interview.

112 *Children's Hospital had established:* Arline Grimes, "'Baby Kennedy' Gets Reception for VIP," *Boston Herald*, August 8, 1963 (p.m.), 1; Jeffrey A. Osoff, "Famed Hospital Mobilizes," *BG*, August 8, 1963, 4.

113 *"quiet authority":* "Dr. Drorbaugh a Man of Quiet Authority," *BG*, August 8, 1963, 6.

113 *Boston Lying-in Hospital:* In 1966, Lying-in became Boston Hospital for Women in a merger, then in another merger in 1980 become part of Brigham and Women's Hospital. "Q. Can you explain the Brigham & Women's Hospital Name?" Harvard Countway Library, asklib.hms.harvard.edu.

113 *"Well," replied the:* Hughes, author interview.

113 *"he managed to":* Ibid.

113 *"The first thing":* Ryan, *Patrick Bouvier Kennedy*, 58 in text; 99 in Ryan interview with Drorbaugh.

114 *"I grabbed my":* Ibid.

114 *"No soup bowls":* Nemetz, "Airman's Admiration Grew as JFK, Jackie Grieved Son," 7.

114 *"was in":* Ryan, *Patrick Bouvier Kennedy*, in Ryan interview with Drorbaugh, 100.

115 *"and grunting":* Lawrence K. Altman, "A Kennedy Baby's Life and Death," *NYT*, July 30, 2013, D3.

116 *"very distressed":* Douglas S. Crockett, "Baby Sped to Boston," *BG*, August 8, 1963 (a.m.), 3.

116 *was better equipped:* AP, "Kennedy Baby Ill, Taken to Boston," *Hartford Courant*, August 8, 1963, 1.

116 *"a precautionary move":* Crockett, "Baby Sped to Boston."

116 *"I learned to anticipate":* Hill and McCubbin, *Mrs. Kennedy and Me*, 11.

117 *"I had to":* Ibid., 242.

117 *"I didn't know":* Landis, author interview.

117 *"He lay on":* Gallagher, *My Life with Jacqueline Kennedy*, 289.

117 *"It was a very":* Ibid.

TEN: "He's a Kennedy—He'll Make It"

118 *"Is that a Cadillac?":* Sanislow, author interview.

119 *"I recall seeing":* Ryan, *Patrick Bouvier Kennedy*, 101.

119 *"Dr. Hughes, are":* Ibid., 124.

119 *"respectful and aware":* Ibid., 125.

120 *"He didn't look":* Hughes, author interview.

121 *"We had to":* Ibid.

121 *"There wasn't all":* Ibid.

122 *"the very best start":* Gallagher, *My Life with Jacqueline Kennedy*, 289.

122 *"They screamed and":* Mary McGrory, "Anxious Father: Shuttling Between Hospitals," *WES*, August 8, 1963, 1.

122 *"unsmiling":* Robert B. Hanron, "Boston Crowds Share President's Anxiety," *BG*, August 8, 1963 (a.m.), 8.

122 *"seemed faintly cheered":* McGrory, "Anxious Father."

122 *"As he stepped":* Crockett, "Baby Sped to Boston," 3.

122 *"Good luck!":* McGrory, "Anxious Father."

123 *"very congenial":* Ryan, *Patrick Bouvier Kennedy*, 119.

123 *"Just like all":* Ibid., 116.

123 *"He used to come":* Jeremiah V. Murphy, "Ritz Puts on Ritz for Sudden V.I.P. Guest," *BG*, August 8, 1963 (a.m.), 5.

124 *"idiopathic respiratory distress":* "Baby Pat Has Bad Turn," *BG*, August 8, 1963 (p.m.), 17.

124 *"a cause for concern":* Ian Menzies, "Peak of Crisis Hard to Predict," *BG*, August 8, 1963 (p.m.), 1.

124 *"make a final diagnosis":* Crockett, "Baby Sped to Boston," 1.

124 *"Is it on":* UPI, "President Keeps Tabs on Ailing Son," *St. Albans* (VT) *Messenger*, 1.

124 *"I would not say":* Crockett, "Baby Sped to Boston," 1.

124 *"I would rather not":* Blair, "2d Son Born to Kennedys; Has Lung Illness," 28.

124 *"The President assured":* UPI, "President Hurries Back to Boston," *Pittsburgh Press*, August 8, 1963, 1.

124 *"remarkably good condition":* Ibid., 6.

125 *"A worried father":* "The Hospital Shades Come Down and Vigil Starts over Patrick Kennedy," *Life*, August 16, 1963, 28–28B.

125 *"Somebody called us":* Hughes, author interview.

125 *"There was nothing magical":* Ibid.

126 *"He's a loveable":* UPI, "Condition Seen as Serious," *Citizen-News* (Hollywood, CA), August 8, 1963, 1.

126 *"I wish I could say":* UPI, "No Irish Red in Baby's Hair," *Vancouver Sun*, August 8, 1963, 15.

126 *"BABY SPED TO":* Details from *BG*, August 8, 1963 (a.m.), 1.

126 *"He's a Kennedy":* Mary McGrory, "'He's a Kennedy—He'll Make It,'" *BG*, August 8, 1963 (a.m.), 1.

126 *"He is only":* Negri, "Whole World Taken by Littlest Kennedy."

127 *news kiosks announced:* UPI, "Europeans Show Deep Concern for Kennedy Infant," *The Evening Herald* (Pottsville, PA), August 8, 1963, 11; Ralph Champion, "Jackie Has a Boy—Ambulance Dash to Save Him," *Daily Mirror* (London), August 8, 1963, 1.

127 *"an abortion might":* UPI, "Europe Shares Concern for Kennedy Baby," *New York Newsday*, August 8, 1963, 21.

127 *"The White House":* UPI, "Europe Shares Concern for the Kennedy Baby," *WP*, August 9, 1963, A6.

127 *"the great leveler":* "Tragic Ending," *Buffalo Evening News*, August 9, 1963, 24.

127 *"prayerful watch":* "U.S. Shares Grief over Kennedy's Son," *Spokesman Review* (Spokane, WA), August 10, 1963, 4.

127 *"The world shares":* "Prayers for a Baby," *NYT*, August 8, 1963, 26.

128 *fifty-fifty chance of surviving:* "Lung Ailment Often Is Mild, Can Be Fatal," *Philadelphia Inquirer*, August 8, 1963, 1.

128 *"His condition was":* Sarah DiGregorio, *Early: An Intimate History of Premature Birth and What It Teaches Us About Being Human* (New York: Harper, 2020), 125.

129 *"both had essentially":* Ibid.

129 *"We were busy, busy":* Ibid.

129 *"You would think":* Ibid., 123.

ELEVEN: Prayers for Patrick

130 *nuclear weapons test ban treaty:* Henry I. Trewhitt, "Rusk to Stop in Bonn, Give Assurances," *Baltimore Sun*, August 8, 1963, 1; Paul W. Ward, "26 Nations to Sign Ban Pact Today," *Baltimore Sun*, August 8, 1963, 2.

131 *"move swiftly":* "Senate Asked for 'Swift' OK to Test Pact," *WES*, August 8, 1963, 1.

131 *"I just wanted":* "JFK Quits Wife's Side, Flies Back to Hub," *BG*, August 8, 1963, 17.

131 *"ghoulishly with":* Mary McGrory, "Helpless As Any Father," *BG*, August 9, 1963 (p.m.).

132 *"He's got leukemia":* Ibid.

132 *"still serious":* Ibid.

132 *"It is the normal":* "JFK Quits Wife's Side, Flies Back to Hub," *BG*.

132 *"The situation remains":* UPI, "President Given Encouraging News," *Evening Tribune* (Cocoa, FL), August 8, 1963, 1.

133 *"the grubby little":* McGrory, "Helpless As Any Father."

134 *"Daddy's in a":* "Daddy's in a Whirl," *Miami News*, August 8, 1963, 12B.

134 *"when we have":* Richard O'Donnell, "President's Day: Helter Skelter," *BG*, August 9, 1963 (a.m.), 4.

134 *"a very good night":* UPI, "Jackie Spends Comfortable Night, Appears Quite Healthy," *Evening Tribune* (Cocoa, FL), August 8, 1963, 3.

134 *"Her post-operative":* Ibid.

134 *"The hospital visit":* O'Donnell, "President's Day."

135 *"She wanted me to":* Gallagher, *My Life with Jacqueline Kennedy*, 290.

135 *"After consulting with"*: AP, "Timetable of Tragedy," *Austin* (TX) *American*, August 10, 1963, 7.

136 *"the most common"*: Donald White, "Doctor Team Guards Patrick Against HMD (Lung Disease)," *BG*, August 8, 1963 (p.m.), 3.

136 *"No action can"*: Menzies, "Peak of Crisis Hard to Predict," 2.

137 *"the prayers of"*: Wire Services, "Kennedy Baby's Difficulties Said to Be Increasing," *St. Louis Post-Dispatch*, August 8, 1963, 1.

137 *"they . . . wanted to"*: Ryan, *Patrick Bouvier Kennedy*, 116.

137 *"because of the situation"*: Ibid.

138 *"It will injure"*: Dr. Donald Null, interview with author.

139 *"remained pretty cool"*: Ryan, *Patrick Bouvier Kennedy*, 124.

139 *"If the baby survives"*: Dr. Robert H. Pass, "A Conversation with Living Legend Dr. Welton Gersony," *Pediheart: Pediatric Cardiology Today*, Podcast 247, April 7, 2023, https://www.spreaker.com/episode/pediheart-podcast-247.

139 *"The longer a baby"*: Null, author interview.

139 *"Mr. President"*: Pass, "A Conversation with Living Legend Dr. Welton Gersony."

140 *"in rough shape"*: Ryan, *Patrick Bouvier Kennedy*, 113.

140 *"something I would"*: Ibid., 114.

140 *"I couldn't possibly"*: Ibid., 113.

140 *"I told him"*: Ibid., 117.

140 *"The president's new"*: UPI, "President Hurries Back to Boston," *Pittsburgh Press*.

140 *"BABY PAT HAS"*: "Baby Pat Has Bad Turn," *BG*, 1.

141 *"You mustn't blame"*: McGrory, "Helpless As Any Father."

141 *"This comes with"*: Jean Dietz, "Children Send Get-Well Cards," *BG*, August 9, 1963 (a.m.), 2.

141 *"It's on the house"*: Mary McGrory, "JFK No Different: Worried Father Stalks Hospital," *BG*, August 9, 1963 (p.m.), 3.

142 *"I want you"*: Rachel Zimmerman, "Tale of the Pediatrician Snatched to Treat the Kennedy Baby," WBUR.org, August 6, 2013.

142 *"Mrs. Levine, I"*: Ibid.

142 *"Scramble!"*: Hughes, author interview.

142 *"Where are you?"*: Lincoln, *My Twelve Years with John F. Kennedy*, 352–53.

142 *"He was just":* Ibid.

143 *"Please find enclosed":* Clarke, *JFK's Last Hundred Days*, 13.

143 *"Tell the bank":* Lincoln, *My Twelve Years with John F. Kennedy*, 353.

TWELVE: "Chances of His Survival Are Very, Very Slim"

144 *"The air in":* Ryan, *Patrick Bouvier Kennedy*, 70.

145 *"His EKG looks":* Owen, *November 22, 1963*, 277.

145 *"was still very":* Ibid.

145 *"slightly improved":* Dorothy McCardle, "Mrs. Kennedy Cheered by News of Son's Gain," *WP*, August 9, 1963, A6.

146 *"brought a glow":* Ibid.

146 *"He's doing very":* Frank Falacci, "Mrs. Kennedy Never Knew Pat Worse 'til JFK Said He Was Improving," *BG*, August 9, 1963 (a.m.), 5.

146 *"Although maintaining her":* Ibid.

147 *"He showed up":* Ryan, *Patrick Bouvier Kennedy*, 118.

147 *"I'm very impressed":* Hughes, author interview.

147 *"I have quite":* Pierre Salinger, press briefing #1189, August 8, 1963, 6:17 p.m., Papers of John F. Kennedy, Presidential Papers, White House Staff Files of Pierre Salinger, Press Briefings 1961–1964, Press Briefings, File 1, 1961–1964, John F. Kennedy, Box 68, 1–4, JFKWHSFPS-068-004, JFKL.

148 *"BABY RALLIES AFTER":* *New York Daily News*, August 9, 1963 (FINAL).

148 *"the double strain":* McCardle, "Mrs. Kennedy Cheered by News of Son's Gain."

148 *"cool and calm":* Gloria Negri, "Mother Cool, Calm in Crisis," *BG*, August 9, 1963 (a.m.), 1.

149 *"I just wanted":* Arthur Stratton, "Father in Hospital Vigil as End Comes," *Boston Herald*, August 9, 1963 (LATE), 6.

149 *"it would be":* "President Silences Cavalcade Sirens," *Boston Herald*, August 9, 1963, 7.

149 *"a trace of":* David Wilson, "President Sleeps at Hospital to Be Near Infant Patrick," *Boston Herald*, August 9, 1963, 7.

149 *"Everything was quiet":* Ryan, *Patrick Bouvier Kennedy*, 116.

149 *"Both of us":* Ibid., 119.

149 *"He was a diligent":* Owen, *November 22, 1963*, 279.

149 *"You gave him the straight":* Ibid.

150 *"We were giving":* Ibid., 277.

150 *"the chances of":* Ibid.

150 *"He understood with":* Ryan, *Patrick Bouvier Kennedy*, 114.

150 *"I think we're":* Ibid., 113–14.

150 *Strategic Air Command:* Bryce Miller, UPI, "Helpless, He Cried Alone," *Miami Herald*, August 10, 1963.

151 *"the President faced solitary":* O'Donnell, Powers, and McCarthy, *"Johnny, We Hardly Knew Ye,"* 280.

151 *"Dave would watch":* Ibid., 305.

151 *"Sometime during the":* Owen, *November 22, 1963*, 278.

152 *"things were not":* Ibid.

152 *"As soon as":* Ibid.

152 *"Each time she":* Hill and McCubbin, *Mrs. Kennedy and Me,* 245.

153 *"Could you tell":* O'Donnell, Powers, and McCarthy, *"Johnny, We Hardly Knew Ye,"* 436.

153 *"Dear Mrs. Cramb":* AP, "Presidential Encouragement," *WP*, November 21, 1972, B3.

153 *"began to feel":* Ibid.

153 *"His tiny arms":* Ryan, *Patrick Bouvier Kennedy*, 78–79.

154 *"there wasn't enough":* Owen, *November 22, 1963*, 278.

154 *"we were losing":* Ryan, *Patrick Bouvier Kennedy*, 120.

154 *"He put up":* O'Donnell, Powers, and McCarthy, *"Johnny, We Hardly Knew Ye,"* 436.

154 *"walked away from us":* Salinger, *With Kennedy*, 140. Some accounts have incorrectly reported that President Kennedy held Patrick in his arms during the baby's final moments. Dr. Drorbaugh, who was inside the chamber with Patrick, set the record straight in an interview with author and registered respiratory therapist Michael Ryan, explaining that no one outside the chamber had access to Patrick at any time before he died or for several hours afterward while the tank was decompressed (Ryan, *Patrick Bouvier Kennedy*, 105).

155 *"He didn't want":* O'Donnell, Powers, and McCarthy, *"Johnny, We Hardly Knew Ye,"* 436–37.

155 *"She's finally gone":* Hill and McCubbin, *Mrs. Kennedy and Me*, 245.

155 *"Patrick Kennedy died":* "August 9, 1963, Press Secretary Pierre Salinger Announces the Death of Patrick Bouvier Kennedy," posted September 27, 2012, by HelmerReenberg, https://www.youtube.com/watch?v=YMe91-KNOCg.

156 *"From that time":* "Salinger Breaks News," *BG*, August 9, 1963 (p.m.), 1.

156 *"I can just take one":* Ibid., 1 and 6.

157 *shouted the headlines*: AP, "Condolences Come from All Over the World," *Cincinnati Enquirer*, August 10, 1963.

158 *"She was devastated":* Hill and McCubbin, *Mrs. Kennedy and Me*, 246.

THIRTEEN: "No Privacy in Their Grief"

159 *"tense stillness":* UPI, "At Otis, Sun Was Shining but Sorrow Clouded Faces," *New York Newsday*, August 9, 1963, 3.

159 *"why such a terrible":* Gallagher, *My Life with Jacqueline Kennedy*, 291.

160 *"rode concealed beneath":* AP, "President Arrives at Wife's Bedside," *Delaware County* (PA) *Daily Times*, August 9, 1963, 1.

160 *"She had been":* Gallagher, *My Life with Jacqueline Kennedy*, 290.

160 *"just out of":* Schlesinger, *Jacqueline Kennedy*, 185.

160 *"just sobbed":* Ibid., 185–86.

160 *"stunned":* Leaming, *Mrs. Kennedy*, 303.

161 *"There's just one":* Manchester, *The Death of a President*, 8. Note: this passage has been picked up by many authors in various forms.

161 *"He was going":* Sanislow, author interview.

161 *"Because we had":* Maud Shaw, recorded interview by Pamela Turnure, April 27, 1965, 11, JFKLOHP.

161 *"He proved himself":* Ibid.

162 *"Caroline was very":* Ibid.

162 *"The news brought":* Shaw, *White House Nannie*, 158.

162 *"was really astounding":* Shaw, JFKLOHP, 11.

162 *"That night":* Shaw, *White House Nannie*, 158.

162 *"There will be":* Pierre Salinger, press briefing #1194, August 8, 1963, 12:20 p.m., Papers of John F. Kennedy, Presidential Papers, White House Staff Files of Pierre Salinger, Press Briefings 1961–1964, Press Briefings, File 1, 1961–1964, Box 68, JFKWHSFPS-068-004, JFKL.

163 *"PRESIDENT'S BABY DIES":* *BG*, August 9, 1963 (a.m.), 1.

163 *"Mrs. Kennedy Unaware":* *Tampa Times*, August 9, 1963, 1.

163 *Condolences:* In addition to the many condolences available online and in files at the John F. Kennedy Library, others are no doubt in Jacqueline Kennedy's JFKL holdings that are currently closed to the public.

164 *"For Bostonians there is":* "The World Sympathizes," *BG*, August 9, 1953, 10.

164 *"So closely":* "Tragic Ending," *Buffalo Evening News*, August 9, 1963, 24.

164 *"Theirs is the":* "A Little Boy," *NYT*, August 10, 1963, 16.

164 *"When he went":* AP, "5 Presidential Children Died in Fathers' Terms," *WP*, August 10, 1963, A6.

165 *"You can't let":* O'Donnell, Powers, and McCarthy, *"Johnny, We Hardly Knew Ye,"* 437.

165 *"the child's death":* Leaming, *Jacqueline Bouvier Kennedy Onassis*, 120.

165 *"One person who":* Alvin Spivak, UPI, "Kennedys Mourn Loss," *Bangor* (ME) *Daily News*, August 10, 1963, 1.

165 *"she was taking":* UPI, "Kennedy at Baby Rites," *The Independent* (Richmond, CA), August 10, 1963, 1.

166 *taking it all "well":* AP, "Patrick Kennedy Is Laid to Rest in Family Plot," *Buffalo Evening News*, August 10, 1963, 1.

166 *"She looks like":* "These People Report the News from Around the World, Write Columns," *The Daily Progress* (Charlottesville, VA), October 18, 1963, 10.

166 *"I doubt it":* Joyce Brothers, "Unloading Grief Best," *Fort Worth Star-Telegram*, August 18, 1963, 55.

167 *"to stay away":* "Grief a Family Affair," *BG*, August 10, 1963 (a.m.), 1.

168 *"excellent":* "A Mother Waits in Grief," *BG*, August 11, 1963, 4.

169 *"Blessed be the name":* Charles T. Burns, AP, "Special Ritual for Kennedy Infant Stresses Eternal Life," *The Times Argus* (Barre, VT), August 10, 1963, 1.

169 *"O God":* "Prayer Composed by the Cardinal," *Boston Sunday Herald*, August 11, 1963, 44.

169 *"It was a":* Francis X. Morrissey, recorded interview #2 by Ed Martin, September 9, 1964, 64–65, JFKLOHP.

170 *"He literally put":* Richard Cardinal Cushing, recorded interview by Edward M. Kennedy, 1966, 19, JFKLOHP.

170 *"He wouldn't take":* Sorensen, *Kennedy*, 367.

170 *"copious tears":* Cushing, JFKLOHP, 19.

170 *"One of the few":* Morrissey, JFKLOHP, 64–65.

170 *"one of the most":* Ibid., 64.

170 *"He is very tired":* James F. Droney, "Patrick Kennedy Laid to Rest," *Boston Sunday Herald*, August 11, 1963, 44.

171 *"Their mien":* Ibid.

171 *"rigid, frozen in":* Edward G. McGrath, "Grief-Stricken President in Sad Farewell to Son," *BG*, August 11, 1963, 1.

171 *"Bow down Your":* Ibid., 4.

171 *"his shoulders rise":* Mary C. Curtis, "To Serve a President," *Charlotte Observer*, November 16, 2003, 11.

172 *"From high in":* Droney, "Patrick Kennedy Laid to Rest," 44.

172 *"to tell me how":* Ibid., 64.

172 *"great love":* Ibid., 65.

172 *"From that sad":* Spoto, *Jacqueline Bouvier Kennedy Onassis*, 215.

FOURTEEN: Lifting Jackie's Spirits

173 *"The degree of":* Forbes, Oral History #1, JFKLOHP, 13.

173 *"Their parenthood bound":* Spoto, *Jacqueline Bouvier Kennedy Onassis*, 216.

174 *"It is so hard":* Fay, *The Pleasure of His Company*, 217.

174 *"This man":* Spoto, *Jacqueline Bouvier Kennedy Onassis*, 215.

174 *"Pregnancy is the waiting":* "He Lived," *Richmond News Leader*, August 10, 1963, 0708-112-119, JFKL.

175 *"I am convinced":* Lincoln, *My Twelve Years with John F. Kennedy*, 354.

175 *"My son didn't":* Curtis, "To Serve a President," 11.

176 *"Was there anyone":* Pierre Salinger press briefing #1196, August 10, 1963, 1:00 p.m., 2, Box 68, JFKWHSFPS-068-004.

177 *"offer prayers that":* William M. Blair, "Caroline, Carrying a Bouquet, and John Jr. Visit Mother in Hospital," *NYT*, August 12, 1963, 44.

177 *"Down in front":* Mary McGrory, "Grieving Kennedy Unspared," *WES*, August 12, 1963, A3.

177 *"The President was":* Andersen, *Jack and Jackie*, 355.

178 *"It is clear":* Victor O. Jones, "Reaction to Tragedy Enhanced JFK Image," *BG*, August 16, 1963, 7.

178 *"was greatly cheered":* Andrew T. Hatcher, press briefing #1197, August 11, 1963, 1:00 p.m., Box 68, JFKWHSFPS-068-004.

179 *twelve-minute flight:* Helen Thomas, UPI, "Mrs. Kennedy Rests at Home," *WP*, August 13, 1963, D3.

179 *"Where's mummy?":* Frank Falacci, "Mrs. Kennedy Has Visitors," *BG*, August 12, 1963, 1.

179 *"JBK pulling herself":* Gallagher, *My Life with Jacqueline Kennedy*, 291.

180 *"first real boyfriend":* Alford, *Once Upon a Secret*, 112.

180 *"He invited me":* Ibid., 120.

181 *"Gad, he's sad-looking":* Lincoln, *My Twelve Years with John F. Kennedy*, 355.

181 *"Very Important Puppy":* *BG* (a.m.), August 14, 1963, 1.

181 *"just adored":* Thomas, "Mrs. Kennedy Rests at Home."

FIFTEEN: "Like a Couple of School Kids"

182 *"The first thing":* Sanislow, author interview.

183 *"Malignant melanomas":* Ibid.

183 *"If she had":* Turnure and Tuckerman, JFKLOHP, 22.

183 *modest hospital bill:* Frances Lewine, AP, "Kennedy's AFB Hospital Bill Is $12.25, (Tucson) *Arizona Daily Star*, August 18, 1963, 10.

184 *"With deep appreciation":* "The Presidency: Home Again," *Time*, August 23, 1963; Thomas, "Mrs. Kennedy Rests at Home."

184 *"You've been so wonderful":* Jan Pottker, *Janet & Jackie: The Story of a Mother and Her Daughter, Jacqueline Kennedy Onassis* (New York: St. Martin's, 2001), 194.

184 *"Just to do":* Hill, author interview.

184 *"Careful":* Martin, *A Hero for Our Time*, 528.

184 *"like a couple":* Frank Falacci, "Jacqueline Ordered to Curb Activities," *BG*, August 15, 1963, 6–7.

184 *"It was a small gesture":* Hill and McCubbin, *Mrs. Kennedy and Me*, 249.

185 *"It was the first":* Martha Bartlett, interview with author.

185 *"By golly":* Sanislow, author interview. Reference to AP story "First Lady Back Home," *Niagara Falls Gazette*, August 14, 1963, 1.

186 *"For the children":* Shaw, *White House Nannie*, 159.

186 *"Dr. Walsh has asked":* Pierre Salinger, News Conferences, #1200, August 14, 1963, 12:00 p.m., 2, JFKL.

187 *"The President's only concern":* Lincoln, *My Twelve Years with John F. Kennedy*, 354.

187 *"Each time":* Ibid., 354–55.

188 *"To the natural":* Jones, "Reaction to Tragedy Enhanced JFK Image."

188 *"a happy man":* Fay, *The Pleasure of His Company*, 218.

188 *"occasional moments":* Ibid., 217–18.

188 *"It has been":* Ibid., 217.

SIXTEEN: A President's Pledge to Save Newborns

190 *"death comes most":* "Hyaline Membrane Disease," August 19, 1963, Subject File, 1960–1963, Hyaline Membrane Disease, JFKWHSFTR-007-009-p0024.

190 *"Little is known":* Ibid., p0025.

191 *"a fund for":* President, 5: Kennedy, Patrick B.: General, 1963: 21 August–17 September, JFKWHCSF-0709-011-p0054.

191 *"a good project":* Ibid., p0053.

191 *"sounds like a good one":* Ibid., p0051.

191 *"Prematurity has been":* Hyaline Membrane Disease, JFKWHSFTR-007-009-p0020.

192 *"two program areas":* Ibid., "Hyaline Membrane Disease: A Status Report," August 28, 1963, 7, JFKWHSFTR-007-009-p0013.

192 *"solid conviction":* Ibid., 8, JFKWHSFTR-007-009-p0014.

192 *headlines brought the issues:* "Baby Disease Baffling in Cause and Effects—Born 5 Weeks Early," *WP*, August 10, 1963, A6; "Premature Infants Subject to HMD," *BG*, August 11, 1963, 15; "Mortality in Infants—Disease That Killed Kennedy Baby Is Biggest Danger in Premature Birth," *NYT*, August 18, 1963, 74.

192 *"The death of infant":* "The Premature Baby Problem," *Tulare* (CA) *Advance Register*, August 15, 1963, 10.

192 *Thousands of American parents:* From JFKWHCSF, Tony Sylvester, 0708-004-060; John Cabot, 0708-006-100; Glenn Seaborg, 0708-003-226; Mrs. Milton Katz, 0709-010-059; Steve Derounian, 0708-003-095.

192 *"We had a similar":* Robin Brown, White House Social Files, JFKL.

193 *"identical" misfortune:* Leonard B. Schlosser, Papers of John F. Kennedy, Presidential Papers, JFKWHCSF, 0708-003-232, PP5: Kennedy, Patrick B.: Executive 19, August 1963.

193 *"Death is not the worst":* Syd Herlong, JFKWHCSF 0707-014-131, 132.

193 *"As the father":* Herb Klotz, JFKWHCSF 0707-014-198, 199.

194 *"It's a terrible thing":* Joe Fox, JFKWHCSF 0709-002-019.

194 *"the double ache":* Justice Arthur Goldberg, JFKWHCSF 0709-001-0002.

194 *"I don't like to argue":* James Reston, JFKWHCSF 0708-006-131.

194 *"I find that as I":* Cecil Sanders, JFKWHCSF 0708-002-143.

194 *"It certainly is":* Senator Birch Bayh, JFKWHCSF 0708-006-0018.

194 *"If there is any":* Walt Rostow, JFKWHCSF 0707-014-290.

194 *"I don't know the President":* Bob Eunson, JFKWHCSF 0708-006-115.

195 *"very sincere sympathy":* Goro Nakajima, JFKWHCSF 0708-007-011.

195 *"pain and anguish":* Abba Eban, JFKWHCSF 0708-007-017.

195 *"We tried our best":* Dr. Peter S. Liebert, interview with author.

195 *"the most sincere":* Peter S. Liebert, JFKWHCSF 0708-001-016.

196 *"You and the resident":* John F. Kennedy, letter, August 16, 1963, provided by Dr. Liebert.

196 *"It will mean":* Nancy Tuckerman, letter to Carol Anne Timothy, August 14, 1963, JFKWHCSF, 0503-020.

197 *"These are for":* Inger Boye, JFKWHCSF 0709-003-p0005.

197 *"Mr. President":* Ibid.

197 *"the kindness of":* John F. Kennedy, Ibid., 0709-003-p0003.

197 *"Dear David and Sharon":* Ibid., p0004.

197 *"a book of David's choice":* Inger Boye, Highland Park Public Library, Children's Department, Report for August 1963.

197 *"There's no record":* Julia Johnas, Highland Park Public Library, email.

198 *"feeling great":* UPI, "Mrs. Kennedy's Recovery Going Well," *BG*, August 18, 1963, 14.

198 *"Caroline was being":* Martin, *A Hero for Our Time*, 528.

198 *"The house was":* Ibid.

199 *"She hung onto":* Ibid.

199 *"I noticed that he":* Hill and McCubbin, *Mrs. Kennedy and Me*, 249.

199 *"This was all":* Ibid.

199 *"As if looking":* Fay, *The Pleasure of His Company*, 168–69.

199 *"My dearest Jacqueline":* Father Leonard Joseph, Mrs. Kennedy's Files, Alphabetical file, Message (Sympathy—Received), L Lenn. JFKWHCSF -0606-013.

SEVENTEEN: They Had Weathered It All

201 *"This was the first":* Benjamin C. Bradlee, *Conversations with Kennedy* (New York: Norton, 1975), 206.

202 *"It was only":* Hill, author interview.

202 *"They'd certainly":* Janet Lee Bouvier Auchincloss, recorded interview by Joan Braden, September 6, 1964, 26–27, JFKLOHP.

203 *"read all the quotations":* Bradlee, *Conversations with Kennedy*, 208.

203 *"a sweet one":* West and Kotz, *Upstairs at the White House*, 247.

203 *"Got to steer":* Bradlee, *Conversations with Kennedy*, 207.

203 *"I could see":* Schlesinger, *Jacqueline Kennedy*, 144.

204 *"As he knelt":* Leaming, *Mrs. Kennedy*, 312.

204 *"that their son":* Clarke, *JFK's Last Hundred Days*, 171.

204 *"It was the first":* Landis, *The Final Witness*, 109.

204 *"Mrs. Kennedy seemed":* Hill and McCubbin, *Mrs. Kennedy and Me*, 251.

205 *"Jack—or really":* Charles Bartlett, letter from Jacqueline Kennedy, September 15, 1963, courtesy of Martha Bartlett.

EIGHTEEN: Jackie's Aegean Adventure

206 *"Immediately I called":* West and Kotz, *Upstairs at the White House*, 248.

207 *"Nothing was said":* Ibid.

207 *"honor the cause":* Bradlee, *Conversations with Kennedy*, 213.

207 *"Except for his love":* Ibid., 212.

207 *"ill-at-ease":* "Politics: Striking the Theme," *Time*, October 4, 1963.

207 *"sometimes rambling speeches":* Julius Duscha, "Kennedy Urges New Advance by Science," *WP*, September 26, 1963, A2.

207 *"the foresight and":* Carroll Kilpatrick, "Kennedy's Aides, 6 Other Scientists Join in Endorsing Test-Ban Treaty," *WP*, August 25, 1963, A1.

207 *"one of the greatest":* Ibid.

207 *"gives us the hope":* Frank Falacci, "Rain Keeps JFK Ashore," *BG*, August 25, 1963, 6.

207 *"No other single":* Sorensen, *Kennedy*, 740.

207 *"as his greatest":* O'Donnell, Powers, and McCarthy, *"Johnny, We Hardly Knew Ye,"* 409.

208 *"We are talking":* John F. Kennedy, "September 26, 1963: Address at the Mormon Tabernacle," University of Virginia Miller Center, https://millercenter.org/the-presidency/presidential-speeches/september-26-1963-address-mormon-tabernacle. See also Beschloss, *The Crisis Years*, 637.

208 *"For the first time":* Richard Reeves, *President Kennedy: Profile of Power* (New York: Simon & Schuster, 1993), 607.

208 *"We've found that peace":* Beschloss, *The Crisis Years*, 637.

209 *"A chance to see":* Bradlee, *Conversations with Kennedy*, 213.

209 *"There was no sexual":* Sally Bedell Smith, *Grace and Power*, 411.

209 *"What I didn't realize":* Alford, *Once Upon a Secret*, 123.

209 *"The President and I":* Ibid., 125.

209 *"It's a testament":* Ibid.

209 *"When I was on":* Ibid.

209 *"The tragic death":* Ibid.

210 *"When I was in":* Ibid.

211 *"Kennedy said to":* Leamer, *The Kennedy Women*, 587.

211 *"Jack went down":* Sally Bedell Smith, *Grace and Power*, 398.

211 *"should be rediscussed":* Turnure and Tuckerman, JFKLOHP, 18.

212 *"He sent me":* Schlesinger, *Jacqueline Kennedy*, 25.

212 *"Mrs. Jacqueline Kennedy":* AP, "Jacqueline to Visit Greece, as a Tonic," *BG*, September 18, 1963, 11.

212 *"White House sources":* Ibid.

212 *"the guest of":* "Mrs. Kennedy to Relax on Onassis Yacht," *BG*, September 25, 1963, 39.

213 *"While they flew":* Landis, *The Final Witness*, 112.

213 *"she was smiling":* AP, "Jacqueline, Weary, Takes Oxygen on Flight," *BG*, October 3, 1963, 12.

213 *"Are you ready":* Hill and McCubbin, *Mrs. Kennedy and Me*, 253.

214 *"Most women have":* Olga L. Wilson, Letters to the Star, *WES*, October 11, 1963, A18.

214 *"Mrs. Kennedy should not": Detroit News*, "The Wrong Yacht for Mrs. Kennedy," Other Editors Say Column, *La Crosse* (WI) *Tribune*, October 23, 1963, 4.

214 *"First Lady's Cruise":* Drew Pearson, "First Lady's Cruise Causes Stir," *WP*, October 17, 1963, G15.

214 *"She would wait":* Manchester, *The Death of a President*, 9.

214 *"This is Washington":* "President's Call Raised Wrong Mrs. Kennedy," *NYT*, October 12, 1963, 22.

215 *"both children":* Bergquist, *A Very Special President*, 125.

215 *"secret door":* Ibid.

215 *"He held out":* Kay (Katherine Murphy) Halle, recorded interview by William M. McHugh, February 7, 1967, 19, JKFLOHP.

215 *"What have we":* Clarke, *JFK's Last Hundred Days*, 220.

216 *"G'omyko!":* Bergquist, *A Very Special President*, 128.

216 *"to romp with":* Lincoln, *My Twelve Years with John F. Kennedy*, 357.

217 *"The President was":* Tretick, JFKLOHP, 47–48.

217 *"Their little legs":* Lincoln, *My Twelve Years with John F. Kennedy*, 357.

218 *"I haven't got":* Cecil Holland, "Nuclear Test Treaty Signed by President," *WES*, October 7, 1963, 1.

218 *"He believed":* Clarke, *JFK's Last Hundred Days*, 215.

218 *"He was still an unknown":* Bergquist, *A Very Special President*, 122.

218 *"was one of the":* Ibid., 123.

219 *"He's going to":* Tretick, JFKLOHP, 44.

219 *"a small news":* Bergquist, *A Very Special President*, 124.

219 *"going out of":* Tretick, JFKLOHP, 44.

219 *"As soon as":* Ibid., 45.

219 *"If she's not":* Laura Bergquist Knebel, Oral History #1, JFKLOHP, 7.

220 *"How do you like":* Bergquist, *A Very Special President*, 125.

220 *"a father can be":* Ibid., 120.

220 *"John-John and":* Bradlee, *Conversations with Kennedy*, 161.

220 *"He felt the loss":* Bergquist, *A Very Special President*, 120.

220 *"Let's go see":* Ibid., 126.

221 *"Yeah, and I've":* Ibid., 127.

221 *"He ran all":* Tretick, JFKLOHP, 48.

221 *"She wasn't mad":* Ibid.

221 *"I got him":* Ibid., 49.

221 *four days before:* Kitty Kelley, "Stanley Tretick Calls the White House," kittykelleywriter.com.

222 *"secret door":* Bergquist, *A Very Special President*, 125.

222 *"act of God":* Ibid., 121.

222 *"I felt that":* Fay, *The Pleasure of His Company*, 216.

222 *"more than anything":* Bradlee, *Conversations with Kennedy*, 167.

223 *"King Hassan is":* Hill and McCubbin, *Mrs. Kennedy and Me*, 260.

223 *"She showed no":* Landis, *The Final Witness*, 125.

223 *"grace and dignity":* Hill and McCubbin, *Mrs. Kennedy and Me*, 262.

223 *"Isn't it wonderful":* Ibid., 262–63.

224 *"Mrs. Kennedy laughed":* Hill and McCubbin, *Mrs. Kennedy and Me*, 263.

224 *"It struck me":* Knebel, Oral History #2, JFKLOHP, 15.

224 *"He was heavier physically":* Ibid., 16.

224 *"That was the":* Ibid., 14.

225 *"one of the most":* Maier, *The Kennedys*, 442.

225 *"When my great-grandfather":* Ibid., 433.

225 *"Jack Kennedy seemed":* Ibid., 442.

225 *"In such a short":* Ibid., 4.

225 *"was disturbed over":* Jack Anderson, "JFK Urged Jackie to Hurry Home," *WP*, October 19, 1963, D29.

226 *"The little ones":* Dorothy McCardle, "Postman's Son Also Walks," *Baltimore Sun*, October 27, 1963, 97.

226 *"Caroline sat":* Muriel Dobbin, "D.C. Fetes Irish," *Baltimore Sun*, October 16, 1963.

226 *"The Irish have":* Reed, JFKLOHP, 75.

226 *"I cried at every":* McCardle, "Postman's Son Also Walks."

226 *"I think one":* Reed, JFKLOHP, 75.

NINETEEN: "He Seems So Alone Here"

227 *"Mrs. Kennedy couldn't":* Hill and McCubbin, *Mrs. Kennedy and Me*, 264.

228 *"The party continued":* Spoto, *Jacqueline Bouvier Kennedy Onassis*, 219.

228 *"In a way":* Ibid.

228 *Jackie's arrival:* Film of Jackie's arrival: "October 17, 1963—First Lady Jacqueline Kennedy Welcomed Home from Greece," posted June 25, 2013, by HelmerReenberg, https://www.youtube.com/watch?v=dSmLicqwPtM.

228 *"Come, here, John":* Dorothy McCardle, "First Lady Is Back Home," *WP*, October 19, 1963, C7.

229 *"Oh, you caught":* Bergquist Knebel, Knebel, Oral History #2, JFKLOHP, 15.

229 *"She was really":* Carl Sferrazza Anthony, *The Kennedy White House: Family Life & Pictures, 1961–1963* (New York: Touchstone, 2001), 252.

230 *"I'll never be":* Ibid.

230 *"I was melancholy":* Maier, *The Kennedys*, 474.

230 *"Americans should be":* Wilfred C. Rodgers, "Exhorts Congress in Hub Speech," *BG*, October 20, 1963, 1.

231 *"would be catastrophic":* James S. Doyle, "Rocky Raps Barry in N.H. Speeches," *BG*, October 20, 1963, 42.

231 *"But," as the* Globe: Richard J. Connolly, "Plaza Crowd's Loss Was Harvard-Columbia Gain," *BG*, October 20, 1963, 64.

231 *"unusually silent":* O'Donnell, Powers, and McCarthy, *"Johnny, We Hardly Knew Ye,"* 438.

231 *"Mrs. Lincoln":* Ibid.

232 *"turned to me":* Ibid.

232 *"the pain you":* The story of the Cura Carpignano boys can be found in the JFK Library in Benjamin Read, memo to McGeorge Bundy, October 1, 1963, and in a series of documents including the boys' letter in JFKWHCSF 0709-007-p0011 through p0018.

233 *"The President just":* David Klein, letter to Cardinal Cushing, October 8, 1963, JFKWHCSF 0709-007-p0015.

233 *"You may be sure":* Fr. Joseph McGuire, letter to David Klein, October 10, 1963, JFKWHCSF 0709-007-p00014.

233 *"from the Parish Boys' Group":* Ibid., p0013.

234 *"Dear Boys":* Evelyn Lincoln, letter to Parish Boys' Group, Church of San Tarcisio, October 31, 1963, JFKWHCSF 0709-007-p0011.

234 *"The President looked":* O'Donnell, Powers, and McCarthy, *"Johnny, We Hardly Knew Ye,"* 438.

235 *"Look who's here!":* AP, "Youth So Surprised He Can't Serve President His Ice Cream in Boston," *Springfield* (OH) *News-Sun*, October 20, 1963, 8.

235 *"Can't you see":* Ibid. See also Jeffrey A. Osoff, "A Protocol Session at Sundae School," *BG*, October 20, 1963, 1.

235 *"Get me a chocolate":* O'Donnell, Powers, and McCarthy, *"Johnny, We Hardly Knew Ye,"* 445.

235 *"a resounding cheer":* Charles E. Claffey, "7500 Cheers for President Make Armory Walls Shake," *BG*, October 20, 1963, 65.

236 *"We don't want":* Rose Fitzgerald Kennedy, *Times to Remember*, 124.

236 *"coughing and unable":* Nasaw, *The Patriarch*, 776.

236 *"transformed from the":* Ibid., 777.

236 *"He would bellow":* Ibid.

237 *"He had been":* Ibid., 782.

237 *"the President went":* O'Donnell, Powers, and McCarthy, *"Johnny, We Hardly Knew Ye,"* 43.

238 *"a tragic figure":* Nasaw, *The Patriarch*, 779.

238 *"He's the one":* O'Donnell, Powers, and McCarthy, *"Johnny, We Hardly Knew Ye,"* 43.

TWENTY: "I'll Campaign with You Anywhere You Want"

239 *"In the gossipy"*: "Jackie," *Time*, January 20, 1961, cover story.

240 *"I remember most"*: Bradlee, *Conversations with Kennedy*, 28–29.

240 *"Jackie was not"*: "Jackie," *Time.*

241 *"seemed much more attentive"*: O'Brien, *John F. Kennedy*, 778.

241 *"When I came back"*: Maier, *The Kennedys*, 474.

242 *"brilliantly lighted"*: Bradlee, *Conversations with Kennedy*, 219.

242 *"Maybe now"*: Ibid., 220.

242 *"I almost fell"*: O'Donnell, Powers, and McCarthy, *"Johnny, We Hardly Knew Ye,"* 2.

242 *"I'll campaign with"*: Manchester, *The Death of a President*, 9.

242 *"She flipped open"*: Ibid.

243 *"I do not think"*: President John F. Kennedy, News Conference 12, June 12, 1961, 1:15 p.m., Palais Chaillot, Paris, JFKL, https://www.jfklibrary.org/archives/other-resources/john-f-kennedy-press-conferences/news-conference-12.

243 *"it was clear"*: Dallek, *An Unfinished Life*, 400.

243 *"wanted to be"*: Turnure and Tuckerman, JFKLOHP, 29.

243 *"she wanted"*: Ibid., 28.

243 *"She would do"*: Ibid., 29.

243 *"I am going"*: Ibid., 28.

TWENTY-ONE: Bagpipes on the South Lawn

245 *"The image of"*: Helen Thomas, UPI, "Kennedys Believe in Togetherness," *Orlando Sentinel*, November 17, 1963, 25.

245 *"so the children"*: Nancy Tuckerman, Sanford L. Fox, Social Events, 1961–1964. Events: 13 November 1963, Perf. of Black Watch Band and Pipers, JFKWHCSF 026-007-p00022.

245 *"It would be hard"*: Peter Lisagor, "Radiant Jacqueline Hears Black Watch," *BG*, November 14, 1963, 4.

246 *"We regard it"*: White House Films, The Black Watch Band and Pipes, November 13, 1963, JFKL, https://www.jfklibrary.org/asset-viewer/archives/jfkwhf-whn11/.

247 "*Mr. President, would*": Preston Bruce, recorded interview by Nancy Tuckerman and Pamela Turnure, June 16, 1964, 10, JFKLOHP.

247 "*It was the last*": Caroline Kennedy, "Kennedy Name Still Resonates in Japan," *60 Minutes*, CBS, April 12, 2015, https://www.cbsnews.com/news/ambassador-to-japan-caroline-kennedy-60-minutes/.

247 "*He sat there*": Bruce, JFKLOHP, 9–10.

247 "*a close family*": Thomas, "Kennedys Believe in Togetherness."

248 "*What would people*": Lincoln, *My Twelve Years with John F. Kennedy*, 361.

248 "*Star light*": Ibid., 362.

249 "*He talked about*": Martin, *A Hero for Our Time*, 539.

250 "*Jack knows I*": Robin Douglas-Home, "Jacqueline Kennedy: A Study in Power: Jackie Knew She'd Hate Texas," *Philadelphia Inquirer*, February 21, 1967, 1.

250 "*drew a crowd*": "Society Steps Out at White House," *Miami News*, November 21, 1963, 50.

250 "*I didn't come*": AP, "Jackie Appears as White House Hostess for 1st Time Since August," *Sacramento Bee*, November 21, 1963, 4.

250 "*She was convinced*": Thurston Clarke, interviewed by Ted Widmer, JFKL, JFK's Last Hundred Days, September 9, 2013, https://www.jfklibrary.org /events-and-awards /forums /past-forums /transcripts /jfks-last-hundred-days.

250 "*I think we're going*": Clarke, *JFK's Last Hundred Days*, 287.

251 "*I had worked so*": Maier, *The Kennedys*, 475.

251 "*I miss you*": Manchester, *The Death of a President*, 55.

251 "*Caroline! John!*": Ibid., 56.

251 "*She liked to make*": Ibid.

252 "*Bye, Daddy*": Ibid.

252 "*As you grow*": Ibid., 56–57. Note to Collins children, November 20, 1963, JFKWH Central Files Chronological_015-007-p0098.

252 "*We're going in*": Gerald Blaine and Lisa McCubbin, *The Kennedy Detail* (New York: Gallery, 2010), 157.

253 "*President Kennedy got*": Hill and McCubbin, *Mrs. Kennedy and Me*, 273.

253 "*I want to*": Manchester, *The Death of a President*, 63.

253 "*It's just a*": Hill and McCubbin, *Mrs. Kennedy and Me*, 274.

253 *"The President kissed"*: Manchester, *The Death of a President*, 63–64.

254 *"he always loved"*: Ibid., 64.

TWENTY-TWO: Texas: Animosity and Adulation

255 *"DV arriving"*: Manchester, *The Death of a President*, 71.

256 *"There it is!"*: Ibid. Newspapers reported the many shows of enthusiasm for the first lady throughout the trip.

257 *"We are confronted"*: John F. Kennedy, "Television Address to the Nation on Civil Rights," June 11, 1963, Historic Speeches, CBS, jfklibrary.org.

257 *"Can you believe"*: Ted Sorensen, *Counselor* (New York: Harper Perennial, 2008), 282.

257 *"one of the most eloquent"*: Telegram from Martin Luther King Jr. to President Kennedy, June 11, 1963, JFKL, https://www.jfklibrary.org/Asset-Viewer/, fXbXxZHwaUmJqbxW_5IrQg.aspx. For more on Kennedy and King's relationship and the president's civil rights evolution, see Steven Levingston, *Kennedy and King: The President, The Pastor, and the Battle over Civil Rights* (New York: Grand Central, 2018).

257 *"God made big people"*: Manchester, *The Death of a President*, 44.

258 *"couldn't resist"*: Hill and McCubbin, *Mrs. Kennedy and Me*, 275.

258 *"She followed the President's"*: Ibid.

258 *"a mutual understanding"*: Maier, *The Kennedys*, 475.

258 *"haunted them and"*: Clarke, JFKL, September 9, 2013.

258 *"acted as a"*: Douglas-Home, "Jaqueline Kennedy: A Study in Power: Jackie Knew She'd Hate Texas," 14.

259 *"I had been"*: Alford, *Once Upon a Secret*, 126. By the time of the Texas trip, Jack's affair with Mimi Beardsley was over. Of course, it was possible, given his known proclivities, that Jack continued to stray. But if he was still philandering, as some Kennedy observers believe, it was also true that he had embraced Jackie as never before and she had renewed her love of him, underscoring that this complicated relationship does not yield to black-and-white analysis. Even Seymour Hersh, who explored Jack's sexual shenanigans in his book *The Dark Side of Camelot*, acknowledged that things had considerably changed between them as Dallas approached, pp. 438–439.

259 *"Welcome, JFK"*: Manchester, *The Death of a President*, 75.

259 *"youthful Commander in Chief"*: Green Peyton, *Fifty Years of Aerospace Medicine*, Series No. 67-180 (Brooks Air Force Base, TX: AFSC Historical Publications, 1968), 234.

260 *"Just as the wartime":* John F. Kennedy, "Remarks at the Dedication of the Aerospace Medical Health Center, San Antonio, Texas, November 21, 1963," JFKL, jfklibrary.org/archives.

261 *"We did tidy": JFK: The Final Hours*, directed and written by Erik Nelson, produced by Robert Erickson, executive produced by Dave Harding, National Geographic Channel, 2013.

262 *"caught the attention":* Peyton, *Fifty Years of Aerospace Medicine*, 236–37.

262 *"I can't tell you how":* Ryan Loyd, "JFK's Day in San Antonio 24 Hours Before His Assassination," Texas Public Radio, July 10, 2103, https://www.tpr.org/arts-culture/2013-07-10/jfks-day-in-san-antonio-24-hours-before-his-assassination.

262 *"gave us a wide smile":* Sal Devivo, "Falls Airman Recalls Chat with Kennedy," *Niagara Falls Gazette*, December 4, 1963, 1.

262 *"He wasn't the":* Loyd, "JFK's Day in San Antonio 24 Hours Before His Assassination."

262 *"He says you are":* Nelson, *JFK: The Final Hours.*

263 *"Here, Jackie":* Clint Hill and Lisa McCubbin, *Five Days in November* (New York: Gallery, 2013), 33.

263 *"taken by":* Devivo, "Falls Airman Recalls Chat with Kennedy."

263 *"Good luck":* Peyton, *Fifty Years of Aerospace Medicine*, 237.

263 *"The death of":* O'Donnell, Powers, and McCarthy, *"Johnny, We Hardly Knew Ye,"* 22.

263 *"Apart from the":* Manchester, *The Death of a President*, 77.

264 *"He wondered why":* Ibid.

264 *"President Kennedy looks":* Hill and McCubbin, *Five Days in November*, 33.

264 *"As a father myself":* Nelson, *JFK: The Final Hours.*

265 *"She saw her husband":* Manchester, *The Death of a President*, 117.

265 *"Two years ago":* Philip Potter, "Kennedy Murdered by Sniper in Dallas," *Baltimore Sun*, November 22, 1963, 5.

265 *"Jackie was saying":* O'Donnell, Powers, and McCarthy, *"Johnny, We Hardly Knew Ye,"* 25.

TWENTY-THREE: Red Roses for Jackie

266 *"This trip is":* O'Donnell, Powers, and McCarthy, *"Johnny, We Hardly Knew Ye,"* 28.

267 *"But in Dallas":* Theodore H. White Personal Papers, Camelot Documents, Item III-A: Copy of White's December 19, 1963 transcript of interview notes, THWPP-059-013, JFKL.

267 *"OK, here we go":* Alexandra Zapruder, *Twenty-Six Seconds: A Personal History of the Zapruder Film* (New York: Twelve, 2016), 35.

267 *"It has been":* "The Zapruder Film," *NYT*, June 23, 1998, A18.

268 *"flesh-colored":* "Testimony of Mrs. John F. Kennedy," Friday, June 5, 1964, "Hearings Before the President's Commission on the Assassination of President Kennedy," U.S. Government Printing Office, Vol. V, 180.

268 *"all the seat":* White, THWPP-059-013.

268 *"He's dead":* Manchester, *The Death of a President*, 163.

268 *"Mrs. Kennedy, please":* Hill and McCubbin, *Five Days in November*, 111.

268 *"Please let us":* Ibid., 112.

268 *"Mrs. Kennedy was":* Bradford, *America's Queen*, 271.

269 *"He's still alive":* Manchester, *The Death of a President*, 185.

269 *"Do you think . . . ?":* Ibid.

269 *"I did not have":* O'Donnell, Powers, and McCarthy, *"Johnny, We Hardly Knew Ye,"* 32.

269 *"I'm going in":* Manchester, *The Death of a President*, 185.

269 *"I'm going to get":* Ibid., 186.

270 *"She leaned forward":* Ibid.

270 *"in a truly wonderful":* McClelland letter from a private collection.

271 *"Miss Shaw":* Shaw, *White House Nannie*, 9.

272 *"Come along, children":* Ibid., 10.

272 *"big and suntanned":* Ibid., 11.

272 *"he looked ghastly":* Ibid., 10.

272 *"The President's dead":* Ibid., 11.

272 *"she retained her":* Manchester, *The Death of a President*, 290.

273 *"The ring . . . would":* Ibid., 293.

273 *"it's the closest":* White, THWPP-059-013.

273 *"Do you think":* Ibid.

273 *"I was not":* O'Donnell, Powers, and McCarthy, *"Johnny, We Hardly Knew Ye,"* 35.

273 *"As soon as":* Bradford, *America's Queen*, 272.

273 *"No," she insisted:* Hill and McCubbin, *Five Days in November*, 121.

275 *"more harassed than":* Shaw, *White House Nannie*, 16.

275 *"Mrs. Kennedy is":* Ibid., 16–17.

275 *"Dear me":* Ibid., 17.

275 *"Our talk with":* O'Donnell, Powers, and McCarthy, *"Johnny, We Hardly Knew Ye,"* 42.

275 *"They must be":* Ibid., 44.

275 *"It almost seemed":* Ibid., 43.

276 *"so alone":* Ibid., 43.

276 *"I'll bring them":* Ibid.

276 *"I summoned everybody":* West and Kotz, *Upstairs at the White House*, 252.

277 *"How are the":* Manchester, *The Death of a President*, 408.

277 *"Caroline":* Shaw, JFKLOHP, 13.

277 *"loved this moment":* Shaw, *White House Nannie*, 20.

277 *"God had taken":* Shaw, JFKLOHP, 13.

277 *"He was there":* Ibid.

277 *"Patrick was so lonely":* Manchester, *The Death of a President*, 409.

278 *"God gives":* Ibid.

278 *"It was a dreadful":* Shaw, *White House Nannie*, 20.

278 *"If she doesn't":* Manchester, *The Death of a President*, 415.

278 *"a talkathon":* Ibid.

278 *"Always the two deaths":* Ibid.

279 *"Jackie, I'm going":* Ibid., 427.

279 *"I want to":* Ibid.

279 *"This is the greatest":* White, THWPP-059-013.

280 *"It has always":* Shaw, *White House Nannie*, 22.

281 *"Mr. Foster":* Blaine and McCubbin, *The Kennedy Detail*, 281.

281 *"We're going to go say good-bye":* Manchester, *The Death of a President*, 542.

TWENTY-FOUR: The Salute

282 *his father's funeral:* "Timetable of the Kennedy Funeral and Procession," *NYT,* November 26, 1963, 4; "John F. Kennedy Funeral," White House Historical Association, www.whitehousehistory.org.

283 *"as close to her":* Manchester, *The Death of a President*, 579.

283 *"Pardon me":* Ibid.

283 "Non, non": Ibid.

284 *"Stay on task":* Blaine and McCubbin, *The Kennedy Detail*, 294.

284 *"Where's my daddy?":* Manchester, *The Death of a President*, 584.

285 *"John, no, son":* Hill and McCubbin, *Five Days in November*, 206.

285 *"Caroline couldn't see":* Manchester, *The Death of a President*, 587.

285 *"May the angels":* Ibid., 589.

286 *"You'll be all right":* Ibid.

286 *"John, you can salute":* Ibid., 590.

286 *"nothing approached":* Ibid.

286 *"Somehow the mood":* Ibid.

286 *"His bearing":* Ibid.

287 *six gray horses:* Gary Schweid, AP, "Kennedy at Rest in Hero's Grave," *Oakland Tribune*, November 26, 1963, 2.

287 *"We're going to visit":* Manchester, *The Death of a President*, 642.

288 *"Daddy always loved":* Ibid., 643.

288 *"I call him":* Ibid.

288 *"Oh Mummy, I'm":* Ibid.

TWENTY-FIVE: "We Were About to Have a Real Life Together"

289 *"Thinking of Patrick":* Manchester, *The Death of a President*, 199.

290 *"Does God know":* Maier, *The Kennedys*, 472.

290 *elaborate stealth mission:* Details of Patrick and Arabella's interments: Wilfred C. Rodgers, "Kennedy Babies Reburied with Him," *BG*, December 5, 1963, 1.

292 *"I have never met":* Dave Powers, "Life Remembers," *Life*, August 1995, 35.

292 *"The pictures":* Ibid.

292 *"the public life":* Clarke, *JFK's Last Hundred Days*, 69.

293 *"Jack just had":* Bradford, *America's Queen*, 101.

293 *"They were both":* Heymann, *A Woman Named Jackie*, 192.

293 *"They folded into":* Andersen, *These Few Precious Days*, 269.

293 *"at her side":* Ibid.

293 *"There had always been":* Ibid., 255.

293 *"It took a very":* Heymann, *A Woman Named Jackie*, 426.

EPILOGUE: Patrick's Legacy

295 *first-person piece:* Holly Jordan, "A Tragedy in the Kennedy Family Saved My Preemie—And I Got the Chance to Thank Them," *People*, November 16, 2022.

295 *"Pete, there's Caroline":* Holly Jordan, interview with author. All subsequent Jordan quotations from two author interviews.

296 *"There was nothing":* Null, author interview.

297 *"What you have to":* Ibid.

297 *two-bill package:* "The Nation: For the Retarded," *NYT*, November 3, 1963, E2.

297 *$594 million:* "Legislative Chronology," National Institutes of Health, history, nih.gov.

297 *$40 million:* "Congress Enacts New Mental Health Programs: Action on S 1576 Action on HR7544", CQ Almanac 1963, *Congressional Quarterly*, https://library.cqpress.com/cqalmanac/document.php?id=cqal63-1316932.

297 *$800,000:* Jerome Wiesner, Presidential Papers, President's Office File, November 6, 1963, JFKPOF-085-011-p0090-92, JFKL. See also Hyaline Membrane Disease, JFKWHSFTR-007-009-p0009.

297 *25,000 babies a year:* Robert K. Plumb, "Fatal Baby Disease Is Reported Cured," *NYT*, October 22, 1964, 1.

297 *50 percent:* "Lung Ailment Often Is Mild, Can Be Fatal," *Philadelphia Inquirer*, August 8, 1963, 1.

298 *"My assignment was":* Joe Palca, "Joe's Big Idea: How a Scientist's Slick Discovery Helped Save Preemies' Lives," *Morning Edition*, NPR, August 3, 2015, www.npr.org.

298 *heard about Clements's work:* "Mary Ellen Avery Oral History," Interview with Lawrence Gartner, American Academy of Pediatrics, April 4, 1998, www.aap.org/pediatrichistorycenter.

298 *"He had never":* Ibid.

299 *"could not live":* "Mary Ellen Avery," Changing the Face of Medicine, National Library of Medicine, June 3, 2015, cfmedicine.nlm.nih.gov.

299 *"Within a year":* Henry L. Halliday, "Viewpoint: The Fascinating Story of Surfactant," *Journal of Paediatrics and Child Health* 53 (2017): 327.

299 *surfactant research:* M. H. Malloy and J. P. McGovern, "Hyaline Membrane Disease (HMD): An Historical and Oslerian Perspective," *Journal of Perinatology* 38 (2018): 1602–6.

299 *so disappointing:* Mikko Hallman and Egbert Herting, "Historical Perspective on Surfactant Therapy: Transforming Hyaline Membrane Disease to Respiratory Distress Syndrome," *Seminars in Fetal and Neonatal Medicine* 28, no. 6 (2023): 101493; J. Usha Raj et al., "Life-Saving Effect of Pulmonary Surfactant in Premature Babies," JCI 100th Anniversary Viewpoint, *Journal of Clinical Investigation* 134, no. 9 (2024): 1; Eric Boodman, "How an Inconspicuous Slaughterhouse Keeps the World's Premature Babies Alive," *STAT News*, March 12, 2018, statnews.com.

299 *human and mammal lung surfactants:* Robert Hentschel et al., "Surfactant Replacement Therapy: From Biological Basis to Current Clinical Practice," *Pediatric Research* 88 (2020): 176–83; Halliday, "Viewpoint," 329; H. L. Halliday, "Surfactants: Past, Present and Future," *Journal of Perinatology* 28 (2008): S55.

300 *"It took forty years":* Palca, *Morning Edition*, NPR.

300 *"one of the greatest":* Hentschel et al., "Surfactant Replacement Therapy," 183.

300 *"They said, 'You' ":* DiGregorio, *Early*, 116.

301 *"It was a different era":* Dr. James deLemos, interview with author.

301 *"morally complex":* DiGregorio, *Early*, 118.

302 *"Newborn intensive care":* Dr. George Gregory, interview with author.

302 *"More than any other":* Anne M. Jorgensen, "Born in the USA—The History of Neonatology in the United States," *NICU Currents*, June 2010, 11, static .abbottnutrition.com.

303 *"the same thing":* Gregory, author interview.

303 New England Journal of Medicine: George A. Gregory et al., "Treatment of Idiopathic Respiratory-Distress Syndrome with Continuous Positive Airway Pressure," *New England Journal of Medicine* 284, no. 24 (June 17, 1971): 1333.

303 *"Gregory's innovation saved":* Christine L. Mai, Myron Yaster, and Paul Firth, "The Development of Continuous Positive Airway Pressure: An Interview with Dr. George Gregory," *Pediatric Anesthesia* 23 (October 5, 2012): 5.

303 *"revolutionized the treatment":* Ibid., 3.

304 *"the workhorse mechanical":* Donald M. Null, Bradley A. Yoder, and Robert A. Geronimo, "Early Neonatal Research at Wilford Hall US Air Force Medical Center," *Pediatrics* 129 (February 2012): S1, S21.

305 *"a 99 percent chance":* Null, author interview.

305 *"It was evident":* Dr. Bradley A. Yoder, interview with author.

305 *"If we had not been":* Parviz Minoo, interview with author.

306 *"own feeling of":* "Letters: Tribute to Robert A. deLemos," *Journal of Pediatrics*, 133 (August 1998): 309.

306 *"I'm sure some of":* Null, author interview.

306 *parameters of prematurity:* "Preterm Birth, Key Facts," World Health Organization, accessed May 1, 2024, www.who.int/news-room/fact-sheets.

306 *odds of survival:* "When Is It Safe to Deliver Your Baby?," University of Utah Health, healthcare.utah.edu/womens-health/pregnancy-birth/preterm-birth/when-is-it-safe-to-deliver.

307 *"We're light-years away":* Yoder, author interview.

307 *"She was really":* Jordan, author interview.

308 *"Jack's life had":* Heymann, *A Woman Named Jackie*, 418.

308 *"Don't let it":* White, "For President Kennedy," 59. *Camelot*, the musical by Alan Jay Lerner and Frederick Loewe, opened on Broadway on December 3, 1960, a month after Kennedy was elected president. The play is based on T. H. White's 1958 novel about King Arthur, *The Once and Future King.* The debut production starred Richard Burton, Julie Andrews, and Robert Goulet and played 873 performances. "Camelot—The Original Cast Recording 1960," https://masterworksbroadway.com.

308 *"So the epitaph":* Heymann, *A Woman Named Jackie*, 419.

308 *"The reason I wanted":* Jordan, author interview.

BIBLIOGRAPHY

Adler, Bill, ed. *The Eloquent Jacqueline Kennedy Onassis*. New York: William Morrow, 2004.

Alford, Mimi. *Once Upon a Secret: My Affair with President John F. Kennedy and Its Aftermath*. New York: Random House, 2013.

Andersen, Christopher. *Jack and Jackie: Portrait of an American Marriage*. New York: Avon, 1996.

———. *These Few Precious Days: The Final Year of Jack with Jackie*. New York: Gallery, 2013.

Anthony, Carl Sferrazza. *As We Remember Her: Jacqueline Kennedy Onassis in the Words of Her Family and Friends*. New York: Perennial, 2003.

———. *Camera Girl: The Coming of Age of Jackie Bouvier Kennedy*. New York: Gallery, 2023.

———. *The Kennedy White House: Family Life & Pictures, 1961–1963*. New York: Touchstone, 2001.

Bergquist, Laura. *A Very Special President*. Illustrated by Stanley Tretick. New York: McGraw-Hill, 1965.

Beschloss, Michael R. *The Crisis Years: Kennedy and Khrushchev, 1960–1963*. New York: Edward Burlingame, 1991.

Blaine, Gerald, and Lisa McCubbin. *The Kennedy Detail*. New York: Gallery, 2010.

Blair, Joan, and Clay Blair, Jr. *The Search for JFK*. New York: Berkley, 1976.

Bradford, Sarah. *America's Queen: The Life of Jacqueline Kennedy Onassis*. New York: Penguin, 2000.

Bradlee, Benjamin C. *Conversations with Kennedy*. New York: Norton, 1975.

———. *A Good Life: Newspapering and Other Adventures*. New York: Simon & Schuster, 1995.

Brinkley, Alan. *John F. Kennedy*. The American Presidents. New York: Times/Henry Holt, 2012.

Brower, Kate Andersen. *The Residence: Inside the Private World of the White House*. New York: Harper, 2015.

Burns, James MacGregor. *John Kennedy: A Political Profile*. New York: Harcourt, Brace, 1960.

Callahan, Maureen. *Ask Not: The Kennedys and the Women They Destroyed*. New York: Hachette, 2024.

Clarke, Thurston. *JFK's Last Hundred Days*. New York: Penguin, 2013.

Collier, Peter, and David Horowitz. *The Kennedys: An American Drama*. New York: Summit, 1984.

Dallek, Robert. *An Unfinished Life: John F. Kennedy, 1917–1963*. New York: Back Bay, 2013.

Damore, Leo. *The Cape Cod Years of John Fitzgerald Kennedy*. New York: Four Walls Eight Windows, 1993.

DiGregorio, Sarah. *Early: An Intimate History of Premature Birth and What It Teaches Us About Being Human*. New York: Harper, 2020.

Fay, Paul B., Jr. *The Pleasure of His Company*. New York: Harper & Row, 1966.

Gallagher, Mary Barelli. *My Life with Jacqueline Kennedy*. New York: Paperback Library, 1970.

Goodwin, Doris Kearns. *The Fitzgeralds and the Kennedys: An American Saga*. New York: Simon & Schuster, 1987.

Guthman, Edwin O., and Jeffrey Shulman, eds. *Robert Kennedy: In His Own Words: The Unpublished Recollections of the Kennedy Years*. New York: Bantam, 1988.

Hamilton, Nigel. *JFK: Reckless Youth*. New York: Random House, 1992.

Hersh, Seymour M. *The Dark Side of Camelot*. Boston: Little, Brown, 1997.

Heymann, C. David. *A Woman Named Jackie*. New York: Lyle Stuart, 1989.

Hill, Clint, and Lisa McCubbin. *Five Days in November*. New York: Gallery, 2013.

———. *Mrs. Kennedy and Me*. New York: Gallery, 2012.

———. *My Travels with Mrs. Kennedy*. New York: Gallery, 2022.

JFK: The Final Hours. Directed and screenplay by Erik Nelson. Produced by Robert Erickson and executive producer Dave Harding. National Geographic Channel, 2013.

Kelley, Kitty. *Jackie Oh!* Secaucus, NJ: Lyle Stuart, 1978.

Kennedy, Edward M. *True Compass: A Memoir*. New York: Twelve, 2009.

Kennedy, Rose Fitzgerald. *Times to Remember*. New York: Doubleday, 1974.

Klein, Edward. *All Too Human: The Love Story of Jack and Jackie Kennedy*. New York: Pocket Books, 1997.

Koehler-Pentacoff, Elizabeth. *The Missing Kennedy: Rosemary Kennedy and the Secret Bonds of Four Women*. Baltimore: Bancroft, 2015.

Landis, Paul. *The Final Witness*. Chicago: Chicago Press, 2024.

Larson, Kate Clifford. *Rosemary: The Hidden Kennedy Daughter*. New York: Houghton Mifflin Harcourt, 2015.

Lasky, Victor. *J.F.K.: The Man and the Myth*. New Rochelle, NY: Arlington House, 1966.

Leamer, Laurence. *The Kennedy Women: The Saga of an American Family*. New York: Fawcett, 1994.

Leaming, Barbara. *Jacqueline Bouvier Kennedy Onassis: The Untold Story*. New York: Thomas Dunne, 2014.

———. *Mrs. Kennedy: The Missing History of the Kennedy Years*. New York: Touchstone, 2001.

Lincoln, Evelyn. *My Twelve Years with John F. Kennedy*. New York: David McKay, 1965.

Logevall, Fredrik. *JFK: Coming of Age in the American Century, 1917–1956*. New York: Random House, 2020.

MacNeil, Robert, ed. *The Way We Were: 1963, The Year Kennedy Was Shot*. New York: Carroll & Graf, 1988.

Mahoney, Richard D. *Sons & Brothers: The Days of Jack and Bobby Kennedy*. New York: Arcade, 1999.

Maier, Thomas. *The Kennedys: America's Emerald Kings*. New York: Basic Books, 2003.

Manchester, William. *The Death of a President*. New York: Harper & Row, 1967.

———. *Portrait of a President*. New York: Macfadden, 1967.

Martin, Ralph G. *A Hero for Our Time*. New York: Macmillan, 1983.

———. *Seeds of Destruction: Joe Kennedy and His Sons*. New York: G. P. Putnam's Sons, 1995.

McDermott, Rose. *Presidential Leadership, Illness, and Decision-Making*. Cambridge: Cambridge University Press, 2007.

Mosley, Charlotte, ed. *Love from Nancy: The Letters of Nancy Mitford*. London: Sceptre, 1994.

Nasaw, David. *The Patriarch: The Remarkable Life and Turbulent Times of Joseph P. Kennedy*. New York: Penguin, 2012.

O'Brien, Michael. *John F. Kennedy: A Biography*. New York: Thomas Dunne, 2005.

O'Donnell, Kenneth P., David F. Powers, and Joe McCarthy. *"Johnny, We Hardly Knew Ye."* New York: Pocket Book, 1973.

Owen, Dean R. *November 22, 1963: Reflections on the Life, Assassination, and Legacy of John F. Kennedy*. New York: Skyhorse, 2013.

Parmet, Herbert S. *Jack: The Struggles of John F. Kennedy*. New York: Dial, 1980.

Pearson, Drew. *Washington Merry-Go-Round: The Drew Pearson Diaries, 1960–1969*. Lincoln, NE: Potomac Books, 2015.

Perry, Barbara A. *Jacqueline Kennedy: First Lady of the New Frontier*. Lawrence: University Press of Kansas, 2004.

———. *Rose Kennedy: The Life and Times of a Political Matriarch*. New York: Norton, 2013.

Peyton, Green. *Fifty Years of Aerospace Medicine*. Series No. 67-180. Brooks Air Force Base, TX: AFSC Historical Publications, 1968.

Pottker, Jan. *Janet & Jackie: The Story of a Mother and Her Daughter, Jacqueline Kennedy Onassis*. New York: St. Martin's, 2001.

Reeves, Richard. *President Kennedy: Profile of Power*. New York: Simon & Schuster, 1993.

Reeves, Thomas C. *A Question of Character: A Life of John F. Kennedy*. New York: Free Press, 1991.

Rubin, Gretchen. *Forty Ways to Look at JFK*. New York: Ballantine, 2005.

Ryan, Michael S. *Patrick Bouvier Kennedy: A Brief Life That Changed the History of Newborn Care*. Minneapolis: MCP Books, 2015.

Salinger, Pierre. *P.S.: A Memoir*. New York: St. Martin's, 1995.

———. *With Kennedy*. New York: Avon, 1967.

Sandford, Christopher. *Harold and Jack: The Remarkable Friendship of Prime Minister Macmillan and President Kennedy*. Amherst, NY: Prometheus, 2014.

Schlesinger, Arthur M., Jr. *Jacqueline Kennedy: Historic Conversations on Life with John F. Kennedy*. New York: Hyperion, 2011.

———. *A Thousand Days: John F. Kennedy in the White House*. Boston: Houghton Mifflin, 1965.

Shaw, Maud. *White House Nannie: My Years with Caroline and John Kennedy, Jr.* New York: New American Library, 1966.

Shorter, Edward. *The Kennedy Family and the Story of Mental Retardation*. Philadelphia: Temple University Press, 2000.

Simon, Carly. *Touched by the Sun: My Friendship with Jackie*. New York: Farrar, Straus & Giroux, 2019.

Smith, Amanda, ed. *Hostage to Fortune: The Letters of Joseph P. Kennedy*. New York: Viking, 2001.

Smith, Jean Kennedy. *The Nine of Us: Growing Up Kennedy*. New York: Harper, 2016.

Smith, Sally Bedell. *Grace and Power: The Private World of the Kennedy White House*. New York: Random House, 2004.

Sorensen, Ted [Theodore C.]. *Counselor*. New York: Harper Perennial, 2008.

———. *Kennedy*. New York: Harper & Row, 1965.

———. *The Kennedy Legacy*. New York: Macmillan, 1969.

Spoto, Daniel. *Jacqueline Bouvier Kennedy Onassis: A Life.* New York: St. Martin's, 2000.

Stein, Jean. *American Journey: The Times of Robert Kennedy*. Edited by George Plimpton. New York: Harcourt Brace Jovanovich, 1970.

Storey, Kate. *White House by the Sea: A Century of Kennedys at Hyannis Port*. New York: Scribner, 2023.

Stossel, Scott. *Sarge: The Life and Times of Sargent Shriver*. Washington, DC: Smithsonian, 2004.

Taraborrelli, J. Randy. *Jackie, Ethel, Joan: Women of Camelot*. New York: Grand Central, 2000.

———. *Jackie, Janet & Lee: The Secret Lives of Janet Auchincloss and Her Daughters Jacqueline Kennedy Onassis and Lee Radziwill*. New York: St. Martin's, 2018.

———. *Jackie: Public, Private, Secret*. New York: St. Martin's, 2023.

Thayer, Mary Van Rensselaer. *Jacqueline Bouvier Kennedy*. New York: Doubleday, 1961.

______. *Jacqueline Kennedy: The White House Years.* New York: Popular Library, 1971.

Thomas, Evan. *Robert Kennedy: His Life*. New York: Touchstone, 2000.

Thomas, Helen. *Front Row at the White House: My Life and Times*. New York: Touchstone, 2000.

Travell, Janet, M.D. *Office Hours: Day and Night*. New York: New American Library, 1969.

Vickers, Hugo, ed. *Beaton in the Sixties: More Unexpurgated Diaries*. London: Phoenix, 2003.

Vidal, Gore. *Palimpsest: A Memoir.* New York: Penguin, 1995.

Von Post, Gunilla, and Carl Johnes. *Love, Jack*. New York: Crown, 1997.

Watts, Steven. *JFK and the Masculine Mystique: Sex and Power on the New Frontier*. New York: Thomas Dunne, 2016.

West, J. B., and Mary Lynn Kotz. *Upstairs at the White House: My Life with the First Ladies*. New York: Open Road, 1973.

White, Theodore H. *The Making of the President 1960*. New York: Atheneum, 1961.

Widmer, Ted, comp. *Listening In: The Secret White House Recordings of John F. Kennedy*. New York: Hyperion, 2012.

Wills, Garry. *The Kennedy Imprisonment: A Meditation on Power*. Boston: Mariner, 2002.

Zapruder, Alexandra. *Twenty-Six Seconds: A Personal History of the Zapruder Film*. New York: Twelve, 2016.

INDEX